# Inside the Business Enterprise

A National Bureau
of Economic Research
Conference Report

# Inside the Business Enterprise

## Historical Perspectives on the Use of Information

Edited by **Peter Temin**

The University of Chicago Press

*Chicago and London*

PETER TEMIN is professor of economics at the Massachusetts Institute of Technology and a research associate of the National Bureau of Economic Research.

The University of Chicago Press, Chicago 60637
The University of Chicago Press, Ltd., London
© 1991 by the National Bureau of Economic Research
All rights reserved. Published 1991
Printed in the United States of America
00 99 98 97 96 95 94 93 92 91   5 4 3 2 1

ISBN (cloth): 0-226-79202-1
ISBN (paper): 0-226-79204-8

Library of Congress Cataloging-in-Publication Data

Inside the business enterprise : historical perspectives on the use of infor-
    mation / edited by Peter Temin.
        p.   cm. — (A National Bureau of Economic Research conference
    report)
    Includes bibliographical references and index.
    1. Business intelligence—Congresses. I. Temin, Peter.
    II. Series: Conference report (National Bureau of Economic Research)
    HD38.7.I54   1991
    658.4'7—dc20                                                    91-27377
                                                                        CIP

♾The paper used in this publication meets the minimum requirements of the American National Standard for Information Sciences—Permanence of Paper for Printed Library Materials, ANSI Z39.48–1984.

# Contents

# Introduction

Peter Temin

All too often business enterprises are considered to be the "atoms" of economics, the irreducible unit of analysis. This is a procedure that works well in many contexts, which is why it persists. When competitive industries are the subject of analysis, for example, then the assumption that business firms are unitary has proven a fruitful starting point. But this approach also has drawbacks, since enterprises are complex organizations. This volume contains essays that explore a different view. They look inside the business enterprise.

The concept of a firm as a simple decision unit has been encouraged by the formal similarity between the analysis of the individual and of the enterprise in elementary economic theory. In each case, the person or the business firm is represented by a function representing either preferences (for individuals) or costs (for enterprises). The description proceeds symmetrically as the parallelism between the preference and cost functions is exploited. The analysis begins to differ only when individuals confront their budget constraints and enterprises seek to make profits.

This symmetry can be overdrawn. Many business enterprises have grown to be vastly larger and more complicated than individuals or even families. They involve the activities of many people, organized into several layers of authority over often diverse locations, product lines, and productive facilities. The modern business enterprise can now rival countries in size.

To understand this complex organization, it is necessary to look inside the business enterprise to examine behavior within the enterprise's boundaries. One cannot assume that a message delivered to one part of a large enterprise will make its way to all others. One cannot assume that information generated at the shop floor will be clear to top management. One cannot assume that

Peter Temin is professor of economics at the Massachusetts Institute of Technology and a research associate of the National Bureau of Economic Research.

plans made in the board room get implemented swiftly and uniformly throughout the enterprise.

Different levels of abstraction are appropriate for different problems. The view of the business enterprise as a "black box" is still useful for many questions. But there are other problems for which the internal operation of business firms matter. If we seek to learn about employee compensation, for example, then a look inside the firm is needed. Simple wage payments are only the most basic way of compensating employees. More complex alternatives are used widely, for reasons related to the internal needs of the enterprise.

Alternatively, if we are investigating how new technology is used by enterprises, we may well want to look inside the firm. As some of the papers in this volume show, enterprises can be organized in ways that allow only certain kinds of information to be used. The absorption of new techniques may be rendered difficult by the established patterns of communication within the enterprise.

Finally, the question of American "competitiveness" hovers around all discussions of economic progress today. American enterprises operate differently from those in, say, Japan. This observation has been widely repeated but not yet analyzed enough to know its importance. We need to characterize the way in which American enterprises conduct their business in order to evaluate the role of internal processes in the fate of nations.

The essays in this book make a start in this direction. They all in various ways direct their attention to activities inside the business enterprise. They try to organize their observations in ways that will be useful to others studying these operations. They provide insights for economics students studying the American economy, guides for business historians chronicling the progress of specific firms, and material for theorists trying to understand how enterprises and countries respond to stimuli.

Even though the essays were written by different people and draw on varied materials, they form a unified introduction to the study of the business enterprise. They are drawn together by two underlying themes.

The first theme is analytic. The essays argue for a specific approach to the study of business enterprises. In this view *information* is the key element to the functioning of an enterprise. The scarcity of information gives rise to institutional arrangements to economize its use. The complexity of information induces simplifications and abstractions, notably in the form of accounting. The use of information evolves as enterprises grow and change, and the ability to retrieve and use existing information increases as well.

The second theme is historical. The modern business enterprise is a creature of the last century. Historical examples from a century ago, from the Gilded Age before the First World War, give us a window on the early years of this unique organization. Most of the essays in this volume concentrate on the years around the beginning of the twentieth century, providing a picture of industry and finance of the time. Individual papers reach back into the early nineteenth century and forward into current events. But the center of attention is the Gilded Age.

These two themes combine to provide a model for the investigation of complex business enterprises. This approach can help business historians see the common elements in the history of any single enterprise. It may inspire theorists to model concrete practices of actual firms. And it should help students of economics and economic history to understand how those large organizations go about responding to the demands upon them.

The papers in this volume were presented at a Conference on Microeconomic History at the National Bureau of Economic Research in October 1990. The conference was organized by Naomi Lamoreaux, Thomas McCraw, Daniel Raff, and myself: two economists and two historians from departments of economics and history and a business school. We all hope that this conference will be the first of a series on related topics of microeconomic history.

The six papers fall into three groups. The first two, by Daniel M. G. Raff and myself and by H. Thomas Johnson, present the underlying themes of the volume. They discuss the agency problems arising from scarce information, and accounting as a primary means of communication within large enterprises. The second two papers, by Margaret Levenstein and JoAnne Yates, discuss the demand for and supply of information in two growing enterprises of the Gilded Age. They show how the use of accounting and other information is conditioned by the overall strategy of the enterprise and the technology of information transfer and storage. The final two papers, by Naomi R. Lamoreaux and J. Bradford De Long, turn to the interaction between industrial firms and financial intermediaries. They show how some of the important financial institutions of the Gilded Age responded to the changing availability of information and how these changes affected the financial environment within which business enterprises operated.

Raff and I argue in "Business History and Recent Economic Theory" that the vertical relations within business enterprises have many important common characteristics. These traits derive from the scarcity of information available to a superior (often called the principal) about the activities of a subordinate (called the agent). Limited information gives rise to what economists call the principal-agent problem, which renders many simple wage contracts inefficient. Raff and I describe various arrangements that have been used to preserve incentives in the absence of full information. We argue that the problems and the solutions are similar at the level of employee compensation, the direction of business units, and the finance of enterprises as a whole. In fact, the solutions to these information problems are important determinants of where the boundaries of business enterprises lie.

Johnson, in "Managing by Remote Control," traces the history of accounting within American business enterprises from the early nineteenth century to today. He finds, rather paradoxically, that nineteenth-century accounting practice was in some ways superior to the accounting techniques that followed it.

As Johnson sees it, accounting serves (at least) two functions. It informs owners and top management about the profitability of the firm and its major activities. And it communicates between these owners and top managers on the one hand and plant managers on the other. These functions are very different, and the modern practice of using the same accounting conventions for both of them has distorted incentives at the plant level. Managing "by the numbers" gives rise to long production runs and large inventories; it reduces the communication between producers and their customers.

These two papers emphasize the consequences to the internal functions of business enterprises of scarce information. The general point is that institutional arrangements can offset but not eliminate the problems of insufficient information. The specific point is that accounting tools have been developed to summarize the available information and that these tools in turn affect how enterprises operate. Examination of principal-agent problems and of accounting provides a way to understand how enterprises respond to new challenges.

Levenstein, in "The Use of Cost Measures," traces the beginning of accounting in the Dow Chemical Company before World War I. She argues that the company's strategy determined its need for information. Cost accounting therefore grew and changed as the company grew and changed its position in the industry. Her study shows the effects of the demand for information within the enterprise. She provides numerous concrete examples of internal reports, interesting both for what they contain and what they omit.

Yates, in "Investing in Information," describes the changing communications within the Scovill Manufacturing Company from the mid–nineteenth century to the early twentieth. She emphasizes the supply of information in a complex organization, noting that information does not exist if you cannot find it. Levenstein documents the effect of changing manufacturing technology on the demand for internal information; Yates analyzes the effects of changing information technology on the supply of internal reporting. She follows the transition from handwritten messages to printed forms, from daybooks to vertical files. Even the limited information assumed by the other authors to be present would not be useful in the absence of the techniques for reproduction, transmission, and storage that she describes.

The two papers by Levenstein and Yates provide detailed case studies of individual enterprises. They show how the general problems outlined in the earlier papers were worked out in particular cases. And they complement each other by emphasizing the demand and supply of information, respectively.

Lamoreaux looks at financial enterprises in "Information Problems and Banks' Specialization in Short-Term Commercial Lending." She traces the development of commercial banks in New England throughout the nineteenth century. Scarcity of information about investments in the early nineteenth century led banks to operate as a primitive mutual fund of investments by bank directors. As information became more plentiful, in part for reasons outlined by Yates, banks changed their function. They loaned less to insiders who now had access to broader markets, and they loaned more to outsiders about whom there was much less information. To reduce the risk of lending on this open market, the banks restricted their loans to short terms. They became modern commercial banks. The changing American market and the resulting change in information availability led banks to shift their role within the financial structure of the United States and separate the concerns of banks and industrial firms. Investment financing was done increasingly outside of commercial banks as the twentieth century opened.

De Long examines investment financing in the Gilded Age in "Did J. P. Morgan's Men Add Value?" He analyzes the institution that replaced the investment function of commercial banks as they specialized in short-term funding. He discusses the conflicting views held by Morgan's supporters and his critics of the balance between his anticompetitive and efficiency-enhancing activities. De Long subjects these views to a test, finding that the presence of a Morgan man on the board of a corporation increased its value by about 30 percent. The higher stock price was accomplished by higher earnings, but the mechanism by which the presence of a Morgan man raised them is unclear. Morgan's men seemed to provide a guarantee to investors of corporate quality. They provided the information that commercial banks no longer could furnish.

These essays provide a view of the business enterprise that exposes some of its internal workings. They suggest a variety of hypotheses and frameworks for further analysis. And they provide a picture of American industry in the Gilded Age. This picture is a rough mirror of the economy today. The accounting rules described by Johnson may constrain American firms from adapting to new technologies and procedures today. The revolution in information technology described by Yates is similar to the revolution going on today with desktop computers and fax machines. And the absence of investment bankers like Morgan may possibly inhibit industrial progress in the United States today.

All of these topics deserve further study. They have been introduced here from a vantage point that stresses the importance of scarce information and the institutions created to utilize and economize it. This approach is designed to be the "atom smasher" of economics and of business history, to provide a way to peer inside the business enterprise and analyze its operation.

On behalf of the operating committee for the conference, I want to thank Martin Feldstein and the National Bureau of Economic Research for financial support.

# 1     Business History and Recent Economic Theory:
## Imperfect Information, Incentives, and the Internal Organization of Firms

### Daniel M. G. Raff and Peter Temin

## 1.1   Business History and Economists

Traditional economic theory—that is, economics as it has been taught to elementary students since World War II—is of only limited use to business historians. Business history is about firms, and there is not much to traditional economic theory's firms or to the problems they confront. The structure of the wants of the consuming public is a given. So is the particular selection of those wants that any particular firm should try to meet. So also are the methods by which inputs are to be combined to produce those goods. Nor are there any difficulties involved in getting the inputs to combine as they are meant to. Most firms are small with respect to the markets they trade in, and there are no intricate reactions or interactions between buyers, sellers, or buyers and sellers together to be puzzled out and manipulated. Altogether, strategic choice (in both the businessman's sense and that of the game theorist) is absent, and the details of organization are never a problem.[1]

This view of the economy represents the outcome of an intellectual struggle almost a hundred years old. Even before World War I, economics was hardly a unified discipline. The contending positions at that time can grouped roughly into two camps. The English school believed in abstract reasoning

Daniel M. G. Raff is an assistant professor at the Graduate School of Business of Harvard University and a research associate of the National Bureau of Economic Research. Peter Temin is professor of economics at the Massachusetts Institute of Technology and a research associate of the National Bureau of Economic Research.

The authors are grateful for helpful comments from Adam Brandenburger, Oliver Hart, Naomi Lamoreaux, and Thomas McCraw and from audiences at the Harvard Business School Interfunctional Lunch Group and Business History Seminar. Raff's work was generously supported by the Business School's Division of Research. The authors alone are responsible for the views expressed.

1. For a careful intermediate account of the traditional theory, see, e.g., Nicholson (1988). For strategic choice, see Learned et al. (1965) and Luce and Raiffa (1957), respectively.

and models along the lines pioneered by Ricardo, Mill, and Marshall. The German school believed in inductive reasoning exemplified by Sombart and Weber.[2]

Both schools of thought have endured, but the English methodology captured the seats of power within economics. German methodology survived in business schools. Economics and management studies both flowered, but along largely independent lines. The developments, however, were not completely parallel. For while economists could and did generally ignore scholarship from business schools, the business schools could not ignore conventional economics.

The relationship between these two strains of thought has become more interactive in our generation. Business historians, firmly rooted in the particulars of the companies under scrutiny, have begun to hazard tentative generalizations about the best way to organize complex economic activities. Led by Alfred D. Chandler, Jr., in a series of books, some business historians have tried to describe the operation of an abstract entity: the modern business enterprise (Chandler 1962, 1977, 1990).

Whether by design or the result of unseen forces, economists began to think at approximately the same time about issues members of the business community and business historians would recognize as managerial. George Stigler's famous article "The Economics of Information," emphasizing that information, like other goods, is costly and that it has consequences for decisions, was published virtually simultaneously with Chandler's *Strategy and Structure*.[3] Stigler's observation is not in itself startling; his contribution was to show how the cost of information might be inserted into economic analysis.

Treating information like another scarce good has many powerful implications. The deepest and most significant is that economic decision-makers will generally not choose to acquire all the information available, any more than they will want to have all of any other good or service in the economy.[4] They may not want, or even be able, to process all the information to which they do have access (Simon 1945, 1955). As a result, business people typically have to make decisions on the basis of only incomplete information.

Institutions have emerged to facilitate decision making in the presence of incomplete information, but they too have problems. Some forms of economic organization constrain reactions to new information and make transactions more costly than they would be in a simpler world.[5] Other forms of organization offer such substantial opportunities for abuse that the activities appear to be better undertaken without any explicit transaction or direct quid

---

2. For the development of early social sciences, see Haskell (1977); Ross (1991).

3. Stigler ([1961] 1968). Although Stigler's observation now seems like a commonplace even to economists, it struck the Nobel Committee as sufficiently momentous to be the centerpiece of Stigler's Nobel prize citation in 1982.

4. That is, information, like all other goods, is subject to diminishing returns at the margin.

5. See Johnson's essay (chap. 2) in this volume.

pro quo at all.[6] Management—in the whole breadth and variety the word conveys in a business school—emerges as an important activity.

In fact, the functions of management are visible at many different levels of business enterprises. There is an isomorphism between the process of making decisions at the level of hiring employees, managing subordinate business units, and deciding about the extent and financing of firms as a whole. The recognition of this commonality has sparked interest in the development of management tools and in the creation of a body of economic theory useful for thinking about this development.[7] There is a meeting ground in this intellectual endeavor for business historians who have long been interested in the questions of management and economists newly attentive to these questions.

There is also, however, a problem of communication—a problem of language. Business historians have adopted a literary style that is short on generalizations. Economists employ mathematics that assumes away details. These vernaculars obviously reflect the interests of the two groups. But they also create barriers to cross-fertilization. They promote insularity, even antagonism, between the two groups of scholars. Oliver Williamson has tried to bridge this gap in a series of discussions that have provided many of the terms that will be used here (1975, 1985). But traffic on this and other bridges has not been heavy as yet.

Economists writing about these issues, for example, are fond of referring to *principals* and *agents*. These are abstract terms designed to identify actors who stand in certain relations to one another, independent of the particular level or circumstances of their relationship. The principal is the manager, owner, or financier who has an asset he or she wants someone else to operate. The agent is the worker, manager, or owner who undertakes to act on the principal's behalf. The same individual may be principal in one transaction and agent in another. And in any given relationship both individuals, principal and agent alike, must be happy with the arrangement if it is to function well. These abstract claims represent the start of economic analysis, but also the outer bounds of traditional historians' interest. What do these abstractions have to do with any specific historical incident?

We contend that business historians and the new industrial organization theorists are looking—in the terms of the old story—at different parts of a common elephant. We believe that the analyses of each would benefit from a view of the animal as a whole. We cannot deliver such a view in any detail in an introductory essay. But we can offer some examples that strongly suggest there is indeed a single beast under scrutiny.

We do this by working through a series of historical examples that have

---

6. Coase (1937). In his analysis the choice is in effect either to buy a service on a market from a stranger whom you will never see again or to have it performed by your personal servant. The alternative to the open market rarely involves such an extreme of trustworthiness. The principle at issue is quite important, however. We develop it at some length in section 1.2.

7. On the new theory, see Levinthal (1988) and Holmstrom and Tirole (1989).

been carefully selected, ordered, and developed. Many of the episodes described below may well seem familiar. But the contexts in which we describe them and the emphases we place and questions we raise probably will not. One of our objectives in laying out the material in this way is to suggest, we hope seductively, a set of concepts business historians might use to organize their data. We feel confident that if they do this, they will reap better than they sow. (The proof of this, in the instance of this paper, will lie in the unexpectedness of our conclusions or the insights our arguments generate.)

Another objective is to encourage historians to turn up material that economists will find anomalous or otherwise beyond the scope of their familiar models. This should provide grist for the theorists' mills, or—to vary the metaphor—grit around which to make pearls. Such ongoing interactions, we feel, would be good for all parties concerned.[8]

Our examples illustrate three levels of managerial decisions: organizing the work of individuals, organizing whole production units, and organizing finance to pay for the enterprise as a whole. Our theme is that these are not in principle three disparate or even particularly distinct realms at all: the one single logic is working itself out, again and again, with only incidental variations. Our essay concludes with some ideas about fruitful ways of exploring the meaning and relevance of these parallels in particular cases.

## 1.2   Relationships with Individuals

We begin with the most familiar vertical relationships within the firm, that is, with workers and the structure of the employment relation. One respect in which labor—considered as a factor of production—is different from machines is that machines are designed to do nothing but perform some task or set of tasks. Once turned on, they steadily and consistently carry out the task. Their standard of performance may degrade over time as parts wear. If the energy supply is interrupted or some part suffers a catastrophic failure, the machine may stop entirely. But the motivation of the machine to do the work is never at issue. Roughly speaking, machines do as they are told. They never shirk. They never cheat. They never pursue their own interests.

It is not necessarily thus with people. One may think of human effort as an input to production and thus a good thing for the firm that employs it. But it is equally plausible that effort is, in the abstract, a bad thing for the employees. All other things being equal, most people would rather work less hard than more. They are not willing slaves. They look out for themselves. They certainly prefer their leisure to what they do to earn their living. This is why

---

8. For example, the economists' recent inside-the-firm and imperfect-competition literatures appear to have developed in isolation from one another. It is plausible that the solutions to the two problems might be connected in interesting ways. (For a hint, see Bernheim and Whinston 1985.) The theorists do not seem to know quite where to start in exploring this systematically (see Tirole 1988, 50–51). Historians could play a useful agenda-setting role by identifying and exploring a few really striking examples.

they are paid to do their work. They have their own preferences, and these are often not the same as those of their employers.

All this may seem obvious. But it develops interesting and sometimes subtle ramifications when it is costly for the employee's manager to know how well the employee's tasks have been executed and how diligently the employee's responsibilities have been executed. It may well be true that the workers on Henry Ford's assembly line—made vivid for us all in Chaplin's *Modern Times*—had very little scope for this sort of shirking.[9] But that was due to the experimental and self-consciously radical division of labor at Ford, which produced jobs of a degree of simplicity and monitorability unknown even in Ford's own industry today. Most production jobs in the economy then and now are not like that. Few managerial jobs have ever been. Generally speaking, where there is a job there is an agency problem.

The simplest example with which to begin analyzing agency problems and the significance of their solutions has been famous to economists from the days of Marshall's *Principles*. The subject is agricultural tenants who pay no set fee for the use of the land they farm, but instead give to the landlord a predetermined share of what they grow. Marshall writes that

> when the cultivator has to give to his landlord half of the returns to each dose of capital and labor that he applies to the land, it will not be in his interest to apply any doses the total return to which is less than twice enough to reward him. If . . . he is free to cultivate as he chooses, he will cultivate less intensively than [under a pure rental system]; he will apply only so much capital and labor as will give him returns more than twice enough to repay himself; so that his landlord will get a smaller share even of those returns than he would have on the plan of a fixed payment. (1961, 644)

The situation is that the landlord cannot work the land himself and needs to find someone else to do it for him. He is a principal in search of an agent. Yet he cannot continually stand over the agent, telling him how hard to work, how much fertilizer to apply, and so forth. The landlord—the principal—must employ a tenant—the agent—whose day-to-day actions he cannot observe and on whose day-to-day actions he depends for his income.

All is not lost for the landlord, however. The agent's inputs into the production process cannot be observed. But the process outputs can be observed, and, in Marshall's story, can be observed costlessly. The story is phrased in terms of a single period (one growing season, say). So the contract is set in terms of shares of the output—the harvest—at the end of the season. The problem is that the tenant, who gets to act independently once the period starts, will not want to invest as much of his energies and his wealth as the landlord would wish. The landlord will get something, but his asset will be underemployed.

---

9. See Raff (1991), especially chapters 3 and 5.

The tenant will make his decisions on the basis of his benefits and costs, and so ultimately on the prices and returns to effort that confront him. Only when the tenant's marginal incentives are the same as the owner's will the two want to make the same decisions. Only when both of these are undistorted will these decisions be the correct ones. The way for the landlord to bring about this desirable coordinated state of affairs (to get his asset exploited in an efficient way) is to charge the tenant a fixed rent for the use of the land, leaving the tenant free to capture all the marginal gains to investment and enterprise. The efficient contract sets the level of the rent so as to extract all the (expected) profits without undesirably distorting the tenant's decision making (Cheung 1969).

Marshall was interested in the divergent returns facing the two contracting parties. To focus on this, he set up his model abstracting away from almost all details of the common actual situation. In particular, he omitted some other important respects in which conflicts between the tenant and the landlord could appear. In the most obvious instance, he assumed—casually as it might seem—that both agent and principal knew exactly how much output there was to divide. However much output there was, it was with absolute certainty to be divided according to the initially agreed-upon rule. We now make the problem more complex by varying that assumption.

Consider instead what happens if the tenant can hide the results of a good year. (Consider, that is, what happens when the deterministic relationship between the farmer's effort and the size of the crop becomes uncertain and hard to verify.)[10] We focus on the verification problem.[11] The tenant might think that, since he works the land while the landlord sits by, he is entitled to the benefits of good rainfall. In the manner of taxpayers everywhere, he might not declare the whole of his output. The landlord, lacking accurate information, is at a disadvantage.

The extent of the landlord's vulnerability to self-serving underreporting depends upon the amount of uncertainty in the harvest. If harvests do not vary much from year to year, it will be difficult for the tenant to conceal very much: the landlord will have a fairly precise idea how big a harvest to expect. But if harvests vary a lot from year to year, then the opportunity for fraud is present.

In this context, partial payment creates a further wedge between the motivation of tenant and landlord. Just as in Marshall's original example, the sharing scheme creates inefficiencies. In this context, partial payment creates a new problem as well. How is the landlord to convince the tenant to be honest about his crop? He may need to break out of the simple share contract that Marshall described and design a new way of monitoring his tenant.

Marshall's assumption about the availability—more precisely, the relative

---

10. This situation has been explored systematically by Stiglitz (1974).

11. Most of the literature of the economic theory of agency focuses on the uncertainty and optimal risk-bearing arrangements.

costs—of different kinds of information was extreme. Once we get away from this, it becomes obvious that a landlord actually has many options open to him. He need not confine his attention to the output itself, but may look also at the acreage planted, the effort expended by his tenant, the materials used.[12] Each of these alternatives, of course, may be observable only with error as well. The landlord consequently has to compare the costs and the ultimate benefits of informing himself by different means.

Each of the landlord's alternatives creates a different incentive for the tenant. Faced with an output test, the tenant may hide his crop. Faced with a land or labor observation, he may sham working in order to fool the landlord. In this case, he is actually expending effort fooling the landlord that would be better spent farming. Monitoring schemes can do more than set up suboptimal incentives; they can set up perverse incentives.

This is peculiarly the case when long time periods are involved. Marshall considers only the yearly crop of the tenant farmer. But let us consider the incentives of the tenant to improve his land, by improving drainage or repairing buildings. The investment could be substantial, and the returns might only come over a long stretch of years.

If the tenant has only a yearly contract, he may not have any incentive to engage in a long-term investment. What is to keep the landlord from evicting him just as the improvements begin to improve the yield? How can he be assured of enjoying the fruits of his labor even in this indirect way?

There are again many options. The landlord might require improvements as part of the yearly contract. He could, under certain circumstances, offer the tenant a long-term lease.[13] He might pay the tenant at the time of investment for the time and materials used to upgrade the irrigation system or buildings. Each of these alternatives, as before, has its costs to the landlord and incentives for the tenant. Both aspects need to be considered in choosing or evaluating a contract.

These considerations apply as well to the development of human capital. Stepping outside Marshall's farming example, an employer may want her employees to engage in self-improvement. She may want her workers to engage in activities that will bring returns to the company only after several years. The timing problem is exactly the same as the landlord-tenant problem with fixed capital. But the intensity of effort and the effects of education are harder to observe than the repair of buildings. The problem, in other words, is doubly difficult. The activities in the present are hard to observe, and the results of these actions come only in the future.

12. Levinthal (1988) identifies and analyzes three distinct strategies for reducing these agency costs. They are improved accounting (i.e., measurement), long-term contracts between principal and agent, and competition among agents (i.e., rank-order compensation). There are business-history examples of each of these in our text and in the other papers in this volume.

13. This, to draw out the point of the preceding footnote, is an example of moving towards the first-best by developing a long-term relationship between principal and agent that allows future rewards for present good behavior. We explore this option further below.

Any owner therefore faces a problem of motivating his or her employees or agents. This problem is most intense when uncertainty is high, monitoring is expensive, and observable outcomes are delayed. It is the function of managers—the modern counterparts to Marshall's landowner—to design compensation schemes that are appropriate to the particular structure of costs and incentives faced by the various parties engaged in production.

One historic pattern in compensation schemes for blue-collar employees exposes the result of this kind of managerial design. It is a particularly interesting example because the sort of systematic, explicit reasoning about costs and alternatives we have been developing explains coherently a set of institutions that otherwise seem entirely capricious.

The story begins with a puzzling fact. There were many manufacturing firms circa 1900 that employed both men and women. The men were far more likely to be paid via time rates and the women by piece rates than vice versa. Why should this have been so?

It emerges upon investigation that the bulk of the jobs in question posed monitoring and incentive problems of the sorts outlined above.[14] When output is easily measurable, as it tended to be in these jobs, a formally simple solution to the shirking problem is to pay by piece rates and simply monitor output.[15] This links compensation to effort in a fairly direct way. It typically is a lot cheaper than intensive monitoring of the effort inputs. The problem is that piece-rate schemes are nonetheless costly to administer. Someone has to count the output.

We have a conflict here. The obvious way to respond to the difference between workers' and managers' objectives creates administrative costs. Managers naturally would prefer to solve the incentive problem without incurring large costs. One alternative was to pay time rates rising over time and to pose—through periodic spot-checks of various sorts—some threat of firing before the rates had risen as high as they eventually would. The employer, in other words, offered deferred compensation for hard work. Monitoring would be spread out over a long time, reducing its cost. It might even be done by evaluating relative performance, further reducing the expense.[16] The rising pay scale would provide a way of motivating each hour of work without monitoring each item produced.

This might seem to suggest that all employees would be paid on the same scheme. But that would follow only if all employees could offer a long-term

14. Goldin (1986) gives facts and a detailed analysis.
15. It is characteristic of the sort of jobs we are discussing, as it is of all jobs implicitly described in the economists' literature on compensation schemes, that the more output any particular worker produces, the better off the employer is. When outputs are complementary, this may not be not so. In that case, when workers produce output in an unsynchronized way, downstream employees, capital, and work in process will stand idle. This is wasteful and may be very expensive (see Raff 1988).
16. We assume that workers do not collude. Allowing worker solidarity introduces another level of complexity to the analysis.

relationship to the firm in which the incentive of deferred compensation would have some meaning. Women were systematically different from men in this regard. Their employment was affected by changes in their marital status and by childbearing: at the turn of the century, women were in and out of employment due to the biological and social impacts of reproduction. A deferred compensation scheme did not provide a way to motivate effort on the job for most women because most women would leave a job before the full bargain could be played out. Managers therefore used a rising time-rate pay scale when they could—with typical male employees—and more costly piece rates when they could not. The observed gender difference in pay modes was the result.[17]

A similar story, with interesting additional elements, can be told about the new executive bonus scheme introduced in the General Motors Corporation by Alfred Sloan in 1923. The basic problem and the basic solution idea will be familiar. The motivational mismatch Sloan confronted derives from the existence of firm-specific (or, more generally, transaction-specific) assets.[18] The assets in question are individuals' knowledge specific to a particular firm's operations and markets. Just as Marshall's landlord wanted tenants to use the land and Goldin's managers wanted workers to expend their effort, Sloan sought to induce managers to exploit these assets for GM's benefit. The question to bear in mind is how the mismatch between GM's and the managers' interests might best be accommodated, given that the mismatch problem cannot simply be wished away.

The salient facts are as follows.[19] GM had been operated as a holding company for some time. Roughly from its inception through the end of the war, executives had been paid salaries plus bonuses that were related to the performance of their particular division of the corporation. This naturally encouraged them to make their decisions with principal reference to the fortunes of their own division. There were circumstances, however, in which such decisions might undermine the prosperity of the corporation as a whole.

The first revision of this scheme was, then, to relate bonuses to corporate rather than divisional performance and to pay them out only when corporate performance was above a stated acceptable minimum. But the compensation still remained entirely a current transaction.

Excessive inventory commitments coincided with a downswing in the business cycle in 1920. The viability of the corporation as a whole was threatened, albeit briefly. Sloan's solution to this problem was to create a centralized corporate staff to plan and coordinate financial commitments and long-term investments. He created this staff and began to reorganize the way GM con-

---

17. Discrimination, of course, may provide another explanation. See Lazear (1979) for a different implication of the possibility of long-term contracts.

18. Becker developed these ideas in his "Investment in Human Capital" (1962). We develop the idea of assets being specific to a transaction or a firm at greater length in section 1.3.

19. This account follows Sloan (1964).

ducted its business to bring long-run planning into the forefront of managerial consideration. The creation of a corporate staff was crucial to the process, but the staff had to be motivated to place GM's interests first. Sloan implemented a significant change to the bonus scheme to solve this problem.

The change involved setting up the Managers Security Company. The Du Pont company, then and for many years thereafter the largest single share-holder in GM, made a large block of shares available for sale to this new entity. The Managers Security Company was, from time to time and as exec-utive performances dictated, to makes its own shares available for sale to the corporate executives. Inducing the managers to hold their wealth in GM equity would in itself have given them the sort of longer-term interest in over-all corporate performance the shareholders had. But Sloan produced two twists that made this much more pronounced. The executives bought the stock on margin: they paid only a fraction of the market value of the shares up front and paid off the rest over time. They agreed to pay off the balance through future bonuses they might earn. And the shares they purchased, though these had all the attributes of ordinary GM shares, were not in fact tradable assets. There were not even procedures in place for managers to voluntarily sell out their positions. In short, the investment was on generous terms. But it could only be liquidated with the approval and assistance of GM.[20]

The reorganization plan created a group of tasks whose successful execu-tion would be crucial to the corporation's short-term viability and long-term success. The jobs involved some novelty, considerable difficulty, substantial monitoring problems, and very long-term consequences for the shareholders. Sloan's 1923 plan gave those who were in a position to carry the tasks out a pronounced long-term interest in seeing to it that the return on invested capital exceeded what the shareholders regarded as an acceptable minimum.

From the perspective of Marshall's landlord, experienced tenant farmers from a given region were probably more or less perfect substitutes. From the perspective of the owners of GM, there were no outside perfect substitutes for these men who came to know much more than anyone else did about the im-portant novelties of running the GM business. As one might therefore expect, participation in the plan was not open to all employees of the corporation or even to all executives. It was restricted to "top" executives who were expected to see out their careers with the firm. When Sloan spoke later in the decade of the scheme, with pride, as having created more than a few millionaires, it seems clear that the main group of employees he had in mind were these sen-ior members of the corporate staff.[21] By comparison, individual blue-collar

20. Even John Raskob, a top GM official who had been for many years previously a senior and trusted officer at Du Pont, discovered this when he wanted to leave GM in 1928. He owned nearly $20 million of the nontraded Managers Security Company shares and had to write, formally and as supplicant, to get these turned into securities he could trade on a market (see Kuhn 1986, 163).

21. It is an interesting but separate question whether it was efficient to offer the possibility of wealth on this scale.

employees had nothing unusual to offer the company. They had no long-lived and difficult-to-replace productive asset, and they could offer no services the corporation could not obtain competitively elsewhere.[22] Unless their cooperation became in itself an important asset, the corporation had no reason to pay them any more than the best they could earn elsewhere. Until that came about, though the company prospered, employees were not particularly well paid even within their industry. When it came about, both relationships changed.[23]

These two examples show the principal-agent problem in a simple form. The principals are the employers; the agents, employees at different levels. The problem in each case was what economists call "shirking." This may have been actual shirking in the case of factory pieceworkers. The term, however, is used to refer to any divergence of interest between the principal and agent. In the case of GM, Sloan was not trying to make his managers work harder. He was trying to align their incentives with the enterprise's objectives. "Shirking" in this context means playing for your own or your own division's gain, not the corporation's.

### 1.3   Relationships with Groups

Our discussion thus far has focused on relations between owner/managers and single employees, that is, on the simplest sorts of organizations. But the sorts of considerations we highlighted also bear on optimal designs for complex organizations. They can be observed at work in historical evolution of such designs, and they can be used to assess the wisdom of particular decisions effecting organizational change (see Chandler 1977).

Expanding our horizons adds additional dimensions to the decisions under study. For the issue is not simply how to align incentives between principal and agent, but also whether to use an agent at all. We assumed in the last section that the decision to hire farmers, workers, and managers had already been made. Here we ask also whether activities should be structured within the business enterprise or belong to the relations between firms.

The limits of the firm can be explored in two dimensions: horizontal and vertical. Horizontal integration refers to the inclusion of many similar elements in a single enterprise. Vertical integration refers to the inclusion of different stages of production within a firm: the "make or buy" decision. We provide two examples of each in turn.

In each case, one example is historical and illustrates the growth or restructuring of a large corporation. The other example is drawn from more recent

22. One sees the same sort of concerns at work in the structure of compensation contract in start-up companies backed by venture capitalists. (See Raff and Crocombe 1989.) Managers carrying heavy and difficult-to-monitor responsibilities are paid relatively heavily, and sometimes even predominantly, in shares and options. Managers in more routine jobs are not.

23. For evidence that this was in fact what the corporation did, see Raff (1989, section 4). Presumably the same obtained for lower-level managers. No data seem to have survived with which one could test the claim.

experience and explores the way in which some firms relinquish activities. Since business history is so often the history of successful enterprises, we have to draw on recent experience for examples of companies that are, in some sense, too big.

Around the turn of the century, it became common to find manufacturing firms that were horizontal conglomerates. The enterprises these corporations owned were diverse as well as complex. Furthermore, the performance of the several component parts was interrelated, not least because there was a common pool of capital and a common credit rating. Since generally speaking there are limits to information-processing capacity, this meant that the owners of the firm and even the managers were in roughly the same situation as Marshall's landowners: they couldn't know as much as they would like—and be able to monitor as well as they would wish—all the operational decision-makers.[24] So whatever the advantages, easily realized or merely potential, behind the new, broader grouping, it posed serious problems of control and motivation.

The common form of organization appropriate to simpler organizations was strictly functional. There was a division responsible for engineering (i.e., design of products and manufacturing processes), for manufacturing, for sales, and for finance (i.e., raising working and investment capital). So long as the shareholders—or at least the top managers—grasped all the major details of the business and the operating circumstances, it was possible for them to assess directly how well all the employees were doing their jobs and to reward them in a way that motivated them to continue or improve as appropriate.

Once the operations grew diverse and complicated, this ceased being possible. In particular, it became extremely difficult to tell whether corporate resources were being used efficiently. Not very much information was available to top managers and shareholders. The information they could easily obtain had too little structure to be very useful. For example, suppose one could actually assess on some absolute scales the average quality of the performances of the engineering group and that of the marketing group. How were they to be weighted against one another in a way that gave their employees helpful incentives?

All this became very obvious to the owners of GM during the inventory crisis of 1920 to which we have referred above. The organization they had invested in so heavily was a sort of holding company of divisions rather than a unitary functionally organized entity (see Williamson 1975, 143–44). But

24. This situation was exacerbated by the absence of helpful accounting conventions and, until the Securities and Exchange Commission Act of 1934, of any statutory obligation to publish even annual balance sheets. There was, of course, some incentive to publish some accounting information in hopes of attracting investors. The scale of fraud in such matters in the 1920s suggests the potential for moral hazard in this situation.

Roe (1990) discusses how various legal changes in the 1930s discouraged active shareholder monitoring even as more information became available.

its divisions were uncoordinated, undirected, and scarcely monitored. There was no systematic financial reporting. Many factory managers were in a position to commit the firm's resources to capital and materials expenditure—indeed, even to executive compensation—without any sort of real coordination or control. When the depression of 1920 struck, the firm was badly overextended. When the new owners wanted to rationalize resource use, they found they had very little appropriate and usable data.

The solution put forward was to restructure operations and information flows so that the firm became tautly divisionalized. That is, it became a collection of divisions, each with its own products, organized internally along functional lines, and substantially self-contained, all formally as before—save for finance. There would be a sort of internal capital market to carry out and monitor resource allocation, and a corporate staff was created with the main tasks of performing the monitoring (via regular and frequent calculations of return on corporate investment in the individual entities) and of planning long-term competitive strategy (i.e., making decisions that implicated future investment plans). Divisional managers were responsible for groups of operations that they could understand and assess. Now their own performance was given a common scale (Johnson and Kaplan 1987, 93–123), and the GM stockholders (or at least those acting in their stead) could compare the performance of Chevrolet and Oldsmobile managers, rewarding the managers and allocating capital appropriately.

All this raises an intriguing question. William C. Durant has often casually been said to have bequeathed this slack divisional form to GM because he liked buying companies but was uninterested in running them. After all, incumbent management was perfectly happy to continue doing that. Perhaps this was indeed Durant's psychological quirk. But he was an active investor. Du Pont bought into GM as a passive investment. The Du Pont executives do not appear to have valued the investment in terms of the personal satisfaction that interfering in GM's affairs might yield. Why then did it make sense for them to keep all these operations grouped together in a single giant enterprise? Why did they not seek to break up GM and select which units of the business they wished to own or control?

Horizontal disintegration would have offered an opportunity to shed risk specific to GM and its particular businesses. The du Ponts and their colleagues might have preferred a more diversified portfolio of investments. And they always could replicate the pattern of the risks and returns offered by their original GM interests by buying and selling shares of the disintegrated component companies on a competitive securities market. By keeping GM unitary, they constrained themselves to owning a controlling interest in all the subsidiary auto companies. They forswore the advantages of making individual investment decisions in order—we presume—to take advantage of other opportunities.

We can, of course, only speculate as to their reasons. But we can speculate in a structured way. Suppose we start from the assumption that investors want in some general sense to maximize the return on their investment.[25] It is then natural to infer that the Du Pont group felt a strategy of horizontal disintegration would not realize the same value. Why might this have been? On the one hand, perhaps there were simply limits to abilities of the mass of Wall Street investors to understand the value of individual firms' long-term investment programs. This does not seem a strong argument, at least on a priori grounds: why should their analytical skills and those of their advisors have been dramatically less good than those of the du Ponts' private investment advisors? On the other hand, it is plausible to suspect that the Du Pont group saw or expected to realize economies of scope from joint operation (see Raff 1989). They thought that the sort of managerial skills and discipline required to run a large, complex manufacturing enterprise were scarce (that is, that the right sort of managers were a scarce resource), that they possessed on their staff in Wilmington some of the right sort of managers, and that they could use their influence in the GM boardroom to move these managers into GM.[26] Perhaps, that is, they had reasons for believing their employees would run the companies more efficiently than those who would otherwise do so.[27]

Issues of control at the plant level are more complex than at the individual level. In addition to the principal-agent problems discussed above, problems of synergy also arise. It is only worth designing appropriate incentive schemes, after all, if there are benefits to be reaped from joint activity.[28] The problems of principles and agents need to be placed in the context of control over specific assets.

The recent experiences of the Canadian entrepreneur Robert Campeau seem to expose, at least in the short run, the costs of joint operation. Campeau came to public attention as a man who had made a considerable fortune in real estate development. He also had established a beachhead in retailing.[29] He observed that a number of major American department store chains were up for sale through the sale of their holding company, Federated Department Stores. There were many common suppliers among these retail outlets. (In fact, there were even a considerable number of common products offered for sale.) The marketing strategies of the stores were in some cases competitive where head-on competition did not seek to maximize joint profits. Each chain also paid considerable sums for overhead expenses duplicated at every other division. Given the tax code, many of the individual stores were sitting on land that would be more valuable to other owners. Campeau also saw profit opportuni-

25. This seems historically apt. Consider the account of the Du Pont board's discussion of the initial GM investment in Chandler and Salsbury (1971).
26. Again, see ibid.
27. Appropriate compensation was needed, of course, to induce these managers to perform. This was discussed in section 1.2.
28. The benefits, of course, need to be net of any costs.
29. The most notable vehicle for the presence in retailing was Campeau's purchase of the Allied Stores group in 1986.

ties in malls. Once the Campeau Corporation added the Federated group to its Allied Stores, it would control a large fraction of the department store chains prominent enough to anchor suburban malls. Campeau hoped to use this position to extract equity from mall owners and to obtain more favorable rental terms.

It is characteristic of several of these items that the incentives facing managers of the isolated stores or groups of stores would lead to less profitable plans than would the incentives facing the managers of the whole. Joint profits would be higher if actions could be coordinated and centralized than if they were designed independently and competitively.

Most of these sorts of economies were increasing in the size of the venture. Campeau was a wealthy man, but his resources certainly would not stretch to simply buying Federated out of pocket. The American financial markets had recently become amenable to buying bonds issued to finance such transactions, providing another avenue toward unified operations. Campeau could buy the stores at a price greater than they were worth to their current owners (as they currently understood how to run the business) if he could borrow the money. This would, of course, commit him to regular payments to the lenders. The idea was to finance these payments out of the increased profits from the realized economies of common management.

Campeau attempted to buy the stores in 1988. He got involved in a bidding war. He did in the end succeed in purchasing the stores, but as a result of the bidding he paid a hefty price. His ability to meet the coupon on the bonds sold to cover this price turned on two factors. The first was that gross sales for the group would continue to increase at something like 5 percent per annum. The second was that the forecast economies of overhead reduction and economies of superior purchasing and planning procedures could be realized essentially immediately.

It appears that Campeau's calculations of the value and cash flows of the conglomerate firm—which were the ultimate basis of the price Campeau offered and the interest he was prepared to pay—estimated these joint economies without analyzing precisely how and when they would be generated. The most striking example is informational. The different department store chains each had idiosyncratic management information (i.e., computer control) systems. Configuring these to give top management integrated data on inventories and sales at the level of detail needed to bargain with suppliers was a project of massive proportions. The economies would be unavailable in the absence of such an investment in the infrastructure of information. Under pressure for short-term cash, Campeau instead squeezed the relevant budgets. His managers consequently were preoccupied with short-run survival, not long-run investments in information retrieval. Unsurprisingly, the economies that might have followed from common ordering were not rapidly forthcoming. Other projected overhead economies seem to have been equally unrealizable in the short run.

In the fall of 1989, the Campeau Corporation was in the news again. First cash flow problems were rumored. Then some of the company's suppliers expressed hesitation at extending trade credit. This was an extremely serious threat, given that the goods in question were for the Christmas trade. For department stores, the months preceding Christmas are the most sales-extensive period of the year. For a store to run out of money and therefore trade credit and therefore goods to sell in this period would spell complete commercial disaster.

Federated had initially been a profitable going concern. If it had remained independent, its managers would have taken care to have the cash and credit for Christmas, anticipating the familiar yearly cycle. As part of the Campeau firm, however, the Federated cash could be taken for other purposes. Campeau, optimistic about realizing the scale economies, took the cash to pay the interest on his bonds. He left the stores and their managers in the lurch. Alas, they lurched back at him.

Sales growth, always uncertain, emerged distinctly lower than expected, as the economy proved sluggish in 1989. There were no substantial cost reductions to cushion the blow. (Operations did not get more expensive, but they did not get cheaper as fast as Campeau and his bankers had been counting on.) The real estate deals contemplated were complex and required careful negotiation, and the whole project fell apart long before any opportunities arose to exploit the undervalued real estate. The point of the Campeau story, at least up to its moment of crisis, is that the existence of horizontal scope economies does not mean that their extent is unlimited or their timing wholly flexible. Abstract incentives are not everything: it only makes sense to talk about incentives in a particular informational context. Information, as we have stressed, is available only at a cost. In this case, it would take a considerable investment in order to make the cost manageable. Given the price Campeau had to pay, the optimal horizontal boundaries of a retailing firm were not obviously larger than those of Allied or Federated Department Stores, the economies of joint operations and assets notwithstanding.

Unlike the GM example, Campeau's experience appears to reveal the absence of incentives to integrate horizontally. We turn now to the problem of vertical integration, where we pose the same sorts of questions.

Firms constantly face the "make or buy" decision. Needing various products as inputs or various services as aids to merchandising, firms have to decide whether to purchase them in the market or produce them themselves. There are distinctive features in each case, of course. But the general problem is obvious. Any business person needs to have a source of supply of inputs to his or her productive process. (He or she also needs outlets, and the problem is symmetrical for "upstream" and "downstream" transactions.) It often makes sense to rely on the market for these inputs. But there are conditions under which the market does not work well. In such a case, it makes sense to make rather than buy the input.

As in the previous examples, these conditions feature uncertainty in a central role. Information is incomplete, and private incentives may be divergent in uncertain conditions. Vertical integration involves transactions whose effects will be realized only over time, and so involve some ex ante uncertainty, just as in the examples of employees at the turn of the century and department stores now. Vertical integration also involves assets specific to the transactions in question, as in the example of GM's management incentives.

The modern economist's theory of vertical integration has as its centerpiece a concept of idiosyncratic assets, that is, assets whose uses are specific to certain transactions. A careful definition may be helpful. An asset is said to be transaction-specific to the extent it has lower value in any other use (Klein, Crawford, and Alchian 1978). As we argued above, for example, long-time top managers have skills and knowledge specific to their companies and jobs, while relatively unskilled workers do not. This distinction turns out to make equally incisive sense applied to inanimate assets.[30]

If production costs would be increased by forgoing the use of a transaction-specific asset with one or the other of these attributes, then the owner of the specific asset acquires power. When there are many people involved, this is called market power. When there are only a few, it often is termed hold-up power. Given the durable nature of the asset, this power could be exploited opportunistically once the capital was in use. To avoid such a state of affairs, the buyer of the services of the specialized asset would have to have a complete contract, that is, one in which provisions had been made for all conceivable eventualities. It is very difficult and expensive to write such contracts. People cannot process all the information needed to formulate such a document in an uncertain world. And even if they could, the time needed to write it, negotiate it, and—if need be—contest it after the fact would be horrendous. When the use of a specific asset is indicated, therefore, some sort of integration is indicated.[31]

Chandler's celebrated account of Swift's successful introduction of centralized modern meat packing illustrates the main point vividly. Before the 1880s

---

30. Three distinct kinds of physical asset specificity have been identified by Williamson (see Williamson 1985, 95–96). The first is locational. The second is the ex ante specificity of the purpose-built capital good. The final type includes those assets that do not have any unique aspects ex ante, but that become dedicated to a particular use. (It will be noted that these categories are not necessarily mutually exclusive.)

31. Statistical tests have confirmed the relationship between transaction specificity of assets and various forms of vertical integration. Monteverde and Teece (1982) report that automobile companies were more likely to integrate backward into the production of components if engineering was important or if the item was made by a single supplier. Masten (1984) discovered that aerospace components were more likely to be made internally if they were highly specialized and complex. Joskow (1985) found that vertical integration between electric utilities and coal mines was much more likely for mine-mouth generating plants than for others. In each case, variables indexing transaction specificity significantly affected the decision whether to obtain the desired products through the market or internally. These three examples illustrate the importance of human capital, physical capital, and site specificity, respectively.

fresh meat went east "on the hoof." Animals were shipped live to local slaughterhouses and sold fresh to urban consumers. The animals' rail journey was stressful and resulted in massive losses of weight. There was a clear gain to be had if some way could be discovered to supply fresh meat without shipping live animals.

The modern refrigerated railroad car was invented in 1881.[32] This made it possible to slaughter animals in the West—that is, Chicago—and ship the meat east. But how was the transition to centralized packing to take place? Would there be market transactions? Would railroads sell refrigerated freight services to meat packers or shippers? Would Chicago meat packers sell dressed meat to wholesalers who would transport and sell it in the East?

The refrigerated freight car in the early 1880s was designed to carry perishable goods, and it was in addition the only way to transport such goods from Chicago to New York or Boston. It was an asset specific to this sort of transaction. It was of markedly less value in any other use, and the cost of shipping dressed meat was higher—much higher—by any other facility.

How would a market for refrigerated freight services have worked under these conditions? The answer clearly is badly. The railroads had only minor interest in Swift's business; they had many, many other customers to consider. Given the transaction-specificity of refrigerated cars, a market in their services would have been a bilateral monopoly. There would have been ample scope for bargaining, exploitation, and double-crossing on both sides. Potential entrants into either the refrigerated freight market or the meat-packing business would have been able to anticipate these problems. They would have been discouraged from entering. Even if the potential for bad bargains could have been eliminated by a contract or understanding, the cost of negotiating a suitable arrangement would have been daunting.

Swift's innovation was to create an integrated enterprise that both slaughtered and distributed meat. He expanded the boundaries of his firm to include the functions of shipping and storing dressed meat, that is, to include all the transaction-specific capital. Instead of trying to buy refrigerated freight services from the railroads, he built and operated his own freight cars. Instead of hiring a firm to use these cars to distribute his meat, he included a distribution function within his firm. Instead of relying on the market to buy ice for his refrigerated cars, he built ice stations along the way.[33]

This last, apparently minor, detail of Swift's operation exposes the point clearly. Ice, after all, does not seem to possess the qualities listed above to make an asset transaction-specific. But Swift could not rely on independent suppliers to provide ice at the time and place he needed. And the cost to him

---

32. It may strike the reader that the passive voice here suppresses the detail of what might be an interesting historical process. But our interest lies in the use of the innovation, not its genesis.

33. One might well ask why Swift did not buy the railroads. Efficiently operated railroads had other valuable uses, and we imagine the purchase cost and the costs of operating such a diversified enterprise would have been greater than the benefits in question here.

of being without ice at that time and place was very great. It was not just the cost of any spoiled meat, but also the damage to the nascent market for his meat from a shortage of supply or a shipment of spoiled meat. Swift could be held up by the owner of an icehouse who had the only ice in the neighborhood. Swift avoided this potential conflict by expanding his firm to the point at which he incorporated all the assets specific to his central activity.[34]

The refrigerated cars were specialized capital goods. The degree of their specialization gave them a great deal of transaction specificity. They illustrate the effect of asset specificity in a dedicated use. An icehouse could be located anywhere. But once it was cited, it became specific to the users in that location. Given a single large user like Swift, the potential for hold-ups was great. As Chandler has written, "the refrigerator car . . . was not the reason Swift became the innovator in high-volume, year-round production of perishable products" (1977, 299). Swift was a successful pioneer, Chandler writes, because he expanded strategically the operations of his meat-packing firm.

A recent episode may balance the historical account of Swift. The issue in this case was disintegration rather than expansion. As before, the choice was where to draw the boundaries of an enterprise, but now within the preexisting boundaries of the firm.

The example concerns the choices made by Charles Brown and the top administration of AT&T on the eve of the agreement to dismantle the Bell System. These men were thinking about the optimal configuration of their firm. They had to make an explicit choice because the historical boundaries of the company were no longer politically viable. AT&T was just too big. The firm's leadership therefore found itself in late 1981 under considerable pressure to decide which of several downsizing alternatives would be best for the firm.[35]

AT&T in 1981 was both an operating and a holding company. It provided long-distance telephone service directly through its Long Lines department. It owned the Bell operating companies (BOCs) that furnished local telephone service. It also owned Western Electric, which manufactured equipment used by AT&T and the BOCs, and Bell Labs, which supplied research and development (R&D) to Western Electric and the Bell System.

The managers' alternatives quickly came down to two. A "horizontal" divestiture would keep AT&T and the upstream Western Electric and Bell Labs together but sever the (horizontal) relationship between AT&T and the BOCs. A "vertical" divestiture would spin off Western Electric and Bell Labs from the providers of telephone service, AT&T and the BOCs. The government in an earlier antitrust suit against Western Electric had tried to effect a vertical divestiture. The suit had been resolved by the 1956 consent decree that left AT&T's structure intact but forced Western Electric to freely license its technology. AT&T's leadership feared in 1981 that Judge Harold H. Greene, who

---

34. See Kujovich (1970). Yates (1986) would term the ice time-specific as well as location-specific assets.
35. On all of this, see Temin (1987).

would decide the antitrust case then coming to a close, was sympathetic to the goals of the earlier suit. They resolved to make the choice themselves first.

AT&T's vertical integration dated from the early 1880s, the same time as Swift's. AT&T's market position was based on its patents on telephone sets. It needed a supply of telephones in order to extend its market and to earn revenue. Bell tried initially to license manufacturers, but this system broke down quickly as the interests of Bell and the manufacturers diverged. Once having tooled up to produce telephones, the manufacturers wanted to cut prices, expand, and sell to everyone.

These manufacturing plants had acquired transaction-specific assets as a result of their dedication to manufacturing for a sole purchaser. Initially general manufacturers, they came into a position of bilateral monopoly with Bell as a result of acquiring licenses and specialized technology. The result was conflict, bargaining, and nonadherence to the license agreements. AT&T decided that it would be cheaper to have direct control over the transaction-specific manufacturing assets. It acquired Western Electric and made it the sole source of supply for the Bell System (see Smith 1985).

AT&T's horizontal structure had evolved in the early years of the twentieth century in response to the transaction specificity of telephone equipment in use. Telephones and telephone switchboards, after all, are used for communicating with other telephones and switchboards. Midwestern companies kept installing party lines because they were initially cheaper, even though AT&T was trying to set uniform standards and phase out party lines. Improvements in telephone systems were not adopted uniformly. AT&T's management therefore decided to go to a system of wholly owned subsidiaries in order to avoid these problems of partial integration with asset specificity. Like the employers of men around 1900, they found that a long-term arrangement minimized the cost of control (Garnet 1985; Lipartitio 1989).

These transaction specificities were still present in 1981. Local telephone companies still interfaced with each other and Long Lines. Western Electric still made all the equipment they used, while Bell Labs had since the interwar period provided the Bell System's R&D. Which putative markets could work the best?

AT&T's management had little doubt that the market for telephone equipment could not work well. If Western Electric was to become a separate company, the old problems of patent control and uncertain supply would reemerge. The R&D done by Bell Labs was highly specific to the manufacturing done at Western Electric. The managers thought that a future AT&T dependent on the market for its equipment would be at a competitive disadvantage. They thought they needed to control their supply in order to continuously adapt to changing needs. In contrast, they reasoned that the problems of asset specificity in the telephone network had decreased as a result of both the establishment of a uniform technology and installed equipment base and by the growth of regulation.

A little reflection on transaction specificity suggests that this conclusion of

AT&T's management was probably not economically optimal. Many firms were already manufacturing telephone equipment in the 1970s. AT&T's patents had been licensed under the 1956 consent decree, and large parts of the market for equipment had been opened up by Federal Communications Commission (FCC) actions. In addition, the technology of telecommunications was undergoing a radical transformation. The electromechanical switches that had been the basis of Western Electric's success were being phased out in favor of electronic switches, and metallic cables were being replaced by fiber optics. Western Electric had been slow to enter the world of digital electronic switches in the 1970s. It is not clear that the Western Electric assets had much useful transaction specificity left by 1981.[36]

Turning to AT&T's horizontal integration, the process of divesting revealed clearly the transaction specificity of telephone switches. In fact, it became a make-or-break issue in the negotiations for divestiture. The Department of Justice was worried that the switches interfacing local and long-distance calls were too specific to AT&T's operations and would impose additional costs on Long Lines' competitors. It took a flurry of last-minute bargaining to work out a solution that would not allow the divested AT&T to benefit from the transaction specificity of the earlier investments. AT&T took a multibillion dollar write-off shortly after divestiture to pay for the cost of disentangling the human and physical capital of the Bell System (Tunstall 1985).

This surely is a paradox. The theory of transaction-specific assets indicates a clear choice for a vertical divestiture. Yet Brown and the other managers of AT&T never spent time even considering it. They were so convinced of the opposite that they never even studied the choice. Their strong conviction therefore cries out for an explanation.

AT&T's leaders thought the costs of horizontal divestiture were worth incurring for three reasons. As we have said already, they overestimated the asset specificity in Western Electric. They looked back at the historical source of their electromechanical equipment, rather than to future supplies of electronic fixtures. They also relied on continuing regulation of the BOCs to prevent the exercise of monopoly power by the local exchange carriers. And they had by 1981 to consider the political as well as the economic implications of any agreement. Relinquishing Western Electric would have reduced AT&T's size only by one-fifth; spinning off the BOCs reduced it by two-thirds. Having politicized the discussion of the firm by introducing a well-publicized but ill-fated bill into Congress, AT&T's leadership was forced to take dramatic action to head off drastic legislative action.

The concept of transaction specificity is a useful tool for the analysis of

---

36. Bell Labs' assets were more specific to AT&T's needs, and AT&T's managements were concerned to maintain their R&D edge. They argued that Bell Labs without Western Electric could not function. This is a harder argument to evaluate because the process of R&D is largely hidden from view. But the steady flow of significant telecommunications innovations from small companies supports the inference that here too AT&T management overestimated the amount of transaction specificity.

business decisions about the extent of firms, but it has its limitations. It provides a framework within which to ask questions about the effects of costly information. It directs attention to conditions where divergent interests can impose costs on operations. It provides a way to generalize the questions of control and motivation from individuals to organizational business units.

But how should we react when the theory predicts one kind of institutional arrangement, and historical managers choose another? Like the other concepts described here, the transaction specificity of key assets cannot predict business history, even though it has some predictive power at the industry level. In any individual case, it is not the only factor. It often is an important one, however, in the history of large and complex firms. And when, as in the case of AT&T, managers go against the tide of transaction specificity, the theory suggests either that noneconomic or nonrational considerations are involved. In the case of divestiture, other factors can easily be identified. They were the congressional bill to tighten regulation of AT&T that was in a horse race with the antitrust case to break the company up and nostalgia for the electro-mechanical past in which Western Electric was the centerpiece of AT&T's patent monopoly and then system integration.

The problems of control seen in the principal-agent relationship at the individual level have reemerged at the business unit level. The problems of reporting and investment that were at issue with individuals are equally difficult at the activity or plant level. We have in this section turned our attention from the design of arrangements for control discussed in section 1.2 to the question of whether to seek or maintain control at all. These questions are intimately related. For only if the incentives are appropriate at the individual level will economies of integration appear, as Campeau discovered when his divisions resisted his attempts to integrate their operations. And only if there are transaction-specific assets will it be worthwhile to design complex solutions to the principal-agent problem, as Sloan understood.

## 1.4  Relationships with Entire Enterprises

Having progressed from individuals to business units, it is time to go to the firm as a whole. Up to now, managers have been the principals who were analogous to Marshall's landowner. They had to deal with their agents, employees, or subordinate managers. Now, when the whole firm is in view, managers become the agents of the suppliers of capital. These suppliers may be owners who possess equity in companies, or they may be renters who lend money to firms, that is, bondholders.

The questions here are the same as before. Will principals choose to employ agents? If so, how will the principals motivate their agents? What kind of financial arrangements can reduce the costs of the interaction between the principals and agents? And, for business historians, how can managers get caught by injudicious bargains or inefficient financial arrangements?

The analysis of industrial finance in the last generation has been dominated by the Modigliani-Miller theorem asserting that the value of a firm should be independent of the structure of its financial commitments.[37] The basic Modigliani-Miller argument, which is related to one we invoked in a heuristic way above, was that different financial structures would indeed influence the riskiness of the firm's shares, but that investors cared about the riskiness of their overall portfolio rather than that of the individual underlying assets. They could achieve whatever level of overall risk they wanted by undertaking the appropriate borrowing and portfolio diversification. In doing this, they could in effect undo any unwanted risk taken on by individual firms' managers. Thus the mix of securities issued by a firm would not matter for its value: increased idiosyncratic riskiness would not make investors pay less for the shares.[38]

The assumptions behind this argument paralleled the common assumptions about competition more generally in the old-style microeconomic theory. Just as ignorance was ruled out in ordinary trades, bankruptcy—the inability to make transactions that resolve conflicts without bringing in third parties—was ruled out here. There was no risk of discontinuous losses. And assets were all traded on markets big enough for the price to be independent of the actions of any individual. There were no new and untried financial instruments. There was no private placement. There were no transactions large enough to convey information about the transactors' financial positions and needs.

In many times and places, however, such radical assumptions seem very far from relevance. The availability of many publicly traded financial instruments is a twentieth-century phenomenon. And even now, financial transactions can involve new securities or risk bankruptcy. Under these conditions, financial structure affects behavior.

The giant merger wave at the turn of the twentieth century offers a case in point. Many factors determined the timing and incidence of the mergers. The growth of vertically integrated firms discussed above in the context of Swift was one influence. The effect of the depression of the 1890s on firms with large fixed capital stocks was another. And a dramatic change in financial markets was a third.[39]

Prior to the late 1890s, the market for industrial securities was very thin indeed.[40] Railroads had been able to borrow by means of publicly traded bonds and, to a lesser extent, equity. The markets for these securities were well established. Governments traditionally had borrowed by means of negotiable bonds, and utilities possessed a quasi-governmental character. English utilities had raised money through organized capital markets. But the situation

---

37. Modigliani and Miller (1958). There are, of course, assumptions.
38. This works only for uncorrelated risks. The investor cannot diversify away "systematic risk" that affects all assets at once. See Brealy and Myers (1988).
39. See Chandler (1977), Lamoreaux (1985), and Navin and Sears (1955).
40. For more detail in this vein, see Baskin (1988).

for private enterprise was much more strained. The placements were entirely private. The securities were not really traded on a market. There was real negotiation over the supply and use of resources.

The late 1890s saw the rise of a public market in industrial securities. This amounted to the invention of financial instruments and informational environments to deal with the incentive problems. Private placements were still required to place the bonds initially. But after that, relatively free trading obtained.

This expanded capital market drew on more participants and more money than the nineteenth-century arrangements it replaced. But it did not make all financial transactions like the purchase of a commodity like wheat. Whenever transactions were large in scale relative to the operating cash needs of the firm raising capital, more traditional problems arose. In a world in which bankruptcy was possible—if not to say likely—investors wanted to have more information before committing their funds.

The parallel is with Swift's icehouse. Initially a general-purpose asset, it became transaction-specific by virtue of where it was located and when its services were needed. So too with capital. Initially fully fungible, if a loan or stock purchase is to provide a major part of the capital for a firm, the capital becomes more specific to this transaction.

Once the capital is committed, the lender and borrower or investor and manager are in the position of bilateral monopoly characteristic of transaction-specific assets. The agent has acquired capital; she now has every incentive to run off with it, that is, to use it for her benefit, not the investor's. The principal therefore has a need to monitor the agent's actions, to make sure that the funds are used to best advantage. The agent is in the position Sloan's managers in charge of GM's divisions.

In the midst of the 1920 stock market crisis, it emerged that William C. Durant had been secretly buying GM stock on the market to prop the price up. Durant had been buying on margin from a large number of stockbrokers. Given a recent steady decline in GM's share price and in share prices generally, he had become impossibly overextended. If Durant defaulted on his loans, as seemed quite likely, the brokers would dump the shares they held as collateral on the market. The blocks of stock in question were large, and the market was already skittish. Such a sale would surely make raising funds for GM capital investment programs more difficult.

In his capacity as head of GM, Durant was supposed to be acting as an agent for the owners of GM stock, his principals. He maintained that he was buying stock to protect the financial interests of friends who had invested in the shares on his recommendation and thus in the interests of all GM shareholders generally. The Du Pont group, on the other hand, suspected that he was merely trying to prop up the value of collateral for other investments—speculative investments—that he had made. They therefore felt that he had pursued his own objectives opportunistically in exactly the selfish way that the possession of transaction- (in this case, enterprise-) specific assets allowed. Durant was acting on his own account, not that of GM's shareholders. He was in effect using GM's assets to bolster his personal position, not the firm's.

The Du Pont group was a principal that had found the existing arrangement to be inadequate to protect it from the opportunities created by transaction-specific assets. The positions in GM and its stock were transaction-specific by virtue of their size, that is, by virtue of Du Pont's large holdings of stock and Durant's pivotal place at the top of the GM's management. Durant's and the Du Pont interest's transactions were too large relative to the size of GM for the market to absorb either of them without effect.

Durant appealed to the Du Pont group for help in his distress. They were willing to bail him out to protect themselves, but unwilling to allow the re-creation of the opportunity Durant had just exploited. They felt his secrecy and evasions regarding personal financial matters were of a piece with his reluctance to share or even regularly generate financial and operating statistics about the firm. They therefore performed in this market the equivalent of vertical integration. They bought Durant out and took control of GM.

By the 1980s, the market for institutional securities was performing somewhat better. Robert Campeau could raise the money for his 1986 acquisition on relatively competitive terms. But in 1989 when the Christmas crisis struck, he was not an anonymous transactor but conspicuously in distress. The market failed again. Almost a hundred years after the birth of the market for corporate securities, with the Dow wire, vast statistical databases, and powerful personal computers sitting on every financial analyst's desk, the market still would not buy Campeau's bonds. Campeau did not need much money. But he needed it very soon, and all the world knew it (see Raff and Salmon manuscript, fig. 2). He could not raise cash from real estate sale-leasebacks because potential buyers knew who would have to find the money to pay the lease. Campeau's very fund-raising transaction told everyone about the corporation's financial position and its riskiness.

In a transaction startlingly similar to Durant's seventy years earlier, Campeau turned to some of his friends. He sold a controlling interest in his firm to Olympia and York, another Canadian real estate firm. Like Durant, Campeau found that a private placement offered advantage (a higher price based on the more detailed knowledge) not present in a market transaction. Like the Du Pont executives, Olympia and York did not want to allow Campeau the liberty of going off and making further mistakes.

But even the infusion of capital from Olympia and York proved insufficient to maintain the Campeau firm. Soon after Christmas, rumors began to fly that various department stores were up for sale (*New York Times*, passim). Unlike GM, where a change of leadership revived an economically sound organization, Campeau's firm had outgrown its economic limits. It had expanded beyond the point where the gains from internal operations outweighed the costs of acquisition and integration. The constraints imposed by the capital market—the extent to which the Campeau company had to borrow to raise the cash it needed for ordinary operations—did not allow time for the anticipated cost savings from integrated operations to be realized. However beneficial these economies would be in a steady state, the investment seemed to be too risky in the current financial conditions. Campeau had gone well over the line. The creditors did not trust him and did not wish to throw good money after bad. Chapter 11 bankruptcy proceedings were initiated in February 1990.

Decisions at this third level are symmetrical to those at the preceding two. Principals have trouble directing agents to do their bidding equally at the farm level observed by Marshall and at the firm level in GM. And the question of hiring and firing, of integrating or not, is mirrored by the question of financing or not. Only when there is mutual advantage will a bargain be struck. But, as these examples show all too clearly, advantage appears only dimly in a complex and changing world. Information is costly and hard to find at all levels. Who knows what and when is a crucial element in the structure of relationships and deals.

## 1.5   Conclusion

The traditional economics of industry assumed that most industries, and more broadly most economic exchanges, were competitive. Two assumptions were therefore central in analyses. First, knowledge was possessed by all. Second, no one actor was important enough to affect the price of any transaction. Under these circumstances, decision-makers would be indifferent whether they participated in any particular activity. Activities would be chosen even if they were only marginally more rewarding than the alternatives. The pay for working would be almost the same in any job as in the next best alternative. The price paid for any asset would be the same price that many other people would be willing to pay. The interest rate for loans to different borrowers would be essentially uniform. There would be no agency problem of any form.

The recent economic theory of industry and firms has turned its attention to conditions of imperfect information and limited competition. Attention has thus turned to those conditions where the two assumptions of the traditional theory are not satisfied. Knowledge is assumed to be partial and costly. Situations arise in which a few individuals struggle for control. It therefore matters for the outcome and structure of these transactions who knows what. Particular structures of information may induce inefficiencies and gross distortions.

Agency theories have suggested certain ways out of the dilemmas and burdens threatened by these empirically ubiquitous conditions, and new empirical work has successfully tested the relevance of these theories in a variety of contexts. The examples presented here show how the basic, underlying reasoning can be used to give explanations in business history. The theories, based as the are on profit maximization, are prescriptive as well as descriptive. They always provide a cogent, systematic set of questions. They often provide a standard against which to evaluate actions. They sometimes suggest outcomes that do not at first seem likely or may not even have happened. Either situation provides food for further, focused thought.

The theories ought, therefore, to be useful to business historians. It is our hope as well that the stories business historians tell will stimulate economists to rethink and extend their theories. When the existing theories do not predict well, this may indicate that the theory needs amendment. When the choices of business people cannot be subsumed under a well-formulated case, there is an opportunity to extend theories.

Historians are good at empathy. Economics can supply a little fruitful alienation. The best relationships have a little tension in them.[41] Business history and economic theory can learn from and enhance one another.

# References

Baskin, Jonathan Barron. 1988. The development of corporate financial markets in Britain and the United States, 1600–1914: Overcoming asymmetric information. *Business History Review* 62:199–237.

Becker, Gary. 1962. Investment in human capital: A theoretical approach. *Journal of Political Economy* 70:9–49.

Bernheim, B. Douglas, and Michael D. Whinston. 1985. Common marketing agency as a device for facilitating collusion. *Rand Journal of Economics* 16:269–81.

Brealy, Richard M., and Stewart C. Myers. 1988. *Principles of corporate finance*. Third edition. New York: McGraw-Hill.

Chandler, Alfred D., Jr. 1962. *Strategy and structure*. Cambridge: MIT Press.

———. 1977. *The visible hand: The managerial revolution in American business*. Cambridge: Harvard University Press.

———. 1990. *Scale and scope: The dynamics of industrial capitalism*. Cambridge: Harvard University Press.

Chandler, Alfred D., Jr., and Stephen Salsbury. 1971. *Pierre S. du Pont and the making of the modern corporation*. New York: Harper and Row.

Cheung, Steven. 1969. *The theory of share tenancy*. Chicago: University of Chicago Press.

Coase, Ronald. 1937. On the nature of the firm. *Economica,* n.s. 1:396–405.

Garnet, Robert W. 1985. *The telephone enterprise: The evolution of the Bell System's horizontal structure, 1876–1909*. Baltimore: Johns Hopkins University Press.

Goldin, Claudia. 1986. Monitoring costs and occupational segregation by sex: A historical analysis. *Journal of Labor Economics* 4:1–27.

Haskell, Thomas L. 1977. *The emergence of professional social science*. Urbana: University of Illinois Press.

Holmstrom, Bengt R., and Jean Tirole. 1989. The theory of the firm. In *Handbook of industrial organization,* ed. Richard Schmalensee and Robert Willig, 1:61–133. Amsterdam: North Holland.

Johnson, H. Thomas, and Robert S. Kaplan. 1987. *Relevance lost: The rise and fall of management accounting*. Boston: Harvard Business School Press.

Joskow, Paul L. 1985. Vertical integration and long-term contracts: The case of coal-

---

41. "Is there no change of death in Paradise? / Does ripe fruit never fall?" (Stevens 1954, 69).

burning electric generating plants. *Journal of Law, Economics, and Organization* 1:33–80.

Klein, Benjamin, Robert Crawford, and Armen Alchian. 1978. Vertical integration, appropriable rents, and the competitive contracting process. *Journal of Law and Economics* 21:297–326.

Kuhn, Arthur W. 1986. *GM passes Ford: Designing the General Motors performance-control system.* University Park: Pennsylvania State University Press.

Kujovich, Mary Yeager. 1970. The refrigerator car and the growth of the American dressed meat industry. *Business History Review* 44:460–82.

Lamoreaux, Naomi R. 1985. *The great merger movement in American business, 1895–1904.* New York: Cambridge University Press.

Lazear, Edward. 1979. Why is there mandatory retirement? *Journal of Political Economy* 87:1261–84.

Learned, Edmund, C. Roland Christianson, Kenneth Andrews, and William Guth. 1965. *Business policy: Text and cases.* Homewood, IL: Irwin.

Levinthal, Daniel. 1988. A survey of agency models of organizations. *Journal of Economic Behavior and Organization* 9:153–85.

Lipartito, Kenneth. 1989. System building at the margin: The problem of public choice in the telephone industry. *Journal of Economic History* 49:323–36.

Luce, Duncan, and Howard Raiffa. 1957. *Games and decisions: Introduction and critical survey.* New York: Wiley.

Marshall, Alfred. 1961. *Principles of economics.* Ninth (variorum) edition. New York: Macmillan.

Masten, Scott E. 1984. The organization of production: Evidence from the aerospace industry. *Journal of Law and Economics* 27:403–18.

Modigliani, Franco, and Merton Miller. 1958. The cost of capital, corporation finance, and the theory of investment. *American Economic Review* 48:261–97.

Monteverde, Kirk, and David Teece. 1982. Supplier switching costs and vertical integration in the automobile industry. *Bell Journal of Economics* 13:206–13.

Navin, Thomas R., and Marian V. Sears. 1955. The rise of the market for industrial securities, 1887–1902. *Business History Review* 29 (June):105–38.

Nicholson, Walter. 1988. *Microeconomic theory.* Fourth edition. Hinsdale, IL: Dryden.

Raff, Daniel M. G. 1988. The puzzling profusion of compensation schemes in the 1920s American automobile industry. Manuscript. Graduate School of Business, Harvard University.

———. 1989. Making cars and making money: Scale, scope, and manufacturing strategy in the American automobile industry between the wars. Manuscript. Graduate School of Business, Harvard University.

———. 1991. *Buying the peace: Wage determination theory, mass production, and the five-dollar day at Ford.* Princeton, NJ: Princeton University Press.

Raff, Daniel M. G., and Graham Crocombe. 1989. Equity capital for industry and Cotag International [A]–[C]. Boston: Harvard Business School Case Services.

Raff, Daniel M. G., and Walter J. Salmon. 1991. *Campeau, Federated, and the Fate of Department Stores.* Mansucript.

Roe, Mark J. 1990. Political and legal constraints on ownership and control of public companies. *Journal of Financial Economics* 2:7–41.

Ross, Dorothy. 1991. *The origins of American social science.* New York: Cambridge University Press.

Simon, Herbert A. 1945. *Administrative behavior.* New York: Free Press.

———. 1955. A behavioral model of rational choice. *Quarterly Journal of Economics* 69:99–118.

Sloan, Alfred P. 1964. *My years with General Motors.* Garden City, NY: Doubleday.

Smith, George D. 1985. *The anatomy of a business strategy: Bell, Western Electric, and the origins of the American telephone industry.* Baltimore: Johns Hopkins University Press.

Stevens, Wallace. 1954. *The collected poems of Wallace Stevens.* New York: Knopf.

Stigler, George. [1961] 1968. The economics of information. In *The organization of industry*, 208–34. Chicago: University of Chicago Press. Reprinted from *Journal of Political Economy* 69:432–49.

Stiglitz, Joseph E. 1974. Incentives and risk sharing in sharecropping. *Review of Economic Studies* 41:219–57.

Temin, Peter. 1987. *The fall of the Bell system: A study in prices and politics.* New York: Cambridge University Press.

Tirole, Jean. 1988. *The theory of industrial organization.* Cambridge: MIT Press.

Tunstall, W. Brooke. 1985. *Disconnecting parties: Managing the Bell system breakup.* New York: McGraw-Hill.

Williamson, Oliver E. 1975. *Markets and hierarchies: Analysis and antitrust implications.* New York: Free Press.

———. 1985. *The economic institutions of capitalism.* New York: Free Press.

Yates, JoAnne. 1986. The telegraph's effect on nineteenth century markets and firms. *Business and Economic History*, 2d series 15:149–63.

# Comment    David A. Hounshell

In their paper, Daniel Raff and Peter Temin offer us a lively and elegantly argued statement on the relevance of newer economic theory to the study of business history. Both the economist and the business historian will find much in their paper to contemplate.

In spite of providing us with a brief but cogent sketch of the two dominant approaches to economic thought—English deductionism and German inductionism—Raff and Temin have short-shrifted their readers in not developing a fuller account of how both economists' and business historians' understanding of the firm has changed in the last three to five decades. For example, they argue at the outset that traditional economic theory's treatment of the firm has been of limited use to business people and business historians. But one should not assume that business historians paid no heed to economic thought, because many business historians worked quite diligently to write firm-based business history that was consistent with or shaped by the evolving theory of the firm—theory to which economists contributed all along. Nor do Raff and Temin lay out how economists contemplating both firm and larger economic behavior responded to the work of business historians in their derivation of the new economic theory that Raff and Temin argue is so valuable to business historians.

Perhaps Raff and Temin believe such a developmental history of these two

David A. Hounshell is the Henry W. Luce Professor of Technology and Social Change at Carnegie-Mellon University, Pittsburgh, PA.

fields is unnecessary given that such an economist as Oliver Williamson, whose work figures heavily in their analysis, has written on the historical development of the new economic theory in both his *Economic Institutions of Capitalism* and the autobiographical sketch he included in his collection of essays, *Economic Organization,* and given Thomas McCraw's portrait of business historian Alfred D. Chandler Jr.'s evolving scholarship first published in *Reviews in American History* and later introducing *The Essential Alfred Chandler.*[1] But I, for one, would have liked to have seen the authors include a much fuller section on how these two fields have developed to the point where they can pronounce the new economic theory of great utility to business historians and, presumably, vice versa.

If I read Raff and Temin correctly, the basis of the new theory they advocate stems from George Stigler's classic paper of 1961, "The Economics of Information," and the body of works that followed from it. These works rejected older economic theory with its assumptions that knowledge was essentially a free good, that most industries were competitive, and that no single actor was big enough to affect the price of any transaction. Information, like other goods, is costly, and how much one has of it has definite consequences for decision making. Raff and Temin seek in their paper to draw out more explicitly the useful and critical connections among the Williamsonian theory of the firm, Stiglerian economics of imperfect information, and Marshallian-inspired agency theory and, in their words, "to suggest . . . a set of concepts business historians might use to organize their data."

They do so by illustrating three levels of managerial decisions: "organizing the work of individuals," "organizing whole production units," and "organizing finance to pay for the enterprise." Within each of these three areas of managerial activity, Raff and Temin use specific historical episodes to demonstrate the utility to business historians of the concepts from the new economic theory. Raff and Temin's articulation of agency theory is extremely helpful, but it also poses some problems. The authors argue that a "single logic" governs principal-agent relations at all three levels of managerial decision making within the firm. Agency theory suggests that the major problem is for the principal to devise incentives and controls to ensure that agents serve completely or "maximize" the interests of the principal rather than serving their own interests to the detriment of their principal's interests. The ideal scheme is, of course, to structure principal-agent relations, systems of controls, and incentives such that the interests of both principal and agent are maximized.

---

1. Oliver E. Williamson, *The Economic Institutions of Capitalism* (New York: Free Press, 1985); Oliver E. Williamson, *Economic Organization: Firms, Markets, and Policy Control* (New York: New York University Press, 1986), xi–xviii; Thomas McCraw, "The Challenge of Alfred D. Chandler," *Reviews in American History* 14(1986): 160–78; Thomas McCraw, ed., *The Essential Alfred Chandler: Essays toward a Historical Theory of Big Business* (Boston: Harvard Business School Press, 1988).

But indeed such a set of conditions rarely exists, and the past is replete with cases in which principals maximized their own interests while not protecting those of their agents (some would call such instances "exploitation") and where agents put their own interests above that of their principals (Raff and Temin call this "shirking"). The critical question for me is, speaking as a historian, what is the ultimate utility of determining whether someone in the past exploited or shirked in a relationship?

What is most problematic about the employment of agency theory, either by the economist or the historian, is establishing an appropriate time frame for analysis. In one of the most frequently cited articles ever published in the *Harvard Business Review* (58 [1980]: 67–77), "Managing Our Way to Economic Decline," Robert H. Hayes and William J. Abernathy charged that corporate managers were making decisions to maximize profits in the short run— that is, for the next quarterly report—rather than taking a longer-run view and pursuing long-term objectives for growth and return on investment. The phenomenon Hayes and Abernathy observed could be explained easily using agency theory. But so what? Beyond allowing the scholar to say whether shirking, exploitation, or optimization has occurred, does the analysis help us answer the questions of why and how? If Thomas Johnson (chap. 2 in this volume) is correct that inappropriate accounting rules have led to short-run maximization in the United States, can agency theory tell us why this happened here and how? For this historian, at least, the new economic theory does not go far enough in explaining what aesthetic, cultural, psychological, and other factors come into play when managers, in the face of imperfect information, pursue particular strategies in managing their workers and their nonhuman assets. In other words, I am frankly skeptical of a "single logic" adequately accounting for or guiding decisions at all levels of the firm.

In particular, the analysis in Raff and Temin's paper ignores one very important area of enterprise altogether—in shorthand, Schumpeterian economics. One of the critical aspects of managerial activity surely must be *deciding what to produce*. Such decision making is part of the larger area of entrepreneurship, which is not addressed in this paper. Marshall's (and, indeed, Raff's and Temin's) assumption that all farmers are equal is essentially a statement that rules out the possibility of innovation and entrepreneurship, phenomena that have played a major role in the history of business.

Raff and Temin discuss relationships with groups and devote considerable discussion to horizontal boundaries. Here is where most of my responses to the paper lie. The authors provide an explication of GM's divisionalization. Such a reorganization produced what might be thought of as an internal capital market, made possible by the establishment of a common scale for the evaluation of economic performance across divisions. Despite their earlier recognition that information is costly and not perfect, their account here assumes perfect information. But the reality is very different. Du Pont's post-1921 history is literally full of instances in which the multidivisional firm did not operate in the way Chandler and Williamson would have it. I cite but two examples.

Raff and Temin might consider Du Pont's New Venture Program of the 1960s, which is discussed at length in the study I published with John K. Smith.[2] Here is an instance in which, despite the company's possession of return-on-investment tools, Du Pont's executives had absolutely no rational way for allocating capital because they did not possess the kind of information necessary to make sound judgments across the firm's divisions. The very idea of an effective internal capital market within a decentralized firm such as Du Pont or GM presupposes better information than perhaps really exists in such firms. Decision making, therefore, must be made on some other grounds. What might those grounds be?

The authors might also ponder transfer pricing deficiencies. In Du Pont in the 1940s and 1950s, some departments selling chemical intermediates to other departments kept two sets of books, the "official books" by which transfer prices were negotiated and the "real books" by which division heads made decisions affecting their division's overall allocation of resources. Within the multidivisional, diversified firm, there has been continual difficulty in assessing Du Pont intermediates' performance because some intermediates are not available on the open market, because those that are available are sometimes not perfect substitutes, and because when market-obtained intermediates are available (and, therefore, a market price is valid), executives have been unwilling to discount potential improvements to intermediate products and processes that might come from R&D pursued by those divisions selling the intermediates.[3] This last point is related to the authors' discussion—and Williamson's analysis—of asset specificity.

Raff and Temin explore the question of why the du Ponts did not break up GM. Here the record is pretty clear—at least to me. First, Pierre du Pont and John Jacob Raskob viewed the automobile industry as the major growth industry of their period. They believed the industry was a promising outlet for their hoard of cash earned from World War I explosives sales. The Du Pont Company itself was investing some of this money to diversify the firm away from explosives, and the architects of the strategy had identified the automobile industry as a major market for the company's new products (paints, lacquers, plastics, artificial fibers, artificial leather, fuel additives, etc.). By buying into GM, Du Pont could obtain a captive market (or so the Du Pont people initially believed and so charged the Justice Department in the antitrust case that eventually forced Du Pont to divest its GM holdings). In reality, the automotive markets were indeed huge and proved to be critical for the growth and performance of Du Pont in the 1920s and 1930s.

2. David A. Hounshell and John Kenly Smith, Jr., *Science and Corporate Strategy: Du Pont R&D, 1902–1980* (New York and Cambridge: Cambridge University Press, 1988), 509–40.
3. Ibid., 580–82.

Finally, GM is not an example of perfect horizontal combination. That is, not all GM units or divisions are identical. GM's divisions, one could argue, were producing different products; a Chevy is not a Cadillac. In fact, this point becomes all the more clear after the du Ponts came into the picture and forced Durant out. Sloan's policy of a car for every purpose and purse, the rethinking of the Chevrolet Division in the 1920s (which lead in 1927 to Chevy blowing the Model T out of the market), and the creation of the Pontiac Division to fill a void in the segmented market, all provide testimony to GM's and Du Pont's long-term investment strategy, their recognition of multiple markets within the automobile industry, and their belief in economies of both scale and scope. Finally, one must remember that GM was also characterized by its verticality, which the authors do not address in any detail in this section of the paper.

The authors also discuss the vertical boundaries of the firm and emphasize the concept of transaction or asset specificity, although they play down one of the four kinds of asset specificity articulated by Williamson,[4] namely human asset specificity. One of Du Pont's major weaknesses in developing a pharmaceuticals business has been its lack of know-how in getting compounds cleared through the regulatory/clearance maze.[5] The recently announced Du Pont–Merck pharmaceuticals joint venture was made in large part because Du Pont needed Merck's experience with Food and Drug Administration and other regulatory-body clearance procedures in order to get some very promising compounds into the market.

I want to suggest an alternative explanation for the manner in which AT&T divested, emphasizing similar human asset specificity. I believe AT&T executives saw transaction specificity not in the way interpreted by Raff and Temin but by their assessment of Western Electric's expertise and capabilities—capabilities they did not believe could be easily secured in the marketplace or grown anew. Here I refer to development capabilities, which are in many ways more critical to successful technological innovation than Nobel-prize–caliber research. The success of Bell Labs as an institution rested as much on its and Western Electric's development capabilities as it did on its research per se. The authors discount far too heavily the perceived value of Western Electric in the minds of AT&T executives.

Unlike Hayes and Abernathy's typical managers, AT&T's executives were seeking long-term goals when they charted how they would carve up the pie. They sought entry into new information-processing markets (integrated information processing in particular), which made Western Electric and Bell Labs appear to be transaction-specific and therefore governed their strategy to divest horizontally rather than vertically. On a short-term basis, this type of divestment might have been nonoptimal, but Brown et al. were not thinking short-term. They were looking long-term and working in an entrepreneurial

4. Williamson, *Economic Institutions of Capitalism.*
5. Hounshell and Smith, *Science and Corporate Strategy,* 464–73.

mode that, as I noted earlier, is not accommodated in the new economic theory, as presented by Raff and Temin. Divestment vertically would have left them, I believe, with fewer long-term development capabilities in areas they perceived as having high potential for growth.

Raff and Temin's assessment of AT&T's divestiture raises the fundamental question about the ultimate goals of the economist and the historian. If economic theory suggests that a company or an executive did not maximize profit, what should be our response as historians and economists? Here, I believe, the goals of economists and historians diverge. Raff and Temin suggest that the historian is merely a teller of stories, a suggestion that grossly underrates what historians do. In interpreting the past, the historian seeks to understand and to explain, not just to tell a story and certainly not to castigate or to correct. The historian is prone to pay special attention to the particularities of past events and to the context in which they occurred. But the best historians are also interested in drawing generalizations from the events of the past. Gauging by Raff and Temin's paper, the economist seeks to test current theories on the past and sometimes to test the past as interpreted by historians with current theories. In some instances the economist seeks to expose and to rectify the past.

Business historians and economists have made substantial progress in the last few decades by looking at each other's work. If this conference serves the purpose of opening a more formal dialogue between the two disciplines, so much the better. Yet we must recognize that our ultimate goals might, in fact, be different.

# 2 Managing by Remote Control:
## Recent Management Accounting Practice in Historical Perspective

H. Thomas Johnson

Businesses need information to operate. Informal methods are adequate as long as enterprises are small enough for a single person to gather and process all or almost all the needed information. But when the industrial revolution gave rise to larger productive units, some way had to be found to communicate information about activities in one part of the business to decision-makers in another.

There are many different ways to organize these information flows. Choices need to be made of which variables to observe, how often to observe them, and how to combine them into summary measures. The route that information takes within the business enterprise needs to be specified, whether horizontally or vertically, generally available or privately held. And the reverse flow of information—feedback—can emphasize or exclude any or all of the information gathered or forwarded.

It should be obvious that the nature of the information system within a company can affect its operation. As Daniel M. G. Raff and Peter Temin explain (chap. 1 in this volume), information is the key to action. One need only think about how a business would fare if it had no information at all about its internal operation—that is, if it had an information system that did not collect or communicate data about operations. This business would not fare well except by chance.

It is also true, although not so obvious, that businesses do not always have the best information system they could. Competitive pressures are not strong enough to ensure that only the fittest survive. It is possible for businesses with

H. Thomas Johnson is the Retzlaff Professor of Quality Management in the School of Business at Portland State University, Portland, Oregon.

For their comments and suggestions on earlier drafts of this paper, the author thanks Anthony Atkinson, Donna Philbrick, and all participants in the 1990 NBER Conference on Microeconomic History, especially Peter Temin and Daniel Raff. None is responsible for the views expressed here.

inappropriate information systems to survive and even prosper for years. If information systems have some uniformity in a country, competition within that country may not press any single business enterprise to change. Only when international trade brings this information system—and other characteristics of production—into competition with others, will Darwinian selection ensue.

This paper demonstrates these propositions by a historical account of the most pervasive information system in business: accounting. It describes how accounting systems in the United States have changed over the past two centuries and how these changes have affected the operations of businesses. It argues that current American management accounting is a poor guide for business decisions, that accounting has lost its relevance for the control of business operations. Only with the opening up of the international economy in the past two decades has this become apparent, as American businesses and their management accounting practices have had to compete with other businesses guided by different information.

## 2.1  Introduction: What Accounting Does

For nearly two centuries, businesses have used accounting and nonaccounting information to direct management decisions at the three levels articulated by Raff and Temin: to direct the work of individuals, to direct subordinate production units, and to plan the extent and financing of the enterprise as a whole. Until about forty years ago businesses generally used financial *accounting* information to plan the extent and financing of the firm as a whole. They used *nonaccounting* information, both financial and nonfinancial, to direct the work of individuals and production units. In the 1950s, however, businesses began to use financial accounting information to direct management decisions at all three levels: to control workers and subunits in addition to planning the extent and financing of the enterprise as a whole. Using financial accounting information to control people as well as to plan financial consequences is what present-day accountants refer to as management accounting (Johnson and Kaplan 1987, 140–42).

Present-day accountants consider it natural and inevitable that a company's financial accounting system should be its primary source of management information. They assume that businesses first created accounting systems to collect and report information on financial transactions, and that businesses began to use that accounting information to manage internal activities when those activities reached a requisite level of complexity, which in most cases occurred, apparently, after World War II.

However, recent historical research casts doubt on the idea that financial accounting systems provided the first source of sophisticated financial management information. Businesses, especially in manufacturing, created very sophisticated financial and nonfinancial management information systems between the early 1800s and the 1920s (Johnson 1987). The financial management information referred to here was not necessarily derived from accounting records—even though it sometimes was reconciled with account data. Rather, it consisted of cost and margin information derived primarily from data about work processes and other activities, and it was used to control workers and to evaluate the performance of companies' subunits.

Historians now believe that following World War II financial accounting information intruded upon and distorted the financial and other information companies had used for decades to manage not only operating activities at the worker and the business unit levels but also strategic product choices at the enterprise level. Contrary to popular opinion, new management accounting developments after World War II do not indicate financial accounting's increased relevance to decision making inside complex organizations; instead, they reflect a fall of management accounting from relevance (Johnson and Kaplan 1987). Indeed, many authorities now believe that using financial accounting information to plan and control business activities contributed to declining competitiveness and profitability in many American manufacturing companies after 1960 (Hayes and Abernathy 1980).

Financial management information arose before World War I primarily to simulate market prices that disappeared when companies internalized and managed transactions at the first two levels—workers and business units. For example, reports showing the cost to convert raw materials into finished products arose as soon as businesses began to manage the work of individuals who previously supplied output at spot prices in the market. Later, systems to forecast cash flows, to budget financial results, and to track gross margins, inventory turnover, and return on investment, appeared when companies began to manage "vertical" transactions between diverse production units that previously exchanged through the market (or not at all).

Before 1920 most businesses—especially manufacturers—felt no pressure to provide elaborate information for managing financing decisions at the level of the company as a whole. The people who financed the company tended to be the same people who managed the company—owner-managers epitomized by business leaders such as Andrew Carnegie, John D. Rockefeller, Augustus Swift, Pierre du Pont, and Cyrus McCormick. These people and their close associates understood a business and its customers. These owner-individuals, perhaps because they were so close to their businesses, seemed to operate as though desired financial results emanated from driving workers and business units to "do the right thing," not from driving them to do things that would achieve desired overall financial targets. While they all kept books from which to periodically compile information about their companies' overall financial results, they kept such information close to their vests. The cost and margin information they used to manage decisions at the worker and the business unit levels was not defined by, nor was it necessarily a by-product of, accounting information used to portray overall financial results.

This gradually changed, however, as companies became more and more concerned with the need to communicate with external financial backers after World War I. External financial reporting became an issue when companies turned to capital markets for financing. Few American businesses, other than railroads, entered capital markets before the early 1900s. But manufacturers turned to capital markets in droves after 1900. To help those companies raise capital at the lowest possible cost, investment bankers urged their clients to give the public annual audited financial statements. The need to design and audit the contents of such statements sustained decades of explosive growth in accounting practice, writing, and education.

The financial cost accounting systems accountants designed in the early 1900s to help manufacturers compile information for external financial reporting would eventually intrude upon and distort the financial information companies used to manage decisions at the worker and business unit levels. Before the era of financial reporting, internal financial information used to organize the work of individuals and to organize production units does not seem to have impaired manufacturers' abilities to identify and pursue sources of competitiveness and profitability. By the 1950s, however, the primary source of information to organize the work of individuals and to organize production units was the financial accounting system designed to supply information about results to external backers. Managing costs at the worker and the business unit level with accounting information designed for reporting financial results at the company level—in other words, managing by remote control—undoubtedly contributed to many manufacturers' declining competitiveness and profitability in the past thirty years.

The research discussed in this paper draws a critical distinction between financial accounting information used to report the global financial results of business activities and management information that influences local actions. These local actions will eventually affect global results, but the connections between them often are not direct. Nevertheless, accounting systems that were designed primarily to report financial results to outsiders provided most of the financial management information companies used after the 1950s. That was not always the case, however, and understanding the difference in financial management information before and after the era of financial reporting adds an important dimension to understanding the recent history of American business.

This paper explores and describes how businesses for nearly two centuries have used financial information to guide the "visible hand" of management. The discussion that follows is divided into four parts: the first part describes financial management information in American companies before financial reporting became important, during the century or so ending in the 1920s; the second part compares pre-financial-reporting cost information with the financial cost accounting information developed in the early 1900s that became the main source of management accounting information after World War II; the third part describes how companies have used this financial cost accounting information to manage costs since the 1950s; finally, the fourth part examines reasons for and consequences of business migrating from pre-1920s management information practice to the post-1950s practice of using financial accounting numbers to manage by remote control.

## 2.2   Financial Management Information in the Era before Financial Reporting

In the era before financial reporting, until World War I, top managers seemed comfortable with having accounting information to portray overall financial results and with not also using that same information to manage the operating activities that produce those results. Managers in charge of nineteenth- and early-20th-century companies seemed to understand the difference between viewing financial results reported in accounting records and managing the underlying activities that cause cost, profit, or return on investment (ROI). Top managers in nineteenth- and early-twentieth-century businesses compiled financial information, especially cost information, to make sense of their efforts to manage resources. Although organizations had carried out trading activities for centuries, the idea of internalizing market activity and managing it inside a company was new in the late eighteenth century. But the concept evolved rapidly, from simply manufacturing establishments that supplied small, local markets in northern Europe and North America around 1800 to complex multi-industry enterprises that served world markets by the early 1920s (Chandler 1977).

Accompanying that evolution of managed business enterprise was the development of virtually all the financial management tools used in modern times—cost records for labor, material, and overhead; budgets for cash, income, and capital; flexible budgets, sales forecasts, standard costs, variance analysis, transfer prices, and divisional performance measures (Johnson and Kaplan 1987). Companies created and modified these tools as needs arose for information to plan and control their actions.

Financial management accounting tools developed from 1800 to the early 1920s largely in response to one force—the transfer of economic exchange from market settings into managed business settings. Before the early 1800s, market prices in "arm's length" transactions between individuals guided virtually all economic exchange outside the household. Then around 1800 people began to "internalize" economic activity and manage it in a business. In the nineteenth and early twentieth centuries, companies engaged in mining, manufacturing, transportation, and distribution decided to internalize numerous opportunities for exchange that went begging in the marketplace. Results of these decisions included, for example, managing workers' time to stabilize and increase output of textiles and metal goods; ownership by steel-making companies of raw material sources; and ownership of distribution channels by producers of oil and processed beef.

As these businesses soon discovered, managing economic activity inside a company destroys price signals that people take for granted when they exchange in the marketplace. Without those signals, managers are at a loss to evaluate the profit consequences of choices in order to plan. The development of financial management information between the early 1800s and the early 1920s reflects efforts by companies to simulate market price information and to judge whether their economic activity is conducted as profitably as it might be in another company or in the marketplace. These developments can be grouped roughly into two categories: first are the systems for cost information to control workers in operating activities; second are systems for information to plan and evaluate the profitability of organizational subunits.

### 2.2.1  Controlling Workers in Operating Activities

Some of the earliest financial management information discovered to date in manufacturing enterprises was in textile factories—establishments where people found it more lucrative to conduct simple raw material conversion in a managed setting than through continual exchanges in the marketplace. Having substituted hired workers for subcontractors to process raw and intermediate materials, these enterprises lacked prices with which to evaluate comparatively their managed processes. Intermediate goods were not purchased on the market. Instead of choosing which type to buy—the cheapest of a given quality—managers had to decide which processes needed improvement. Lacking a clear price signal, they developed systems for compiling information about the cost of converting raw materials into finished output. These systems produced summary measures such as cost per hour or cost per pound produced for each process and for each worker. The chief goals of the systems were to identify different costs for the output of the company's internally managed processes and to provide a benchmark to measure the efficiency of conversion processes.

Examples of these systems come from the records of American textile companies, many of which copied the Boston Manufacturing Company's innovative management methods. One such company was Lyman Mills Corporation, an integrated water-powered cotton textile establishment built during the 1840s in Holyoke, Massachusetts. From its inception, Lyman Mills used cost information to manage the processes by which they converted raw cotton into yarn and finished fabric (Johnson and Kaplan 1987, 30–31). Lyman Mills drew information from manufacturing cost statements to evaluate and control the one aspect of their operation not governed by market exchange prices, the conversion of raw materials into finished goods. The company did not need information systems to derive the market prices beyond their control, such as prices for finished goods, raw cotton, supplies, and workers' time. They used cost information to evaluate and control their main managed activity—workers converting raw cotton into yarn and fabric. Such information included the labor and material cost per pound of output by department (i.e., picking, carding spinning, weaving) for each worker.

Information from the Lyman Mills cost statements also offered incentives and controls to mitigate slack behavior that might otherwise dissipate the productivity gains inherent in mechanized, multiprocess systems. Workers had a natural inclination to use their time efficiently when paid in the market for each unit of output they produced; they had no automatic incentive to pursue the same goal when paid a fixed wage per period. Periodically, Lyman Mills managers used cost information to monitor employee performance. They compared productivity among workers in the same process at the same time. In addition, they compared productivity for one or more workers over several periods of time. This comparative information helped managers evaluate internal processes and encourage workers to achieve company productivity goals.

The transportation industry provides other examples of nineteenth-century companies that developed financial management information to evaluate their internal activities. Railroads such as the Pennsylvania and the Erie invented systems to compile costs per ton-mile, operating margins, and other statistics to evaluate the efficacy of their far-flung and diverse operations. The railroads, like manufacturers, devised cost reporting systems to evaluate and control the internal processes by which they converted intermediate inputs into transportations services. Using the ton-mile as a basic unit of output, they created complex procedures to calculate the cost per ton-mile.

Perhaps the first railroad manager to use cost per ton-mile information was Albert Fink, general superintendent and senior vice-president of the Louisville & Nashville in the late 1860s (Johnson and Kaplan 1987, 36–37; Chandler 1977, 116–20). Fink constructed sixty-eight sets of accounts grouped into four categories according to the different ways that costs varied with output. One category included maintenance and overhead costs that did not vary with the volume of traffic; another category included station personnel expenses that varied with the volume of freight, but not with the number of miles run; a third included fuel and other operating expenses that varied with the number of train-miles run; the fourth included fixed charges for interest. In the first three categories, Fink kept track of the operating expenses on a train-mile basis for each subunit of the railroad. With formulas he worked out to convert costs in each category to a ton-mile basis, Fink not only could monitor costs per ton-mile for the entire road and each of its subunits, but he also could pinpoint reasons for cost differences among the subunits.

The great complexity and geographic scale of a railroad suggest why managers such as Fink felt compelled to develop more elaborate cost reports than one finds in manufacturing concerns before the 1800s. The railroads did not simply appoint one person to manage the integration of several specialized processes in one physical location, as was the case with early textile factories. In railroads, the division of specialized tasks was carried out on such a vast and complex scale that there also had to be division of management tasks as well. American railroads were the first businesses in the world in which there was a hierarchy of managers who managed other salaried managers. Cost information in the railroads became, then, more than just a tool for evaluating internal conversion processes; in the hands of Fink and those who followed him, it also became a tool for assessing the performance of subordinate managers.

Still other examples of nineteenth-century businesses that developed cost-reporting systems to control internal processes come from the distribution industry (Johnson and Kaplan 1987, 41). Like the cost management systems devised by manufacturers and railroads, the distributors' systems simulated market prices with which to evaluate the efficiency of internally managed processes—in this case, processes for reselling purchased goods. Giant urban and regional retailers such as Marshall Field's and Sears compiled gross margin and turnover statistics to measure the effectiveness and efficiency of their purchasing, pricing, and selling activities.

Field's, for example, collected departmental information on both gross margins and inventory turnover. The information on gross margins (sales receipts minus cost of goods sold and departmental operating expenses) was analogous to the information railroads used to calculate operating ratios. Gross margin information measured each department's performance and provided a means of comparing departments with each other and with the company's overall performance. The information on turnover, however, was probably unique to mass distributors. Inventory turnover (cost of sales divided by inventory) was for the mass distributor a crucial determinant of profitability. Unlike the traditional merchant, who considered markup on cost as the determinant of profit margins, the new mass distributors were driven to make profit on volume. Hence, they placed enormous importance on the rates at which departments turned over their stock each period.

### 2.2.2   Planning and Evaluating the Profitability of Organizational Subunits

These nineteenth-century financial management developments were largely independent of companies' financial accounting systems. Almost all companies kept a transaction-based bookkeeping system that recorded receipts and expenditures, and they often produced periodic financial statements for owners and creditors—usually distributed privately, but sometimes publicly. Before the 1920s, however, no rules or laws shaped the contents of those statements. Management information systems and financial accounting systems could operate independently of each other, or they could be one and the same—a company was free to decide for itself.

Top managers in most companies before World War II would have blanched at the idea of using financial accounting information to control operations

(Johnson and Kaplan 1987, chaps. 2 and 4–6). They often used it to plan and evaluate results. But financial plans and budgets were secret documents that top management usually kept under lock and key. Their contents were not used to control the actions of subordinates. Managers below the top level were not made to think about conducting operations with an eye to overall profitability. At most, plant and departmental managers were apprised of direct operating costs and were pressed to keep them under control. But it went without saying that those cost-control efforts would not be at the expense of customer satisfaction, employee morale, or product quality.

Indeed, nineteenth- and early-twentieth-century top managers usually were intimately familiar with their companies' customers and technologies. They did not have to hide behind a facade of accounting information to converse with subordinates. They could use financial accounting information to plan and make decisions and at the same time use nonaccounting information to control operations.

A case in point is Andrew Carnegie. Carnegie was obsessed with production costs and output. He drove his plant superintendents to continuously improve their costs and their output (Wall 1970, 337). But he did not drive for high output in order to achieve low costs. He knew that low costs and high output were no guarantee of profits without satisfied customers. "Carnegie insisted . . . that he be provided with a quality product to sell, for he knew that one adverse comment on his rails circulated by word of mouth among the railroad offices could offset a dozen testimonials in writing that he might distribute throughout the country" (ibid., 350). There was little chance that plant managers would achieve cost savings by cutting corners that might risk quality. Moreover, Carnegie could inform his plant people about customers' expectations because he knew his customers very, very well and understood what they expected. "There was not a railroad president or purchasing agent in the entire country with whom he was not personally acquainted and few with whom he had not had business in some capacity or other" (ibid., 348). And he also knew the steel- and iron-making processes so well that he could evaluate his plant managers' cost-cutting efforts and, in turn, keep them apprised of new developments in the world. "The daily communiques [to his partners and superintendents], dealing with every detail of the manufacturing process from the amount of limestone to be used in the blast furnace charge to the relative merits of hammered versus rolled blooms for rails, left no doubt in their minds that Carnegie knew his product probably better than most of the workmen" (ibid., 352). In short, a keen concern for his company's financial condition never led Carnegie to manage operations by remote control, by driving subordinate managers to achieve financial targets at any cost.

The same spirit was voiced many years later by Alfred Sloan, chairman of General Motors from the 1920s to the 1950s, when he said, "The chairman's job is to control the purse strings, not guide the hands of the artisans" (Lee 1988, 90). Sloan, like Carnegie, obviously appreciated the value to top managers of having a broad financial view of a company's affairs. Like most of his contemporaries before World War II, however, Sloan also seemed reluctant to focus the attention of operating managers on the same financial targets.

Three sets of cases, drawn from opposite ends of the time spectrum from the early 1800s to the early 1900s, indicate how companies in the era before financial reporting used financial accounting results to provide a window for top management, but different information to provide marching orders for operating personnel. The earliest example comes from the records of Lyman Mills, the Massachusetts cotton textile manufacturer discussed above (Johnson and Kaplan 1987, chap. 2). The company's top managers, located in the Boston home office, prepared fully articulated income statements for each of the mills located in Holyoke. However, top management does not appear to have shared the information in those statements with the mill managers in Holyoke. Only the treasurer and his peers in Boston saw the mill revenue and net income figures. Correspondence between the home office and the mill manager suggests that top managers focused the mill managers' attention on local mill operating costs, meeting customer delivery schedules, the condition of cotton inventories, mill safety and housekeeping, the condition of workers, and mill productivity measured in terms such as output per worker and labor cost per pound (or yard). It seems the mills were not viewed as profit centers, nor even as cost centers.

As we noted previously, the cost information reported to mill managers at Lyman Mills focused almost entirely on the mill's consumption of cotton and labor time. The mill cost reports paid no attention to so-called fixed costs. Consequently, the mill manager had no incentive to produce output for output's sake, simply to minimize total costs per unit. He had no incentive to influence reported costs by building inventory. His main concern was to run the mill efficiently, not to use its capacity fully. Top management in Boston seems to have assumed responsibility for the impact of excess capacity on profitability.

Over seventy years later, around 1910, one finds similar differences between the financial information viewed by top management and the operating information used by subordinate managers in the company that virtually invented modern management—E. I. du Pont de Nemours Powder Company (Johnson and Kaplan 1987, chap. 4). A notable feature of the Du Pont management information system was the way it used and transformed the cost information devised earlier in the nineteenth century by companies engaged in single functions. Thus, Du Pont's manufacturing units compiled regular information with which to evaluate the costs of converting raw materials into gunpowder and dynamite. And its marketing units compiled information on gross margins and inventory turnover. But having integrated these functions into one company, Du Pont pushed further and developed a unique formula that combined margin and turnover information into a global analysis of ROI.

In effect, the information in Du Pont's ROI system simulated market prices for capital in a complex company that had internalized the market for capital. To simulate market prices with which to evaluate a diverse internal market for capital, the Du Pont Powder Company developed systems before World War I to plan and monitor ROI in every corner of its complex business. Vertically integrated enterprises such as the Du Pont Powder Company, having concluded that their top managers could allocate capital among diverse operating functions more efficiently than the marketplace, proceeded to design information systems that simulated information provided by the capital market itself.

However, Du Pont seems not to have controlled operating managers with the financial information from its early ROI planning budgets. In the decade before 1920, top managers at Du Pont had detailed monthly statistics on the net income and ROI of every operating unit in the company. But they seem never to have imposed net income or ROI targets on managers of their explosives manufacturing plants. Instead, plant managers followed targets dealing with direct operating costs, timeliness of delivery to customers, product quality, plant safety, customer training (to use a very dangerous product), and comparative physical (not dollar) consumption of labor, material, and power among plants. Secure in their knowledge that plant managers would look after those key determinants of competitiveness, top managers took responsibility for the company's financial performance.

Companies by 1925 put these ROI-based systems for monitoring capital allocation decisions to a new use—evaluating managerial prowess in organizations that had, in effect, internalized the market for managers. In the early 1920s the Du Pont ROI system was modified and used to evaluate and control a decentralized market for managers at both Du Pont and General Motors. Du Pont, for instance, faced the need after World War I to administer a diverse array of new product lines created in large part by the company's efforts to use by-products of their wartime smokeless gunpowder production. By 1919 the company no longer made just explosives. Now they were on the way to producing paints, plastics, synthetic fibers, and gasoline additives. However, they found it too complicated and chaotic to manage such diverse technologies and product markets inside the explosive company's old departmentalized functional structure. So they partitioned the organization into multiple multifunctional divisions, each defined by a distinct product line or technology (Chandler 1966, chap. 2). A similar reorganization, orchestrated largely by Du Pont executives, occurred at General Motors between 1921 and 1923 (Chandler 1966, chap. 3; Johnson and Kaplan 1987, chap. 5).

In the new multidivisional arrangement, managers of divisions performed the same role as top managers did earlier in the multifunctional vertically integrated companies. The difference was that divisional managers did not answer to the capital market—they reported to a still higher group of managers who answered, ultimately, to the capital market (Chandler and Redlich 1961). But top managers began using financial accounting information—especially

ROI information—to monitor the performance of divisional managers. Here is the first time top managers unequivocally used financial accounting information to control the actions of subordinate managers. Managers of very large multifunctional enterprises—corporate divisions—were now hired, trained, and disciplined by other managers—not by the capital market or its representatives. To insure commitment and companywide loyalty among divisional managers, top managers also created incentive devices, such as the Managers Security Company bonus plan at General Motors that Raff and Temin describe in chapter 1.

## 2.3 Cost Accounting for Financial Reporting after 1900

As mentioned above, companies in large numbers began to disclose financial information to third parties after 1900, when manufacturers turned to financial markets for capital for the first time. In disclosing financial information, companies ultimately followed reporting rules mandated by accountants—auditors—and by public agencies. In the United States these rules evolved in the 1920s and 1930s in somewhat different details among various agencies (e.g., the Securities Exchange Commission, the Internal Revenue Service, and numerous regulatory authorities); however, the public accounting profession's rules for audited public statements provided the framework for most financial reporting by World War II.

Most public financial reports contain at least two items—a statement of financial condition, popularly known as the balance sheet, and a statement of financial results, usually referred to as the income statement. A balance sheet lists the stock of assets and claims on those assets at one moment—usually the last day of an accounting period. An income statement reports the total flow of revenues and expenses over a period of time. Net income reported in the income statement usually equals the change in balance sheet net worth (assets minus claims) from beginning to end of the period.

Public accountants' rules for financial reporting affect management cost information in two important ways. First, they require costs to be classified in the income statement by functional areas of the business (e.g., purchasing, production, marketing, selling, administration, and finance). Those functional classifications usually conform to subdivisions in a company's organization chart. They do not reflect underlying categories of work, or activities, that cause costs. In other words, these classifications tend to identify costs with locations where accounting transactions occur, not with locations where activities occur that cause the costs. However, companies tend to sort costs used for all purposes according to these ubiquitous financial accounts classifications. As we shall see later, transaction-based cost information is not as relevant and reliable as activity-based cost information for making most management decisions.

The second major influence public accountants' rules have on cost information results from two rules for preparing balance sheets and income statements. First, balance sheet assets must be valued at historical cost, not current market price (unless market price is lower than cost). Second, production expenses deducted from revenue in an income statement must relate specifically to (i.e., "match") revenues generated in the period. To fulfill the historical cost rule, accountants derive all cost information for financial reports from original transactions recorded in a company's double-entry accounts. To fulfill the matching rule, they attach those original transaction costs to manufactured products, using cost accounting systems they designed around 1900.

Accountants designed product costing systems in the early 1900s to divide manufacturers' production costs between goods sold (an expense deducted on the income statement) and goods still on hand (an asset listed on the balance sheet as inventory). If expense deducted on the income statement includes outlays to produce goods sold in prior or later periods—violating the matching rule—then income for the period is misstated. This need to divide production costs between output sold and output still on hand does not arise in service organizations, where output is produced and sold at the same moment, or in a manufacturing establishment that never has any inventory of unfinished or unsold production at the end of an accounting period. In those cases all production expense incurred during a period is deducted from revenue as a cost of the period—a simple matter requiring no special accounting system. Therefore, accountants did not develop product cost accounting systems for industries that do not manufacture products, such as service companies in banking, insurance, telecommunications, health care, and so forth. Presumably they would not have developed product costing systems even for manufacturers, except that a manufacturer's production in one period almost never equals the amount sold in the same accounting period.

To value unfinished and unsold inventories of manufactured products at their original (i.e., historical) transaction costs, accountants after 1900 devised product costing systems to attach direct and indirect production costs to products. Procedures for attaching direct costs are straightforward, since each product's consumption of direct resources (e.g., raw materials, purchased components, and touch labor) is clearly visible. Indirect production costs (often referred to as production overhead), where the consumption of resources in production is not visibly connected with a specific product, are attached to products using various arbitrary—but relatively inexpensive—allocation procedures, the most common procedure being to prorate them over the direct labor hours expended on each product. For convenience, businesses often use a single plantwide rate for allocating overhead to products, regardless of the diversity of their products and processes.

It is interesting to observe that manufacturers before the era of financial reporting concerned themselves very little with the subject of product costing—arguably the topic that contributes most to managerial accounting's fall from relevance after World War II. This inattention occurred simply because they did not feel compelled to "cost" products for financial reporting purposes. Indeed, to prepare in-house financial statements they were content to value unsold and unfinished inventories at market prices. Nevertheless, they did experiment with techniques for estimating product costs—especially near the end of the nineteenth century—for reasons other than financial reporting.

The development of managerial costing systems passed through three stages between the early 1800s and the 1950s (Johnson 1987). In the first phase, to about 1885, manufacturers' systems for monitoring factory conversion costs were not also used to cost products. From a managerial standpoint this is understandable. Although these companies often managed several internal conversion processes, they tended to produce fairly homogeneous lines of output that were sold in competitive markets. They did not require product cost information to evaluate profitability. To assess the profitability of alternative choices facing them, managers simply needed good information about conversion costs in processes, and that is the information their cost management systems were designed to deliver.

Although not required to report financial information to outsiders in this period, manufacturers often prepared financial statements for internal use. As we noted previously, their efforts to prepare these statements did not include costing products. Their income statements simply deducted from revenues all production costs of the period, adjusted by the change in market value of unsold and unfinished inventories from the beginning to the end of the period. By valuing inventories at market, they had no need for systems to attach costs to products. An obvious and simple solution to valuing inventories and to matching costs with revenue, market-price valuation was a casualty to historical cost rules that twentieth-century accountants imposed on financial reporting in the name of consistency and objectivity.

In the second phase, between 1885 and World War I, managers in some industries showed enormous interest in the issue of product costing. However, this interest did not reflect any desire to compile product cost information for financial reporting. Rather, the interest reflected a need for information to evaluate prices and profitabilities of diverse, often custom-made products made in complex metalworking shops. Facing diverse lines of products that consumed resources at widely varying rates, managers in those firms sought accurate product cost and profitability information, primarily to help them bid on custom orders.

A noteworthy aspect of this search for reliable product costs is the careful treatment these late-nineteenth-century metalworking firms gave to overhead costs. Epitomized by the writings of A. H. Church, a contemporary of Frederick W. Taylor, they advocated meticulously tracing resource costs to the products that cause the consumption of resources (Vangermeersch 1986, passim). Unlike accountants who were beginning to write about product costing for financial reporting at this time, Church and his peers were not content to simplistically prorate overhead costs over the direct labor hours in products.

The accountants and Church, of course, had very different reasons for costing products. Accountants merely wanted an easy and low-cost way of attaching overhead costs to products in order to match historical costs against revenue. Church and other managers of complex machine shops wanted reliable cost information to use in bidding.

After a few companies failed at trying to implement his costing concepts, Church's proposals for tracing overhead costs to products fell out of favor and were relegated to the dustbin of history after World War I. The cost of gathering and compiling such information made Church's costing procedures prohibitive in the early 1900s. However, historians have noted how Church's costing methods resembled activity-based costing techniques made possible in the 1980s by the advent of powerful personal computers.

The third phase in the development of managerial product costing between the early 1800s and 1950s began around 1914. At that time, companies in some industries desired product cost information to make decisions, but their wishes were thwarted by the high cost of processing information. These companies, all producing diverse lines of products, faced a dilemma. They knew not to use accountants' financial cost information to evaluate product mix and pricing decisions. But the high cost of processing reliable information precluded installing alternative product costing systems, such as the ones advocated by Church (Yates 1989). Instead, these companies resolved the problem with alternatives other than costing systems.

A solution for some companies, especially hardware-making and metalworking companies, was to ignore product cost information and charge ahead with a strategy of producing and selling "full product lines." They did not question an individual customer's special product demands as long as total profitability of the entire company seemed assured. To know total profitability did not require information about costs of separate products—only the total cost information that was already available at no extra cost in the financial accounting system.

Other companies in the 1920s, especially large firms whose product diversity cut across technological lines (e.g., Du Pont) or industry markets (e.g., General Motors), solved the problem of high information-processing costs by creating decentralized multidivisional organizations. Du Pont, as discussed above, divisionalized to cope with the complexity brought on by new product technologies at the end of World War I; General Motors, as discussed by Raff and Temin, divisionalized by creating a strong corporate staff to coordinate and direct a diversity of product offerings. Both companies coped with the complexity of product diversity by placing the activities of each distinct product line into separate compartments that were subject to the financial discipline of a strong corporate staff. By lowering the cost of coping with diversity, divisionalization extended the horizontal boundaries of companies such as Du Pont and General Motors.

These multidivisional structures were an alternative to investing in a system, such as A. H. Church's, that could reliably trace costs to separate product lines. Presumably it was less costly in the 1920s to restructure than it was to implement a Church-style costing system. However, modern computer technology probably makes the information-processing alternative less costly than restructuring as a way to manage the complexity of diversity today. The unbundling of many diverse conglomerates in the 1980s suggests that is the case. Perhaps multidivisional structures would never have become popular if the computer hardware and software technology of the 1980s—the wherewithal to make A. H. Church's product costing scheme practical—had been available in the early 1900s.

## 2.4    Managing with Financial Accounting Information after 1950

Businesses in the past forty years have used financial accounting information not only to plan the extent and financing of the business as a whole and to report results to outsiders, but also to manage operations inside the company. Thus, accounting information intended primarily for reporting the financial *results* of business operations is used to shape decisions and actions that determine those results. This use of financial accounting information may not be surprising. Unlike management information, which is subjective and process-oriented, financial accounting is objective and rules-oriented. Indeed, financial accounting information provides "an aggregate test of the efficacy of the operational control systems in achieving their objectives," and financial accounting systems "provide the aggregation and summary necessary to reduce complex operations data to comprehensible scores of performance" (Armitage and Atkinson 1990, 141).

However, financial results do not "provide the basis for understanding what needs to be changed and how." They merely "provide a diagnostic of whether there has been a failure in the operations control systems that needs to be discovered and corrected" (ibid.). Consequently, the practice in the past forty years of using accounting information to manage operating activities is problematic. As many believe, the practice may have impeded competitiveness and impaired profitability in recent years. For evidence to support this claim, consider two managerial tasks that have been particularly affected by the practice of managing activities with remote accounting information: planning and decision support, and control of operations.

### 2.4.1    Planning and Decision Support

In running a business, managers need information about the financial consequences of intended actions. As a guide for planning, and to choose among alternatives, managers need profitability information. They especially need reliable cost information. Cost information serves in many planning and decision support roles, such as estimating profit margins of products and product lines, evaluating decisions to make or buy components, preparing departmental cost budgets, and charging administrative services to production departments.

An important source of cost information in American business since the 1950s has been the financial cost accounting system. As we mentioned above, these costing systems were designed originally to attach production costs to manufactured goods in order to divide an accounting period's total production costs between products sold and products still unfinished or unsold at the end of the period. They were not intended to provide information about costs of individual products. Moreover, companies rarely used them to gauge individual products' costs before World War II. But companies everywhere used information from the financial cost accounts to evaluate costs of products after the 1950s.

An example can be drawn from this history of a regulated public utility. AT&T was a regulated monopoly for many years during which accounting techniques were designed to measure the overall rate of return of the company and, as time went on, to separate revenues and costs into interstate and intrastate categories. Competition was allowed into a small corner of AT&T's business in 1959. AT&T responded by cutting its prices for the affected services, and the new entrants complained to the regulators.

The regulators asked AT&T if the new prices covered AT&T's costs. The problem was that no one had ever calculated the cost of an individual service before. The question had not arisen in the previous eighty years of AT&T history. AT&T had followed the pattern of selling a full product line, as described above. This large and sprawling business had been managed by a variety of specific indicators that did not involve the allocation of overhead to specific activities. There consequently were no rules or guidelines with which to allocate AT&T's huge fixed costs to individual services. The quest for a solution to this problem—still controversial today—would consume vast amounts of legal and regulatory time of the next twenty years (Temin 1990).

Financial accounting systems provide poor information to evaluate product costs in manufacturing as well as in regulated telecommunication companies (Johnson and Kaplan 1987, chap. 8; Cooper and Kaplan 1988). The manufacturing cost accountants' traditional approach to allocating overhead costs, in proportion to direct labor hours, systematically distorts the costs of individual products. Attaching overhead costs in proportion to volume of output is a convenient and economical way to insure that production costs are properly matched against revenues at a macrolevel in financial statements. But at the microlevel of the individual product this allocation technique provides reliable cost information only if we assume most overhead costs are caused by or vary in proportion to units of output (Cooper 1990).

This assumption is probably never true, and certainly was not in American manufacturing companies after the 1950s. Indeed, a steady—some would say explosive—growth in manufacturing overhead costs after the 1950s accompanied an equally steady *drop* in the usual overhead allocator—manufacturing direct labor hours. Moreover, products that consume relatively large chunks of direct labor—established lines of commodity-type products that are mass-produced with older labor-intensive technologies—did not cause overhead to grow after the 1950s. Causing overhead to grow were less labor-intensive products that were custom-made with newer, less familiar, and more expensive materials and equipment, as well as rapidly proliferating varieties of new products that demanded expensive design, scheduling, and rework time—all sources of overhead cost. By allocating overhead on direct labor hours, products that caused indirect costs to increase were systematically undercosted, and products not responsible for the increase were systematically overcosted.

These distortions tend to cancel out at the macro level and therefore do not affect income and asset totals reported in financial statements. But they give a misleading picture of individual products' margins, as many American and European manufacturers discovered in the 1970s and 1980s when, using financial cost accounting information to measure product costs, they erroneously assumed they could improve their company's profitability by proliferating varieties of newer "high-tech" lines. In one well-documented case a manufacturer of automotive components in the 1970s, Schrader Bellows, added a dizzying array of complex new products that its accounting system said were quite profitable. In fact, the strategy depressed earnings and led the company to the edge of bankruptcy by the early 1980s (Cooper 1985).

Recognition of this problem grew during the 1970s, and a solution to the problem, known today as activity-based costing (ABC), began to appear in the early 1980s (Cooper 1987; Johnson and Kaplan 1987, chap. 10). Advocates of ABC tell companies, in effect, to cost products differently for financial reporting information than for planning and decision-support information. For strategic planning information, ABC costs the activities, or work, that cause overhead costs and then assigns overhead costs to products by adding up costs of activities that each product consumes. Simple in concept, ABC was a practical impossibility until the advent of low-cost microchip technologies in the 1970s made it economic to collect and compile activity-based cost information.

### 2.4.2   Control of Operations

Companies always had used accounting information to view results of operations, but accounting targets generally were not considered a tool for controlling operations until after World War II. By the 1950s, companies began to evaluate and motivate the performance of operating personnel at all levels in terms of accounting results such as costs, net income, or ROI.

An analogy that helps clarify the difference between using financial accounting information to "see" results and to "manage" results is the giant electronic display board controllers use to monitor activities in a modern oil refinery, chemical plant, or power-generating station. If they followed the logic implicit in managing by the numbers, top managers of power-generating stations or oil refineries would tell personnel in each department to come in from the plant and run things "by the lights" on their respective sections of the control board. Following those instructions, which people are likely to do if an incentive scheme links their compensation to the performance of lights on the board, people will forget what they must do to fulfill the plant's original purpose. Instead, they will take to conducting operations in the plant with an eye to manipulating their department's lights on the board. While that does not portray how electronic control boards are used in processing plants, the following two examples suggest it may accurately depict how companies used accounting information to control operating performance after the 1950s.

The first example shows how cost accounting information often confounds efforts to manage costs simply because it shows only where money was spent, and how much, not why it was spent. A hypothetical company's production department in Cleveland records costs in two separate lines for resin and maintenance incurred in running extrusion machinery. These cost accounts do not indicate, however, that resin and maintenance consumed in the production department reflect a policy, carried out by the company's purchasing department in Baltimore, to "buy in large quantities from vendors that quote the lowest price." A dumpster full of defective extrusions and extra maintenance to unclog gummed-up extrusion machines simply show up in the accounts as extra costs of production in Cleveland, not as the price paid for a Baltimore purchasing agent's efforts to win a bonus by acquiring raw material at the lowest cost. Attempts to manage the costs recorded in such accounts will not affect purchasing policies executed in Baltimore. Instead, favorable price variances on raw material purchases will encourage more of the same policies, while unfavorable production cost variances will focus attention on "inefficiencies" in Cleveland, perhaps prompting a decision to reduce costs by outsourcing extrusion to a Third World country.

The second example showing how "managing by remote control" caused harm after the 1950s involves the use of standard cost targets to control the performance of operating personnel (Hall, Johnson, and Turney 1990, chap. 3). Almost all American manufacturing companies for the past forty years have used cost targets from top-level planning budgets to set standards for operating personnel. These cost targets are seen as an important tool to control the operating performance of plant managers and department supervisors. Like the setting for desired room temperature on a thermostat, cost targets are a setting to compare against actual costs. Variances between actual and desired costs provide "feedback" that is supposed to prompt operating personnel to adjust what they are doing, as a furnace adjusts in response to feedback from the thermostat.

Standard cost variance systems monitor costs in each and every process of a company's production system. For direct costs, labor and machine tracking schemes report direct costs per hour or per unit of output. For overhead costs, reporting schemes track the percentage of overhead "covered" or "earned" by units produced. The goals of these reporting schemes is to have all recorded direct labor or machine hours go toward production of standard output and thereby "absorb" or "cover" direct and overhead costs—a condition referred to as "efficient."

Department managers beat this system by scheduling workers and machines to produce output in long runs, so less time is charged to categories of indirect or "nonchargeable" time such as changeovers or setups. Because output enables a department to "earn" the direct hours incurred each reporting period, supervisors keep workers and machines busy producing output. Every unit produced—including the equivalent of full units in partially finished work—entitles the department to a standard allotment of machine or person hours. If a department produces enough equivalent finished output to "earn" all the direct hours reported in the period, it is declared "100 percent efficient." It does not matter if the output is saleable. In fact, hours spent on "allowable" rework are often considered to be "efficiently covered." With so flawed a system, people sometimes put in hours creating defects, just to build inventory and to create more rework.

Ironically, managers' efforts to achieve high standard cost efficiency ratings have tended over time to increase a company's total costs and to impair competitiveness (Johnson 1990; Kaplan 1985). Achieving standard direct cost efficiency targets leads to larger batches, longer production runs, more scrap, and rework—especially if incentive compensation is geared to controlling standard-to-actual variances. Pressure to minimize standard cost variances, by encouraging department supervisors to keep machines and people busy producing output, regardless of market demand, often causes unnecessary inventories of finished and in-process merchandise to accumulate, product lead times to increase, and dependability at keeping schedules to decrease. Standard cost systems reward personnel for meeting independent finance-driven targets, not for satisfying customers, internal and external. Indeed, customers scarcely fit into the world of standard cost performance. The customer is merely someone the company persuades to buy the output managers are driven to produce, at prices it is hoped exceed variable costs.

Managing costs with accounting information in standard cost systems impedes companies' competitiveness and long-term profitability primarily because it motivates people to sustain output in order to achieve cost targets. It encourages managers to achieve financial cost targets by producing output for its own sake, instead of encouraging them to focus on the one key to competitive operations and long-term profitability—namely, empowering people to efficiently satisfy customer wants.

This impetus to produce output for its own sake, rather than to concentrate on the work needed to satisfy customers, also results from using net income or ROI targets to control operations—another example of managing by remote control that appeared in the 1950s. Moreover, managing profit or ROI goals, just as managing cost numbers, also motivates managers to produce output for its own sake because of the "matching" rules that require accountants to attach production overhead costs to manufactured goods. Only overhead costs attached to products sold are deducted against revenue in the income statement. Therefore, the more units of output produced in a period and the more of those units that remain unsold (but marketable) at the end of a period, the less overhead cost is deducted from revenue in the period. Smart managers who need to temporarily boost income know what to do: go into overtime, rent temporary warehouse space, and get busy producing output.

Obviously this practice has a backlash. In the next period, unless selling prices rise, income is reduced by prior period's costs carried forward in inventory sold in the next period. But managers usually assume they can build inventory to boost income in one period and then spread the effect of the backlash over several future periods, meanwhile hoping no one notices the added inventory carried over from the first period.

Actions taken by operations managers who are driven by remote financial controls will impair companywide competitiveness and long-term profitability not just because accounting rules drive them to produce output for its own sake. Other steps they take to manipulate financial performance that impair a company's long-term economic health include deferring discretionary expenditures for research and development, postponing maintenance programs, encouraging employee turnover as a way of holding down direct labor costs, cutting back employee benefit programs, purchasing materials and supplies only from vendors who bid the lowest prices, cutting employee training programs, postponing capital investments in expensive new technologies (i.e., scrape by as long as possible on old, fully depreciated assets), and more.

The practices spawned by using accounting numbers to manage business operations culminated by the 1970s in people viewing a company as a "portfolio" of income-producing assets. Strategists who adopted that view saw top managements' job as maximizing the value of a company by properly balancing the risks and returns of a company's asset portfolio. While appropriate for managing portfolios of marketable securities, such strategies are totally misapplied when used to manage a business. Managers of conglomerates who followed such strategies turned their attention completely away from internal operating activities and customer satisfaction and attempted to create value out of thin air by "acquiring stars," "milking cash cows," and "divesting dogs."

The consequences of managing operations with financial targets are revealed in the recently published history of a company swallowed up in the conglomeration boom of the 1970s. The company, Burgmaster, was the largest American machine-tool maker west of Chicago when it was bought out by a conglomerate in the mid-1960s. Fifteen years later the conglomerate became the nation's first large leveraged buyout. Burgmaster's history falls into two phases: twenty years of excellent growth and profitability in the hands of a brilliant, customer-focused engineer who founded the company, followed by twenty years of decline into bankruptcy in the hands of finance-driven, numbers-oriented professional managers. Burgmaster's demise, mirrored by countless other companies whose stories have yet to be documented, can be attributed in no small way to the disinterest in people and customers associated with an obsessive push to manage operations with accounting numbers by remote control (Holland 1989).

## 2.5   Management Accounting's Lost Relevance after 1950: Reasons and Consequences

Underlying modern management accounting—and the cause of its lost relevance—is the belief businesses can both plan and control their affairs with financial accounting information (Johnson 1988). This belief was not widespread before the 1950s. Indeed, before World War II companies rarely viewed financial accounting information as anything other than a compilation of results (after-the-event information) or as data that could be used to project, or simulate, the financial consequences of proposals and plans (before-the-event information). Financial accounting information was almost never used to set targets for operating performance.

Businesses have suffered because managers began to take accounting numbers seriously as an object to manage rather than considering them as passive measures of results. By the 1960s, for example, top managers had begun to impose ROI and net income targets on subordinates other than just divisional mangers. They were not content simply to budget and plan based on these financial targets. Instead, financial planning targets were used to control the actions of subordinate managers and operating personnel. Companies drove the profit center concept of responsibility lower and lower into organizations and thereby made it necessary to evaluate growing numbers of people with short-term financial measures like ROI. "Tight financial controls with a short-term emphasis" inevitably impair long-term profitability because they will "bias choices toward the less innovative, less technologically aggressive alternatives" (Hayes and Abernathy 1980, 70, 77).

Top managers after the 1950s took a fateful leap that their nineteenth- and early-twentieth-century predecessors had resisted. They began to use accounting information for a purpose it was not intended to serve. They began using accounting information "to guide the artisans' hands." That practice, more than any other, defines management accounting's lost relevance in recent years. In effect, the decline into irrelevance of management accounting was a case of putting the cart before the horse. Financial information about business results—the cart—became the prime object of managers' attention. Managers quickly lost sight of the horse, that is, the underlying forces that produce financial results. The rest, as they say, is history. Financially oriented managers were poorly equipped to lead companies through the competitive wars of the 1970s and 1980s.

What caused the change that we notice by the 1960s? Usually people blame either the accounting profession, for reporting rules that cause perverse consequences, or Wall Street, for pressuring top managers to achieve market-pleasing quarterly financial results. However, financial reporting information and Wall Street pressures may simply shoulder blame for a much deeper problem; namely, the gradual but relentless power of accounting systems to conquer and shape managers' attitudes. As I said before, accounting is more than just a neutral, technical tool that measures financial outcomes. It also influences the decisions that determine outcomes. Indeed, the history of management accounting in the last fifty years is the story of accounting systems taking on a life of their own and shaping the way managers run businesses.

By the 1960s, the intrusion of financial accounting into management accounting systems was causing top managers' to abdicate their strategic responsibilities. Instead of being broad-gauged integrators—conversant in production, marketing, and finance—many American senior executives by 1970 were forced excessively on the financial dimension of business. They had adopted a "newly managerial gospel" that encourages "a preference for (1) analytic detachment rather than the insight that comes from 'hands on' experience and (2) short-term cost reduction rather than long-term development of technological competitiveness" (Hayes and Abernathy 1980, 68).

In trying to explain how the top managers in American industry migrated during the past century from the likes of Andrew Carnegie to the type of individual just described, one must place a great deal of emphasis on the growing influence accounting information has had on managers since World War II. The proximate origins of this influence probably lie in the increased use of ROI information that accompanied the spread of the multidivisional form of business after the 1920s. In multidivisional companies, the "increased structural distance between those entrusted with exploiting actual competitive opportunities and those who must judge the quality of their work virtually guarantees reliance on objectively quantifiable short-term criteria" (ibid., 70). These diversified organizations were, as suggested earlier, "nurseries" for top-level corporate managers—graduate training grounds, as it were, before there were many graduate business schools. Having been schooled in the virtues of managing through accounting systems, division managers took the same lesson with them when they rose to the top. Eventually, financial reporting dominates managers' attention to the point where they no longer know, or care, about the production, technological, and marketing determinants of competitiveness.

The multidivisional organization is not, of course, the only influence that reinforced and justified the practice of remote management through accounting systems. Another influence was business education itself. Following World War II American business schools adopted the economist's model of the firm as the paradigm for teaching business decision making. Writers of management accounting textbooks also used the model to show how financial accounting information could be made "managerially relevant," largely by separating fixed from variable costs. This model was appropriate for studying price behavior in market settings, but it was not relevant to understanding the workings of a managed enterprise. Nevertheless, thousands of managers by the 1960s were trained to work with a version of economics that does not deal with activities inside managed firms.

Teaching this economic theory to business students and using it to rationalize management by remote accounting controls tended to reinforce in managers' minds the virtues of the mass-production/mass-market mindset that had shaped the way companies organized their operations since early in the century. A mass-production/mass-market mindset that took root in the last quarter of the nineteenth century was nourished and promoted after World War II by the new management accounting practices.

This mindset tends to be linked to a vertical-hierarchical approach to managing that focuses on the performance of individuals, not groups. It also is associated with the poor competitive performance and falling profitability of American manufacturers in the last twenty years (Aoki 1990). The approach is reinforced, but not necessarily caused, by using financial accounting numbers to control operating activities. An alternative horizontal/team-oriented approach (often associated with Japanese companies) is seen as more conducive to competitiveness and profitability in the global economy. It reaches for enhanced flexibility by building to smaller scale and encouraging people to move constraints, not optimize within them. This approach to management overcomes the real short-term bias, which is not simply thinking in terms of next period's income statement, but refusing to move constraints and believing that the best results are had by "optimizing" inside existing constraints.

To get from the vertical to the horizontal approach, companies must change the way they do business and change the way they organize operations. The lost market share, closed plants, and other ills that we associate with American manufacturing in the 1970s and 1980s were not caused by poor-quality management accounting numbers as much as they were caused by an approach to management that was reinforced by the habit of controlling operations with accounting numbers.

## 2.6    Conclusion

In short, patterns of production are shaped by accounting information flows in business enterprises. Using financial accounting information to control operations has encouraged the vertical organization of businesses and mass production. Managing by financial accounting and mass production have become intertwined and mutually reinforcing.

This approach was very successful in the years after World War II. American mass production dominated world production. But accounting information can impede managers' comprehension of changing competitive conditions. American firms by the 1970s were saddled with a management accounting system that did not help them produce for global markets.

It sounds paradoxical to say that managers choose to look at the wrong information. But organizational structures and information systems are fixed investments as durable as any building (Yates, chap. 4 in this volume). Management accounting systems may outlast their usefulness, and it may be hard for practitioners to realize that a massive new investment is needed. The historical examples in this paper suggest that a precondition for an American industrial resurgence is a sharp turn away from existing management accounting practices and toward a new model that focuses operating managers' attention on processes and people (especially customers, employees, and suppliers), not on financial accounting results.

# References

Aoki, Masahiko, 1990. Toward an economic model of the Japanese firm. *Journal of Economic Literature* 28 (March):1–27.

Armitage, Howard M., and Anthony A. Atkinson. 1990. *The choice of productivity measures in organizations: A field study of practice in seven Canadian firms.* Hamilton, Ontario: Society of Management Accountants of Canada.

Chandler, Alfred D., Jr. [1962] 1966. *Strategy and structure.* Garden City, NY: Doubleday.

———. 1977. *The visible hand: The managerial revolution in American business.* Cambridge: Harvard University Press.

Chandler, Alfred D., Jr., and Fritz Redlich. 1961. Recent developments in American business and their conceptualization. *Business History Review* 35 (Spring):1–27.

Cooper, Robin. 1985. Schrader Bellows. Boston: Harvard Business School Case Services.

———. 1987. The two-stage procedure in cost accounting: Part one. *Journal of Cost Management* (Summer):43–51.

———. 1990. Cost classification in unit-based and activity-based manufacturing cost systems. *Journal of Cost Management* (Fall):4–14.

Cooper, Robin, and Robert S. Kaplan, 1988. Measure costs right: Make the right decisions. *Harvard Business Review* (September–October):96–103.

Hall, Robert W., H. Thomas Johnson, and Peter Turney. 1990. *Measuring up: Charting pathways to manufacturing excellence.* Homewood, IL: Richard D. Irwin.

Hayes, Robert H., and William J. Abernathy. 1980. Managing our way to economic decline. *Harvard Business Review* (July–August):67–77.

Holland, Max. 1989. *When the machine stopped: A cautionary tale from industrial America.* Boston: Harvard Business School Press.

Johnson, H. Thomas. 1987. The decline of cost management: A reinterpretation of 20th-century cost accounting history. *Journal of Cost Management* (Spring):5–12.

———. 1988. Let's return the controller to relevance: A historical perspective. In *Cost Accounting of the '90s: Responding to Technological Change*, 195–202. Montvale, NJ: National Association of Accountants.

———. 1990. Performance measurement for competitive excellence. In *Measures for*

*Manufacturing Excellence,* ed., Robert S. Kaplan, 63–90. Boston: Harvard Business School Press.

Johnson, H. Thomas, and Robert S. Kaplan. 1987. *Relevance lost: The rise and fall of management accounting.* Boston: Harvard Business School Press.

Kaplan, Robert S. 1985. Accounting lag: The obsolescence of cost accounting systems. In *The uneasy alliance: Managing the productivity-technology dilemma,* ed. Kim B. Clark, Robert H. Hayes, and Christopher Lorenz, 195–226. Boston: Harvard Business School Press.

Lee, Albert, 1988. *Call me Roger.* Chicago: Contemporary Books.

Temin, Peter. 1990. Cross subsidies in the telephone network after divestiture. *Journal of Regulatory Economics* 2:349–62.

Vangermeersch, Richard, ed. 1986. *The contributions of Alexander Hamilton Church to accounting and management.* New York: Garland Publishing.

Wall, Joseph Frazier. 1970. *Andrew Carnegie.* New York: Oxford University Press.

Yates, JoAnne. 1989. *Control through communication: The rise of system in American management.* Baltimore: Johns Hopkins University Press.

# Comment    Peter Tufano

Johnson's essay "Managing Costs by Remote Control" details how accounting information has been used and misused to manage American businesses since the early nineteenth century. He chronicles the early search for relevant data to measure the performance of people and processes, and the later adoption of flawed financial reporting targets. Johnson's work clearly demonstrates how information, incorporated into incentive systems, can dramatically affect managerial decisions.

Accounting systems produce imprecise and sometimes misleading clues to performance. Investors have long recognized this fact. In the nineteenth century, major investment guides gave potential railroad bondholders detailed operating, as well as financial, data with which to judge the performance of the roads. In the late twentieth century, financial reporting and disclosure are extensive, but much of the well-compensated work of security analysts is to look through and beyond financial statements produced by companies. Thus, the financial markets respond to accounting data, but also search for other measures of performance, and use judgment in interpreting audited annual reports in order to make investment decisions.

Contrast how skeptical investors use accounting data with how modern managers use financial information, according to Johnson. Modern managers use *too little* information, specially management accounting information based upon financial reporting data. These data are technically *flawed* in that they improperly allocate costs. Finally, modern managers *mechanically* use these bad measures to produce decisions and create incentives.

Peter Tufano is assistant professor of business administration at Harvard Business School.

The historical evidence that Johnson cites in sections 2.2 and 2.3 suggests that, until World War I, these three problems were avoided. Managers used a great deal of information, much of it operating statistics, to control firm activities. Thus they did not overlook important nonfinancial variables like product quality. The financial information embedded in operating statistics was not constrained by generally accepted accounting principles such as those that dictate the use of historical cost as a basis for valuation. The most complicated element of the historical picture that Johnson paints is the apparent tension between owners monitoring minute operating details yet providing proper incentives for managers to achieve a wide range of operating goals. Johnson uses the example of Lyman Mills, which apparently developed a useable cost information system that was communicated to mill managers. Somehow, the home office and top managers "focused" the mill managers' attention not only on costs, but also on schedules, inventory levels, safety and employee conditions, and mill productivity.

The example of Lyman Mills suggests that owners must have given managers broad marching orders. Without a better appreciation for how early incentive systems worked, it is impossible to ascertain the impact the quality of data had upon the decision-making process. For example, Johnson condemns modern management accounting for motivating managers to produce excess inventories, in part because it measures costs incorrectly and in part because incentive compensation is tied to standard-to-actual variances. A mill manager intent on meeting all customers' orders and on increasing output per worker may also be guilty of producing high levels of inventories.

People facing multiple objectives must make trade-offs among conflicting goals. They are guided explicitly by orders from top management, or implicitly through compensation, hiring/firing, or investment decisions made by firms. Johnson's historical evidence tantalizes us by suggesting that managers were instructed to address a wide range of concerns, but stops short of telling us how they made decisions.

Johnson claims that financial accounting information was not used to "control" but rather only to "plan and evaluate." First, the distinction between uses of information is quite vague. Second, the prima facie evidence supporting his claim that financial targets were not used to manage firms is that financial results were not communicated to operating managers. However, data that are not directly observable can still influence decisions. For example, a child may never learn her IQ, but that measure can affect child development profoundly if her parents react to their unrevealed knowledge of the score. Much more concretely, Levenstein's work on Dow Chemical, presented in chapter 3 in this volume, suggests that operating managers were indeed evaluated based on financial performance—and acted accordingly—even though they could not directly observe the financial data. This research suggests that companies were indirectly "run by the numbers" well before Johnson suggests our current accounting malaise began, although arguably the numbers used may have been more relevant. Thus, if top executives were concerned with financial reporting results that measured the changes in their own wealth, they may have transmitted this concern to their subordinates even though the specific data were not revealed.

Sections 2.3 and 2.4 chronicle changes in management accounting practice, specifically the development and use of cost accounting systems. According to Yates's work in chapter 4 in this volume, changes in the cost of collecting information provide a powerful explanation for management accounting developments. In the early period, managers measured what was cheapest to measure; that is, the physical amount of inventories or the throughput of processes. Two trends influenced the cost of information gathering and spurred the adoption of financial reporting information as the basis for management accounting. Over time, production technologies became more complicated, especially in multiproduct firms with many joint production costs. As a result, direct measurements of physical processes became more expensive and less informative. At the same time, investors, auditors, and regulators demanded more standardized financial information. For example, the investment community at the turn of the century began to focus more on a corporation's earnings than on its assets as a basis for valuation. This trend manifested itself in new forms of securities, such as debentures, but in turn required that more information be available so that earnings could be measured. These demands for financial information made the marginal cost of using financial reporting data for management accounting nearly zero. In other words, financially oriented management accounting was a low-cost byproduct of the financial reporting system, just as modern activity-based costing is a by-product of lowered computing costs.

In section 2.4, Johnson contends that management accounting systems are not neutral measurement tools. When flawed metrics are used to mechanically motivate managers, wrong decisions are made. Johnson discusses cases where costs are not properly allocated to products or externalities are not identified. He cites field evidence and prior research to support the claim that poor management accounting information leads to incorrect decision making, but he seeks to go far beyond the implications of management accounting for poor shop floor and product-pricing decisions.

It is difficult to draw sweeping conclusions about the impacts of managerial accounting on a company's profitability or a nation's competitiveness. Johnson obviously recognizes this, and therefore in section 2.5 he broadens his focus considerably. He speculates upon the sociological causes for the rise of "finance-driven, numbers-oriented" managers, bound by accounting systems that measure their businesses. Furthermore, he uses these ideas to explain the declining competitiveness of American business. While I find the discussion stimulating, a few pages cannot begin to prove Johnson's arguments regarding the impacts of misguided business education, misused economic thinking, or the development of a new managerial mindset.

In conclusion, Johnson's paper is a valuable contribution that summarizes the changes in management accounting systems over time and that lays out consequences of using poor and narrow accounting measures. As Johnson turns his attention away from history and toward contemporary practice, he offers a provocative set of assertions to account for perceived changes in the performance of American history.

Johnson concludes by exhorting managers to pay attention to processes and people, not to financial accounting results. This advice, while intuitively appealing, seems very difficult to implement. Even a perfect multidimensional measurement system—one that correctly identifies long-term costs of poor quality, customer dissatisfaction, or economic externalities—requires rules to arbitrate how trade-offs will be made when inevitable conflicts arise. The existing system, however flawed, adopts the perspective that financial reporting numbers are meaningful indicators of firm value, which in turn reflect something about the wealth of the owners of the enterprise. Incentive systems that tie managerial rewards directly to value creation as measured by stock prices avoid using imperfect accounting measures, but do so at the cost of introducing a great deal of noise into the system. Giving managers instructions to take care of people and processes, that is, to "do the right thing," may provide managers insufficient guidance and may not result in value-maximizing behavior.

# 3

# The Use of Cost Measures:
## The Dow Chemical Company, 1890–1914

Margaret Levenstein

## 3.1 Introduction

This paper examines the evolution of the measure and use of cost data in a medium-size chemical company in the American Midwest from 1890 to 1914. This was a period during which there was significant innovation in the techniques of cost measurement.[1] It was also a period of experimentation on the part of manufacturing firms in the design of their information systems.[2] These changes reflected new demands arising from the growing size and complexity of firms. In the small, vertically disintegrated manufacturing firm common in the early part of the nineteenth century, the demand for the generation of formal measures of internal firm activity was limited, first, by the availability, through direct observation, of virtually costless "informal" information, and, second, by the relatively restricted set of choices available to managers given the level of technological development. With the growth in the size of the firm and the increasing separation of ownership from management, direct observation of employees and production processes was more costly, if not physically impossible. With the introduction of new, mobile, and inanimate sources of power, firms had much more flexibility in their choice of location and pro-

Margaret Levenstein is assistant professor of economics at the University of Michigan.

The author wishes to express her gratitude to E. N. Brandt, Margaret Lyon, Delores Goulet, and Barbara Brennan, all of the Post Street Archives, for invaluable assistance in guiding me through the Herbert H. Dow Collection in the Post Street Archives. She also appreciates helpful comments on earlier versions of this paper from Naomi Lamoreaux, Peter Temin, David Weiman, and participants in the Yale Economic History Workshop and the NBER Conference on Microeconomic History. This research was supported by a fellowship from the Arthur Andersen and Company Foundation.

1. See Chatfield (1977) and Garner (1976) for surveys of the introduction of new techniques in cost measurement and accounting.

2. See, for example, Johnson (1975); Kistler, Carter, and Hinchey (1984); Loveday (1980); Lubar (1984); McGaw (1985); Tyson (1988); and Yates (1989).

duction method.[3] Vertical integration gave firms greater control over the marketing of their products, and greater responsibility for setting their own prices.[4] These changes led to an increase in the demand for formal data collection for use in firm management and decision making.[5]

Managers, of course, did not simply haphazardly increase the quantity of data collected. These various decisions required different kinds of information. Historically, there is a typical order to the introduction of new uses of formal information systems in manufacturing firms.[6] This order reflects in part the preexistence (i.e., the existing supply, as discussed in Yates, chap. 4 in this volume) of certain information-gathering and aggregation techniques, in particular those developed over the previous several centuries by merchant firms, which I will refer to as "mercantile" accounting techniques. These techniques were appropriate to certain needs, particularly preventing and detecting fraud, that manufacturing firms had in common with their mercantile predecessors. This common order also reflects a similarity in the evolution of demands placed upon formal information systems during this period.

In this paper I focus on the shift in demand for information associated with changes in firm strategy. The strategic shifts observed in this case study are fairly characteristic of nineteenth-century "Chandlerian" firms. In the early years of our story the firm is small and single-product and markets its entire output through exclusive wholesale agents. Later it pursues a technologically innovative, multiproduct strategy that catapults the Dow Chemical Company into a large, modern, vertically integrated firm. By following the evolution of the firm's information system over this period, we can observe the changes in the types and uses of information demanded as a result of this strategic shift.[7]

---

3. While technological change in the production of power is perhaps the most dramatic change observed during this period, many other innovations also presented firms with new choices. See, for example, McGaw's (1985) article describing the use of costing data in choosing between rags and wood in the production of paper.

4. For example, Chandler's (1977) description of the information system at the Lyman textile mills suggests that it was used to control waste of labor and materials. But, "these statistical data were not used in pricing or in making investment decisions. . . . Such decisions remained almost entirely with the firm's selling agent" (247). Until the firm integrated forward and controlled its own sales, there was no managerial demand for cost data to inform pricing decisions.

5. This presumes, of course, that there was an elastic supply of information-gathering techniques. See Yates (chap. 4 in this volume) for a discussion of the innovations in mechanical and managerial techniques of data collection and processing that gave rise to this elastic supply.

6. For a more detailed chronology of the changes in information systems during the nineteenth century, see Levenstein (1991, chap. 2).

7. This assumes that the supply of information is perfectly elastic and itself stable, so that all observed changes trace out shifts in demand. Of course, neither of these assumptions is correct. As the Yates paper (chap. 4 in this volume) makes clear, there were exogenous shifts downward in the supply of information as a result of technological innovation. And despite these declines in costs, the collection and processing of information undoubtedly continued to display increasing marginal costs. This affected not only the quantity of data collected, but the type as well. In order to economize, firms would force data to do "double duty," choosing to produce a measure that could be used for more than one purpose, even if it was not the optimal measure. I examine both how firms made these compromises and what the implications were for decisions taken.

## 3.2  The Functions and Forms of Information

In the discussion that follows it will be useful to make distinctions as to both form and function in describing the data produced by a firm's information system. Included in the "form" of data are features such as units of denomination (e.g., dollars, kilowatts, etc.), frequency of production, degree of aggregation, and whether estimated measures (e.g., standard costs, allocated overhead) are included.

The functions of these data in a manufacturing firm can be divided into two categories: monitoring and planning (see fig. 3.1). The primary distinction between information used to monitor and that used in planning is the timeliness with which it must be produced. Information available only at the end of the period, that is, after a decision has been taken, is still helpful in monitoring. For information to be used in planning, the system that generates it must do so prior to the time when the decision is made.

We may further distinguish between two types of monitoring: monitoring people and monitoring processes (fig. 3.1).[8] Monitoring a process, say to determine whether it is "in-control" or not, is, at least theoretically, a relatively straightforward statistical control problem. Monitoring people is a more complicated problem. In a typical principal-agent problem, the outcome reported by the information system does not perfectly distinguish information about the state of the world from information about the effort and ability of the person monitored. However, the knowledge that one is being monitored influences the behavior of the agent. Thus the form and content of the data gathered must be selected to both inform the principal and provide the appropriate incentives to the agent.

Two different kinds of accounting techniques are used to monitor people. Mercantile accounting procedures were developed, in part, to monitor the honesty of those entrusted with the principals' investment.[9] These techniques provide information on transactions between the firm and outsiders to the firm. During the late nineteenth century new techniques were developed to inform the principal as to the effort and ability of an agent. Like those used to monitor processes, these techniques focused on activity internal to the firm. These techniques were sometimes, though not always, a part of a firm's cost accounting system.[10] These techniques included such measures as time cards

8. See Demski and Kreps (1982) and Baiman (1982) for further discussion of the different uses of information.

9. See Littleton (1933) and ten Have (1976) for survey histories of accountancy. Greif (1989) gives an example of another method developed by merchants to ensure the honesty of their agents when they could not easily be monitored.

10. In chapter 2 in this volume, H. Thomas Johnson distinguishes between "cost accounting" systems, which produced measures of average total cost to be used as input into the firm's financial accounts, and "managerial accounting," which produced various measures, possibly including cost of product, in response to managerial demands for information. During the period under discussion, there was no general agreement as to whether cost and financial accounts should be integrated (see, e.g., Arnold 1899). Thus the line of demarcation is quite fuzzy.

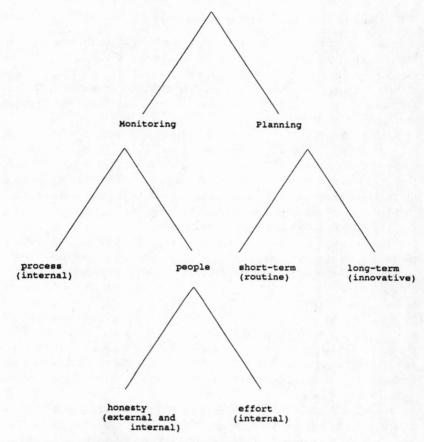

**Fig. 3.1    Functions of information in a manufacturing firm**

and time clocks, which were introduced widely during this period.[11] Frequent reporting of cost, profitability, and other aggregate measures of firm success was used to inform investors of managerial quality.[12]

The planning function can be broken down further into long- and short-term decision making. Short-term decisions include choosing output levels of goods already in the firm's product line, choosing inputs to production, including make or buy decisions that do not involve a large fixed capital investment, making minor modifications to an existing production process, and so

11. An early example is Metcalfe (1885). See Jacoby (1985) for a discussion of the introduction of labor-monitoring techniques in this period.

12. While the calculation of profits was not an invention of the late nineteenth century, periodic reporting was (see Previts and Merino 1979).

forth. Many short-term decisions are made repeatedly (e.g., deciding how much to produce each month). Thus the data necessary to inform these decisions are produced regularly, and the decision rule (the decision as a function of the reported data) can be made routine.

The most important aspect of long-term planning is the making of capital allocation decisions. In a multiproduct firm, comparative measures of profitability may be used to allocate capital among different product lines. However, because the investment decision is inherently prospective, and data produced by a firm's ongoing information system are inherently retrospective, a firm that is innovative in its investment decisions (e.g., considers new product lines) will also rely on ad hoc data to inform its investment decisions.

In general, the purpose of the first formal, systematic use of accounting data in firm management was the use of mercantile accounts to monitor managers' (as well as customers' and suppliers') honesty (monitoring people for honesty, in fig. 3.1). During the nineteenth century, firms began to use accounting and cost data to monitor activities internal to the firm (monitoring processes and monitoring people for effort). Once these data were being produced to monitor internal firm activity, managers began to use them to inform *short-term planning* decisions. As managers faced new strategic and technological choices, they adapted these measures and produced new ones. It was only in firms with already well-developed internal information systems that we observe the use of such data for *long-term planning* (see Levenstein 1991, chap. 2).

## 3.3   Very Brief Organizational History of the Dow Chemical Company

The Midland Chemical Company was incorporated in 1892 on the basis of an invention by Herbert Dow for the electrolytic production of bromine from brine. Its financial backers were a group of Cleveland businessmen, none of whom had a background in chemistry. It was located in Midland, Michigan, where there were underground springs with a relatively high bromine content.

Despite the advantages of Herbert Dow's new technology, there were both technological and marketing bugs to be worked out. The bromine market was at that time controlled by a cartel. This cartel was essentially run by two large fine chemical manufacturers, Powers and Weightman of Philadelphia and Mallinckrodt Chemical Works of St. Louis, who were the only wholesale distributors of pharmaceutical bromides in the United States.[13] Dow, as general manager of the new firm, advocated that the Midland Company operate independently of the cartel. He believed it could supply the entire American mar-

---

13. For a more detailed description of the structure of the bromine cartel in this period, see Levenstein (1989).

ket at a lower cost than the current producers.[14] This proved impossible because of the established reputations of the older firms.[15]

With a variety of technical problems and nowhere to sell the output Midland was producing, finances became extremely tight. They were a continual source of friction between the Cleveland investors and Dow. In late 1893, B. E. Helman, the company treasurer and largest stockholder, fired Dow from his position as general manager. He was replaced by Henry S. Cooper, a less innovative but also less obstinate man, with a background in manufacturing but not in chemistry. In 1894 the Midland Chemical Company contracted with Powers and Weightman and Mallinckrodt Chemical Works to sell all of its output to them at a fixed, and very profitable, price. In return it agreed to limit its output to a predetermined amount, about 50 percent of its capacity.

Dow remained in the employ of Midland, nominally as its secretary. Most of his time was devoted to developing processes for extracting the chlorine and magnesium that remained in the waste brine after the bromine was extracted. After an explosion in the experimental chlorine bleach plant, Helman vetoed further development of a bleach process, and Dow left the employ of the company he had founded three years before.

The Midland Chemical Company continued to produce bromides, selling them through the cartel, but engaged in little or no further research and development and reinvested little of its profits. It had no incentive to invest in increased capacity or improved quality, given its relationship with Mallinckrodt and Powers and Weightman. In summary, Midland adopted a very successful "adaptive" strategy of living off the profits of Dow's initial innovations, but without engaging in the more risky technological or marketing strategies associated with continued innovation.[16]

In 1895 Herbert Dow, again with the backing of Cleveland investors, formed a new company, the Dow Process Company, in Navarre, Ohio, to develop an electrolytic process to extract chlorine from brine. This company never produced chlorine on a commercial scale and was taken over in 1897 by the newly formed Dow Chemical Company. The Dow Chemical Company's plant was adjacent to the Midland Chemical Company. It received the Midland's waste debrominated brine, and from this extracted chlorine for bleach manufacture.

Unlike the Midland Company, Herbert Dow's new company pursued a policy of investing in the development of new products and processes to take

14. See letter from H. H. Dow to B. E. Helman, 9 December 1892, file 920021-Ax, Herbert H. Dow Papers, Post Street Archives, Midland, MI.

15. See letter from H. H. Dow to F. G. Trimble, Asst Sec'y Manistee Development Co., Manistee, MI, 20 September 1905; "Some 12 or 15 years ago we attempted to dispose of some Bromide on the open market, and we went all over the country offering it at about 60% of the recognized market value and could not dispose of it although our Bromide was better than the competing article. The wholesale Drug houses told us they had no demand for KBr [potassium bromide] of an unknown make" (file 050039x, Dow Papers).

16. See Lazonick (1988 and 1990) for further discussion of innovative and adaptive strategies.

advantage of both its natural resource and human capital bases. The ultimate decisions regarding the company's investment policy were still made by a Cleveland board of directors, but Dow's intention from the beginning was to pursue an innovative strategy. He wrote to M. B. Johnson on 5 June 1897, offering him the position of superintendent of the new plant: "We expect with your assistance to beat the world on bleaching powder in the next year or two and on numerous other substances in years to follow" (file 970073c, Dow Papers). By 1914 the Dow Chemical Company was producing at least a dozen other chlorine-consuming products and a dozen different kinds of bromine compounds, and was embarking on research into organic synthesis that made it the first U.S. company to synthesize indigo dyes.

In 1898 Herbert Dow regained control of the Midland Chemical Company and was named its president. Helman's stock was purchased by other Cleveland investors and a new treasurer, H. E. Hackenberg, was elected. Hackenberg was the treasurer of the National Carbon Company, a much larger chemical company based in Cleveland.[17] The general manager of the Midland was replaced by a Dow Chemical Company employee, James Graves. In 1900 the two companies were merged. Herbert Dow was named general manager and James Graves superintendent of the new firm. Hackenberg became its secretary.

Continued innovation in its production processes gave the Dow Company access to technologies with large economies of scale. Continued innovation in product development led it into new markets and encouraged it to develop closer ties to the final consumers of its products. In each case, Dow's strategy of technological innovation led it into conflict with the existing distribution organizations in the pharmaceutical and chemical markets. In most cases, these organizations divided up market share, restricted output, and kept the manufacturer at arm's length from its customers. Thus in 1902, the Dow Company withdrew from its long-standing arrangement with Mallinckrodt and Powers and Weightman. In 1904, it canceled its exclusive agency agreement for the distribution of its bleach. In 1905, it established its own sales organization.

Despite periods of very slim profits, largely the result of a series of severe price wars in the various markets in which the Dow Chemical Company sold its products, the company pursued an aggressive strategy of both absolute growth and product diversification in the period up to World War I. There were other trace elements left in the brine after the bromine and chlorine were removed. The company was continually engaged in research to identify new, inexpensive ways to extract these elements, and to find or create new sources

---

17. Hackenberg was secretary of the National Carbon Company (of Ohio) until 1899. In that year he became treasurer of the National Carbon Company (of New Jersey). That firm was created in 1899 as the result of a nationwide merger of carbon companies. In 1917 it merged with Union Carbide to found Union Carbide and Carbon. See letter from H. E. Hackenberg to H. S. Cooper, 26 January 1899, file 990047x, Dow Papers, and Chandler (1977, 355).

of demand for their consumption. The company was also engaged in research to find new uses for the bromine and chlorine that it could produce in much greater supply than could be consumed in existing markets.

## 3.4˙ Accounting and Strategy at Dow

The design of the accounting system, and the kinds of information that it produced, reflect both the changes in the organizational structure and the strategic posture of the company over this period. The order of the introduction of these changes was similar to that of other manufacturing firms described above. More specifically, I find that, from 1892 to 1898, the design of the accounting system of the Midland Chemical Company (1892–1900) was essentially mercantile. By that I mean that it was designed to keep track of transactions with outsiders to the firm (in fig. 3.1, monitoring people for honesty). The only regularly produced internal report, the general manager's weekly report to the treasurer, mimicked the account statement of an outside supplier to the firm (fig. 3.2). While this system provided necessary information for the provision of funds to the manufacturing plant, it was not used on a regular basis to inform decision making at the plant level or for the monitoring of plant management by the board of directors (i.e., neither for monitoring people for effort nor for monitoring processes nor for planning). The small size of the firm (itself the result of the strategy pursued) did not require it to develop formal systems for monitoring employees. The noncompetitive market in which the firm sold its products permitted, if it did not actually encourage, a relatively lax attitude toward cost saving.[18]

When the Dow Chemical Company began operations in 1897, it adopted a more aggressive, innovative attitude both toward the improvement of production technology and the development of new output markets. This was accompanied by the systematic calculation and use of several measures of production efficiency. This included weekly estimation of the average (variable) cost of bleach, as well as several nonmonetary measures of technical efficiency and quality. During the first four years of the company's existence, this measure (of average variable cost) was used primarily by the company's board of directors as a device to monitor plant management (i.e., monitoring people for effort). The nonmonetary measures were more important in plant-level decision making (i.e., short-term planning).

After the merger of Midland and Dow Chemical in 1900, a new set of reports gave not only average product costs but also average profit on the firm's two primary products, bleach and potassium bromide. In 1905, at the urging of a public accounting firm, the Dow Company modified its costing system to permit a calculation of net income for each of its ten products. At the same

---

18. For a similar case of high profits diminishing the demand for information, see Yates's discussion of Illinois Central (section 4.1 in this volume).

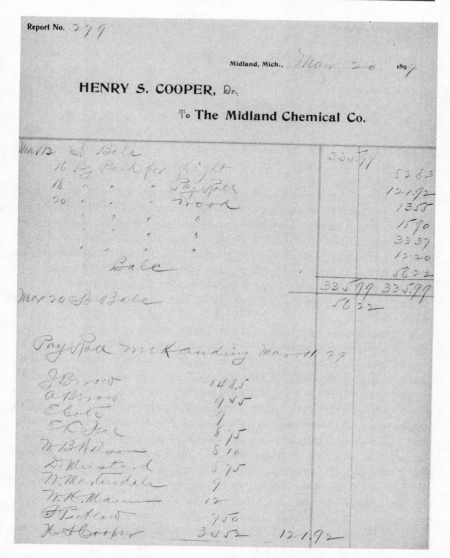

**Fig. 3.2   General manager H. S. Cooper's weekly report, Midland Chemical Company, 1894–99**

time, it resisted the suggestion of its auditors to calculate measures of average total cost by allocating its fixed costs among its products.[19] While the account-

19. The practice of allocating fixed costs to determine average total cost of product is perhaps the defining characteristic of those information systems that Johnson refers to (chap. 2 in this volume) as "cost accounting" systems. These measures of average total costs are used to value

ing and information system went through several modifications between 1901 and 1914, each facilitated the calculation and comparison of net income on an increasing number of products. This measure was used both as a monitor of managerial performance at Midland (i.e., monitoring people for effort) and, more informally, to aid the board of directors in making decisions regarding which product lines to pursue (i.e., long-term planning).

Unlike the procedure adopted at Du Pont during this period, the Dow Company did not regularly or systematically calculate or compare rates of return on each of these products.[20] Rather it treated the largest costs of the firm, the fixed, joint costs of the wells, power plant, and so forth, as essentially sunk costs. These costs were not allocated to any products. Separate accounts were established to keep track of the development expenses of new products; informal comparisons between expected net income and the cost of development were frequently made. These measures were included in discussions by the board of directors of product development policy, capital allocation decisions, and so forth, though no rule was formulated specifying minimum expected returns on the incremental investment in a particular product (as was the case at Du Pont). That is to say, these data were used to inform long-term planning decisions, but there was no attempt to make these decisions a *routine* function of these data.

In summary, like other manufacturing firms of the period, Herbert Dow's chemical companies initially relied on mercantile accounting techniques, which focused on transactions with outsiders to the firm. The only internal information produced was designed to perform a similar function, that is, monitoring people for honesty. Later, as the companies began to pursue a more innovative strategy, more information was required. In the first phase of this new strategy, the focus was on developing new products and new production techniques. Information on product costs and technical efficiency was collected to satisfy this new demand. This information was used first to monitor people for effort and to monitor processes, and soon after to aid in short-term planning decisions. The company soon realized, in typical Chandlerian fashion, that in order to successfully pursue the product diversification strategy adopted in the first phase, it must revise its marketing and distribution strategy. This required a new kind of information, and we soon observe the production of data on price-cost differentials and net income for individual products. These new measures allowed the board of directors to better monitor plant management's performance of this more complex strategy (i.e., moni-

---

inventories in the financial accounts, thus providing the link between the costing system and the financial accounting system. See Levenstein (1991, chap. 5) for a more detailed description of Dow's capital accounting procedures and the influence of accountancy thereon.

20. For a more detailed description of Du Pont's use of rate of return measures in capital allocation decisions, see Chandler (1977) and Johnson (1975).

toring people for effort) as well as make better-informed long-term planning decisions.

## 3.5   The Evolution of the Information System at Midland

### 3.5.1   Stage I: Accounting for Cash

In the early years of the Midland Chemical Company, before bromides were being produced and sold at a profit, the company's record keeping focused on estimating and reporting cash flows over short lengths of time (i.e., days and weeks). These measures were used for two purposes. The first was to inform Treasurer Helman, in Cleveland, of the cash needs of the production unit in Midland. The second was to inform both the management in Midland and the stockholders in Cleveland of the achievement or proximity to profitability, that is to say, whether the firm was producing bromides regularly and cheaply enough that the business was profitable. Each of these purposes required somewhat different information.

The only systematic reporting of information to Cleveland was a weekly report that Herbert Dow sent to B. E. Helman. This report was first produced in April 1892 (see file 920021-Ax, Dow Papers). No copies of this report have been found, but correspondence indicates that it included all of the cash expenditures made during the week at Midland. These expenditures included payroll and any other small, inexpensive items purchased. Invoices for more expensive items were sent to Helman for payment.

These reports gave the Cleveland office information about the cash expenditures at the plant, but in and of themselves gave little information about whether or not Herbert Dow's process was going to be profitable (about which there was some question) or what the future demands for cash would be. In the period before the contract with Powers and Weightman and Mallinckrodt Chemical Works was signed, demands for cash frequently meant demands on the pocketbooks of the Cleveland investors, since receipts for sales were few and far between. Ad hoc reports were prepared to fill this gap.

At the end of 1892, Helman visited Midland, and Dow and Helman estimated the daily expenses of the company. Helman included in this estimate an amount for depreciation and 7 percent interest on capital invested. Dow wrote to another investor, J. H. Osborn, that "profits would not be counted at all unless they exceeded 7%."[21] This suggests that the reason for the determination of daily expenditures was to give an estimate of the required daily income for the firm to be earning positive economic profits, that is, covering both its actual and its opportunity costs. On the other hand, in this letter to Osborn, Dow gives an estimate of the daily expenses, without interest, suggesting that

21. H. H. Dow to J. H. Osborn, 16 December 1892, file 920021-Ax, Dow Papers.

this is how much they needed to "see us through." Dow's estimates do include a daily charge for depreciation, which did not reflect a cash expenditure. Thus the estimate of daily expenses was intended both to give an idea of future cash needs and the proximity to profitability; it did both only with some mismeasurement.

In the terms of figure 3.1, these systematically produced data were not amenable to use in short-term planning. This is not to say that there was no cost consciousness at Midland during its early years. Quite to the contrary, the lack of funds led to a preoccupation, on the part of both plant and Cleveland management, with minute expenditures.[22] Rather, the weekly reports were not designed or used to aid in cost cutting. They were used to some extent to monitor the activities, as reflected in the list of expenditures, of plant management, but did not provide sufficient information to the Cleveland stockholders to evaluate the wisdom of those expenditures. For example, Helman wrote on 6 November 1893, "I must ask you to cut down on every expense and keep it as low as possible. Can you figure out for me the following. 1. What can you make the average weekly output? Give me a safe figure. 2. To make this what would be your expense? Itemize it. If we can save on the fuel item we must do it. I only wish I had the $200 for you" (file 930007c, Dow Papers). Despite weekly reports and frequent letters, this information was not readily available.

### 3.5.2    Stage 2: Information in an Adaptive Firm

After the contracts with Powers and Weightman and Mallinckrodt Chemical Works were signed and the profitability of the company was assured, Midland had to decide whether it would continue to pursue an innovative strategy in other product areas, as the gains to innovation in bromine were limited by the output restrictions in the new contract, or whether it would "consume" the high profits generated by the new contract. There was a brief period during which the company supported Herbert Dow's further research into chlorine and magnesium production, but the stockholders (and particularly Helman) were not willing to accept either the risk or the reinvestment of the firm's surplus that such a strategy required. Dow's research support was cut off, and he left the full-time employ of the company.

This set of decisions, to refrain from significant investment in improving the bromine process, to allow other firms to market its product, and to restrict its product line to crude potassium bromide, had several significant implications for the development of the information system over the following years.

First, the high profitability itself (the company paid monthly dividends of 2–3 percent) seems to have lessened concern for cost cutting. There is certainly less discussion of such matters in the correspondence between Midland and Cleveland during the following years.

22. See, for example, letters from H. H. Dow to B. E. Helman, 13 June 1892, 31 June [*sic*] 1892, 5 July 1892, 13 July 1892, and 9 December 1892, file 920021-Ax, in which he responds to Helman's criticism of his purchase of a lock and expenditures for ashes for potash.

Second, the nature of the sales contract, which inhibited competition among bromide producers and prevented any contact between Midland and its customers (and therefore the establishment of any reputation associated with its brand), provided no incentive for the firm to produce a higher-quality product. Hence, information regarding product quality was not produced as regularly as would be the case later on, and such information as was produced was usually not forwarded to Cleveland.

Third, the need for secrecy to protect its negotiating position vis-à-vis the cartel came to outweigh any benefits to the systematic production of cost data. Years later, Herbert Dow wrote, "If a pound of pure Bromide cost the same in the old Midland Chemical Co. plant a pound of its commercial Bromide would have cost [$].0846. This is about what the actual cost was but I think Mr. Hackenberg will be able to give the exact figure. We were so particular about our costs not being made public that I have not been able to find any document in which it is given" (about May 1904, file 030044x, Dow Papers).

Thus the quantity of information produced for managerial use during this period was limited. In terms of the *functions* of information, the data were used primarily to monitor people for honesty, in both internal and external relationships.

Three different reports were produced during this period, each of which will be discussed in more detail below. Cooper continued the practice, begun by Dow, of submitting a weekly statement of his "personal" account with the company (fig. 3.2). Helman produced annual (and then semiannual) financial statements (fig. 3.3). And for approximately one year, Cooper prepared and submitted to another important Cleveland stockholder, J. H. Osborn, a weekly report on plant activity.

The limited number and content of these reports reflected the strategic attitude of the firm. None of these reports included measures of the monetary cost or technical quality of product. While the weekly reports sent to Osborn did include physical measures of output and input consumption (per week), these data do not appear to have been used by plant management (i.e., for short-term planning), and their production was shortly discontinued. Helman's financial reports were not produced frequently enough, or even with enough continuity of content, to be very useful in evaluating managerial success or failure (i.e., monitoring people for effort). The lack of such data both reinforced the existing managerial attitude toward the importance of cost cutting, particularly relative to the enormous concern displayed regarding renegotiation of the exclusive sales contracts, and denied managers information that would have aided in more aggressive cost cutting.

### 3.5.2.1  Henry Cooper's Weekly Report

After Henry S. Cooper replaced Herbert Dow as manager of the Midland plant in November 1893, he submitted a weekly report to Helman that showed cash received (from Helman) and dispensed (fig. 3.2).[23] The report was designed to mimic the statements of account prepared for outsiders to the firm (i.e., the firm's suppliers). The form itself is identical to that used for suppliers' accounts. The amounts spent in Midland appear exactly as if they were items supplied by Cooper to the firm (e.g., "By Paid for freight," "By Paid for Pay Roll," and "By Paid for Wood"); the amounts received by Cooper[24] appear as if they were payments made to him.[25] Thus while it was the only systematic communication to Cleveland on the internal activity of the firm, the form of the report constrained it to reporting "mercantile" information (i.e., monitoring Cooper for honesty). Occasionally the report would disaggregate the weekly payroll, as in the bottom half of the form shown in fig. 3.2. There were no folio numbers or any indication that these costs were aggregated into subsidiary accounts. There was no information about production or sales activity, though Helman was notified of shipments to Mallinckrodt and Powers and Weightman by the submission of a copy of the invoice. Cooper also occasionally wrote notes to Helman at the bottom of the form indicating his expected cash needs, for example, "Will need about $250. per week for wood for a while."[26]

The continued use of a general manager's personal account, to which all of the Midland expenditures of the firm were credited on the company's ledger, made it impossible to calculate input costs or fluctuations therein. Expenditures included in this account do not appear to have ever been disaggregated into accounts breaking down the cost of product. Thus when Cooper, after Helman's departure from the company, asked the new treasurer for information about the cost of potash, Hackenberg could not easily extract this information from Helman's accounts. Cooper had not, in his own capacity as general manager, kept records that would allow him to measure these input costs.[27]

Thus while this report was produced with frequency and regularity, its content and method of aggregation did not lend themselves to use in the "planning" functions discussed above. This report did permit Helman to monitor Cooper's dispensation of the cash sent to him, and thus detect gross fraud (i.e., monitoring him for honesty), as suggested by the mercantile form, but it did not facilitate an evaluation of his performance as general manager (i.e., monitoring him for effort). However, since Cooper (and his brother) had a

23. See files 980053x and c, 990039c, 990038c, and 000050c, Dow Papers.
24. By chance, no such receipts appear on the report shown in fig. 3.2, as Cooper had received no check from Cleveland during the week covered.
25. It should be clear that Cooper's account is fictitious. Cooper was an employee, not an inside contractor. He was not the residual claimant to this account (i.e., to the amount of $56.22 listed "By Balc"). The local bank accounts to which these amounts were deposited and charges drawn were in the name of the Midland Chemical Company, not Cooper.
26. See report no. 265, 5 December 1898, file 980053x, Dow Papers.
27. See letter from H. E. Hackenberg to H. S. Cooper, 26 January 1899, file 990047x, Dow Papers.

sizable stockholding in the company, the use of a direct performance measure was probably considered unnecessary.

### 3.5.2.2   B. E. Helman's Financial Statements

Helman produced financial statements, from a set of ledgers kept in Cleveland, on an annual and sometimes semiannual basis (fig. 3.3). The first such

BALANCES   JUNE 9th, 1894.

| | | | |
|---|---:|---:|---:|
| Capital Stock, | | | $100000 00 |
| Patents, | $ 22563 | 39 | |
| Real Estate, | 1000 | 00 | |
| W. W. Cooper, | 1437 | 75 | |
| Thos. Percy, | | | 145 85 |
| J. H. Osborn, | 2400 | 00 | |
| H. H. Dow, | 1900 | 00 | |
| Treas? Stock, | 17000 | 00 | |
| Commission, | 33700 | 00 | |
| B. E. Helman, | 56 | 23 | |
| Bills Payable, | | | 1102 00 |
| H.H.Dow, Personal, | | | 36 16 |
| Plant M. C. Co., | 23453 | 48 | |
| Cases, | 152 | 19 | |
| Fuel, | 1115 | 72 | |
| Fixt.& Movables, | 45 | 80 | |
| Laboratory, | 150 | 18 | |
| Expense, | 2270 | 36 | |
| Labor, | 2187 | 42 | |
| Bromine Purifier, | 292 | 79 | |
| Insurance, | 289 | 79 | |
| Interest & Discount, | 296 | 88 | |
| Postage, | 19 | 30 | |
| Salary, | 1000 | 00 | |
| Freight, | 447 | 43 | |
| Cash, | 128 | 21 | |
| Crude KBr., | | | 13781 73 |
| Potash, Bot., | 1331 | 05 | |
| Ashes, | 454 | 30 | |
| Brom. Potash, Crystals, | | | 703 36 |
| Ferric Bromide, | | | 388 26 |
| Dr. Salisbury, | 3 | 00 | |
| Commission, | 311 | 37 | |
| H. S. Cooper, | 337 | 75 | |
| Loss & Gain, | 33 | 43 | |
| Undivided profits, | | | 37 78 |
| Brom. Pur? Accts., | 21 | 85 | |
| Brom. Pur. Accts., | 517 | 58 | |
| Accts., due us, | 2803 | 34 | |
| Accts. Due from us, | | | 1559 45 |
| Iron Scrap, | 5 | 00 | |
| | $117754 | 59 | $117754 59 |

**Fig. 3.3   Midland Chemical Company annual report 1894**

statement known to have been produced, though no copy still exists, was dated January 1894.[28] The June 1898 report was the last produced by Helman.[29] Copies of these statements were distributed to the board of directors of the company.[30]

The statement displayed in figure 3.3, the earliest one produced, consists of a one-page balance sheet. The assets and expenditures of the firm are listed in the left-hand column. The liabilities, equity, and income are listed in the right-hand column. Most of the accounts listed (e.g., cases, fuel, ashes, "Potash, Bot.") represent the cost of goods and materials that the firm had purchased during the period. The accounts listed by individual name (except for Dr. Salisbury, who was an independent pharmaceutical sales agent) represent loans to and from the firm to its principal stockholders. Note that Dow has two accounts listed, one of which is his personal account and the other of which represents his account as manager of the company, as described above. The account listed for H. S. Cooper represents his account as general manager following Dow's dismissal. While the statement is at variance with modern standard accounting procedures in many ways, some of the accounts listed are quite familiar to modern readers. The asset side of the balance sheet includes patents, real estate, plant and equipment, and accounts "due us." The liability side of the balance sheet includes the capital stock (though the amount of $100,000 is incorrect) and accounts "due from us."

These statements always included a balance sheet, and sometimes included sales, inventory, and "loss and gain" statements. No separate income statement was ever produced during Helman's reign as treasurer. Instead, sales are listed as liabilities on the balance sheet (e.g., "Crude KBr., [$]13781[.]73"). The cost of product already sold is included with the cost of materials inventories, labor, and so forth, still in stock as an asset of the firm (e.g., the account "Potash, Bot." might include the cost of potash currently in stock as potash, the cost of potash now stored as potassium bromide inventories, and the cost of potash in potassium bromides already sold). Thus, the value of the potash account on the balance sheet did not report the (historical) value of the potash stock of the firm.[31] Rather it aggregated the cost of potash consumed during the previous year and the value of the existing stock. The cost of potash consumed in producing the previous year's output was never disaggregated. Thus, even on an annual basis, it was nearly impossible to estimate fluctuations in the cost of inputs. This was true as well for estimates of the total cost of production and, therefore, for the profitability of the firm.

28. See letters between B. E. Helman and H. S. Cooper, January 1894, file 940001c, Dow Papers. There are still in existence annual and semiannual financial statements produced by Helman from June 1894, January 1895, June 1896, December 1896, January 1898, and June 1898. See files 940017x, 950080x, and 960111x.

29. File 960111x, Dow Papers. See letter from J. H. Osborn to H. H. Dow, 10 June 1898, indicating that this was the last report produced by Helman (file 980013c).

30. See letter from H. H. Dow to H. S. Cooper, 24 January 1896, file 960027c, Dow Papers.

31. Because of Helman's peculiar method of keeping the accounts, it did not report the entire cost of potash during the previous year, which might also have been useful.

These statements, distributed only to the board of directors of the company, provided very general information about how funds had been spent, the indebtedness of the company, and so forth. The information was not available to most plant managers, except for Dow and Cooper, and therefore would have been of limited use in short-term planning even had the report been produced frequently enough for such a purpose. Because of the unusual aggregation of the accounts, inhibiting the measure of costs over time, the data were not amenable for use in evaluating the performance of plant management (i.e., monitoring people for effort). Thus, the frequency, the type of aggregation, and the degree of dissemination of these reports, like Cooper's weekly report, reflect a focus on monitoring people for honesty, rather any use in monitoring people for effort or providing information for short- or long-term planning.

### 3.5.2.3   J. H. Osborn's Report

The only indication of any systematic reporting of plant operations to Cleveland during this period is found in correspondence between Cooper and J. H. Osborn, the first vice-president of the company, during 1895 and 1896. After making a series of requests for information about plant activities and costs in letters, Osborn asked that Cooper send him a regular report.

> Some time ago Mr. Dow gave me some figgures [*sic*] refering [*sic*] to amount of product per amount of current . . . Have you or can you verify these figgures. Do you keep account of the [     ] current used daily I presume you keep a record of shipments made if so I wish you would send me a complete list of shipments since Jan first of this year; and also amount of labor and salary up there and if you have the record the one amount of current used. I have not heretofore had any regular reports nor indeed know very much about how things were running up there as I never could get any reports from Herbert [Dow]. I should like to have monthly report if you can find time to make it out and in order to make as little work for you as possible I think perhaps I will make out a form and have some printed and sent you so that you will simply need to fill in the figgure and mail it to me. I am often at a disadvantage when talking with Mr. Helman and I know very little about what is going on unless he chooses to tell me. I am of the opinion which I think I expressed when there that you should keep a careful record there of all that is done day by day because it might be useful sometime—another thing I would like to know if possible that is exactly how much potash there is in a pound of KBr as you make it. (10 September 1895, file 950019c, Dow Papers)

Osborn had the form printed in Cleveland and sent to Cooper.[32] There is no indication that Cooper ever sent copies of this report to Helman. No copies of this report still exist, but correspondence indicates that it included potassium

---

32. See letter from J. H. Osborn to H. S. Cooper, 14 November 1895: "I sent you by mail a few days since a package of blank reports. I expect you have received them ere this. I was a long time getting them they were in the printers hands for some time" (file 950019c, Dow Papers).

bromide produced, inventoried, and "in works" per week, and daily power consumption.[33] It did not include any measure of technical efficiency akin to the "bleach output per ampere day," which would later be calculated at the Dow Chemical Company. Osborn did, himself, use the data to calculate output (pounds of potassium bromide) per kilowatt.[34] The report did not include any measure of average cost. The reports were produced for about a year, until November 1896. While Osborn occasionally made comments suggesting his pleasure or displeasure at the results achieved by Cooper (i.e., used the data to monitor effort), his primary use of these data was in formulating the company's position in contract negotiations with the bromine cartel. That winter Osborn went into semiretirement, and there is no indication that the reports were continued in his absence from Cleveland.

The Midland's accounting system in this period (1892–98) was quite typical of nineteenth-century manufacturing firms.[35] The techniques (i.e., the reports and account books) did not innovate on those used by mercantile firms. Thus the information available was useful in monitoring people for honesty but in none of the other potential functions of information discussed above. Given the strategic posture of the firm and the market in which it was operating, this information was sufficient to sustain a very profitable enterprise.

### 3.5.3    Stage 3: Information in an Innovative Firm

While the Midland Chemical Company was pursuing a strictly adaptive strategy, in terms of production technology, product line expansion, and marketing, Herbert Dow was taking the Dow Process and then the Dow Chemical Company on a different path. This meant being more innovative in terms of product and process but, for the first five years, did not mean deviating from the historical norms in the distribution of product.[36]

The changes in the information system were similarly gradual. Thus, during the Dow Process Company period (1895–97), the "mercantile" form of the general manager's weekly report was adopted from Midland Company practice (see fig. 3.4). However, daily time cards, which gave both plant and Cleveland management more detailed information about internal plant activity, were also introduced. When the Dow Chemical Company was founded,

33. See letters from J. H. Osborn to H. S. Cooper, 5 December 1895, file 950019c, 4 March 1896, and 20 March 1896, file 960001x, Dow Papers.
34. See letter from J. H. Osborn to H. S. Cooper, 5 December 1895, file 950019c, Dow Papers.
35. See, for example, Chandler's (1977) description of the Lyman textile mills or McGaw's (1985) description of the Berkshire paper manufacturers.
36. The question of the optimal degree of vertical integration was already an item of discussion at both Midland and Dow. Herbert Dow continued to argue that the Midland should sell its product independently of the bromine cartel. When Hackenberg became a stockholder of the Dow Chemical Company in 1900, he also began to urge that it consider forward integration. He wrote, "I do not wish to be considered presumptuous, especially at this early stage, in again suggesting to you the advisability of making all sales direct instead of through Sales Agents, and hope this matter will be considered in the near future" (June 1900, file 000055x, Dow Papers).

May 22",1897.


REPORT NO. 47.  FOR WEEKS ENDING AS BELOW.

H. H. DOW, IN ACCOUNT WITH THE DOW PROCESS CO.

---

DR.

To check from  THE DOW PROCESS CO.                              $500.00

CR.

```
By balance from last report                       1354.87
Labor vouchers for week ending Mar.20"   61.85
  "        "        "    "      "   27"   55.73
  "                      "      Apr. 3"   54.85
  "                      "      "   10"   62.88
  "                      "      "   17"   59.65
  "                      "      "   24"   57.03
  "                      "      May 1"    74.48
  "                      "      "    8"   47.85
  "                      "      "   15"   92.25
  "      "   To May 22" not"inclusive     51.89    618.46
Postage                                             2.00
Expense, trip to Alpena & return                   17.09
4 Barrels Alpena lime                               2.45
Freight on lime  (receipts enclosed)                .94
Expense 4 trips to Cleveland & return              58.15
Apparatus used in Cleveland                         3.40
Receipts for options                               15.00
Express amounting to                                1.80
Receipts for telegrams                              1.65
Attorney (preparing report for tariff committee)   5.00
Stenographer                                        4.50
Draying lime,etc.                                    .75
Expense (trip to Saginaw & return                  1.55
Livery(Co. work)                                    2.00    2089.61

                  Overdrawn Acct.                          1589.61

                                                            500.00
```

Fig. 3.4   General manager's weekly report, Dow Process Company, 1895–97

while the firm certainly continued to keep financial accounts, the general manager's "personal" account report was dropped. It was replaced by a report that included measures of technical efficiency and product cost (fig. 3.5). For the first time, the firm's formal information system was being used by the board of directors to monitor and evaluate plant management (i.e., monitoring for effort), and by plant management to make short-term planning decisions.

Similar changes were enacted at Midland after Dow regained control of the firm. The general manager's weekly "personal" account report was replaced by one modeled on the Dow Chemical Company report (fig. 3.6). Hackenberg also introduced the production of uniform monthly financial statements (fig.

3.7).[37] These changes reflect the influence of Hackenberg's greater background in accountancy than that of earlier management as well as the more aggressive strategy of the firm in both minimizing costs and improving quality.

### 3.5.3.1  Information at the Dow Process Company

While the Dow Process Company had a very short life and never produced bleach on a commercial scale, its record keeping procedures represent an important transition period, in which Herbert Dow demonstrated, for the first time, an interest in using formal costing procedures in company management. The primary systematic communication between the plant (in Navarre, Ohio) and the investors (in Cleveland) remained, as at Midland, a weekly statement of the "personal account" of the general manager (fig. 3.4). However, a new information-gathering device, the daily time card, was introduced at the plant. These cards were introduced primarily to improve "accountability" (i.e., monitoring employees for effort, providing an incentive for greater effort) on the part of the employees but, once produced, were also used to calculate and compare costs over time. Thus, they were amenable for use by Herbert Dow in making short-term planning decisions about changes in the developing bleach process.

The weekly report Herbert Dow sent to Cleveland was similar to those he and H. S. Cooper sent to Helman for the Midland.[38] It focused on cash transactions at the plant. The first report is dated September 1895, the last May 1897; thus it covered the entire period of the company's existence. The form is a one-page, double-entry list of the receipts and expenditures made at the plant in Navarre. The receipts, reported as "To check from THE DOW PROCESS CO.," are debited to Herbert Dow's "general manager's account" on the books of the Dow Process Company. That account is credited with the expenditures made at Navarre (e.g., labor costs, postage, freight, etc.), which are listed individually below.

These reports were sent to James Pardee, the secretary and treasurer and Herbert Dow's former classmate at the Case School.[39] They were entered by him into the financial books of the company, which, like the Midland's, were kept in Cleveland. If any financial statements were prepared from these books, they have not been located.

After receiving Dow's first report, Pardee suggested that he modify his record keeping for payroll. He wrote, "Your report is all right only that you had better make out a payroll for your labor and have the men sign it. This might

37. As described by Yates (chap. 4 in this volume), the attempt to achieve greater uniformity in reports was accomplished by the replacement of a typed report with a printed blank form into which the month's entries were made.

38. See files 970086 and 950034, Dow Papers.

39. Pardee became vice-president of the Dow Chemical Company in 1901 and chairman of the board in 1935.

be done in a book which you can keep and make copy and send to me. What are the items for your labor account of $59.61 to September 17."[40]

Dow went further than simply having his employees sign the payroll book. He instituted a system of daily time cards for all employees.[41] The use of these time cards is the first instance of any interest displayed, on Dow's part, in the use of accounting or cost data in management. A similar system was used in the Dow Chemical Company throughout the entire period of this study. His reasons for introducing these cards were discussed in a letter to H. S. Cooper, in which he urges Cooper to do the same. "We have every man fill out a labor time card. I think men are more liable to make a showing if they have to account for all their time in detail and it enables us to know what each thing costs by referring back to cards even if a separate account is not kept" (13 November 1895, file 950023c, Dow Papers). That is, by monitoring effort the cards provided workers with an incentive to increase their effort. The information, once produced for its monitoring and incentive functions, was used to calculate costs for short-term planning. Unfortunately, none of these cards appear to have survived.

### 3.5.3.2  Information at the Dow Chemical Company

When the Dow Chemical Company was formed, the "personal" account of the general manager was dropped. The new account books were designed to allow periodic calculations of the cost of plant activities. The weekly report form (fig. 3.5) included data on the cost of these activities (e.g., cost per pound, fuel cost, lime cost) and on various measures of technical efficiency and the quality of product (e.g., barrels of bleach produced, pounds of bleach per ampere day, and percentage of chlorine in escaping gas). The latter measures were calculated with the greatest frequency and appear to have been most important in the day-to-day management of the plant. The report usually included brief discursive remarks on plant events (shutdowns, etc.). The report included total value of sales but did not report an average price received.

The average dollar cost of product was, however, more easily comprehensible to the nonchemist stockholders and was added to this form shortly after it was introduced. Cost per pound is equal to the sum of lime cost, fuel cost, payroll chargeable to manufacture, and all other expenditures chargeable to manufacture, divided by pounds of bleach manufactured. Thus there were no "depreciation" or allocated machinery charges included in this measure of costs. This was a measure of average *variable* costs.[42]

40. 22 September 1895, file 950043c, Dow Papers. See file 950034x, report no. 1.
41. Card-based cost systems were becoming increasingly popular during this period (see Arnold 1899).
42. Herbert Dow confirms this understanding of the measure of cost in a letter to James Pardee, in which he says, "Enclosed please find a statement of average cost per pound making bleach for a number of weeks past. As more bills for current expenses are paid some weeks than others, a

Report No 2      Mr. Dow's Copy.

THE DOW CHEMICAL COMPANY

Midland, Michiga, May 24 1898

SUMMARY FOR WEEK ENDING 12 P. M. 5/21 1898

No of Machine hours, 5-23 ½

Barrels Bleach produced, 31 = (10123#)

Lime used 6940 pounds @ .0028 ---- 19.43

Fuel,
72 Cords Wood @ .90 ---- 64.80

Tons Coal ----

Pay Roll,
Chargeable to equipment, ---- 238.62

Chargeable to manufacture, ---- 259.86

All other expenditures, ----
Chargeable to equipment, ---- 980.55

Chargeable to manufacture, ---- 215.43

Barrels of Bleach for which
Orders have been received, 2

Barrels of Bleach shipped 2

Barrels of Bleach in stock, 438

Total amount of sales, ---- 11.86

Remarks We were shut down first half of week to make apparatus explosion proof.

---- [illegible] Gen. Mgr.

Cost per lb 5.54

**Fig. 3.5 General manager Herbert Dow's weekly report, Dow Chemical Company, 1898–1900**

This report included a summary report on the previous week's expenditures. These expenditures were divided between those chargeable to manufacture and chargeable to "equipment."[43] The inclusion of the latter item reflected the expectation that the company would continuously invest in its plant and equipment. This was a decidedly different strategic position than that of the Midland Chemical Company; the latter distributed its surplus (and probably some of its capital, given its nonexistent depreciation procedures) to its stockholders, rather than reinvesting in the firm.

This format, with various modifications, usually new measures of production efficiency (e.g., pounds of bleach per ampere day, apparent cost per ampere day, percentage of chlorin in escaping gas, etc.), continued in use until the merger with the Midland Company.

During the first two years of its operation the Dow Chemical Company struggled to achieve profitability. While within the plant this meant monitoring chlorine losses and the efficiency of traps and tanks (monitoring processes), discussions between Herbert Dow and Cleveland stockholders focused on the proximity of average costs, included in the weekly reports, to selling price (a proxy measure of Dow's effort and ability, as well as indicator of when the firm would cease to be a drain on the pocketbooks of its stockholders and instead fill them). For example, A. W. Smith, a large stockholder and Case Technical School chemistry professor writes,

> I was quite disappointed in the showing made, as I had hoped very much to hear by this time that the cost was below the selling price. It seems that this much desired state of affairs has never yet been reached. It is very essential, it seems to me, that every effort be made to bring this about at once, or we shall have a fine row on our hands with Mr. Convers [the Dow Chemical Company's president and largest stockholder] and Co. Just what is the cause of the large difference between your estimated output and that obtained? (30 April 1899, file 990003c, Dow Papers)

However, perhaps because of the lack of profitability, Dow does not include average selling price or average profits in the weekly report during this period. He prefers to emphasize their production of electric power at low costs or the

---

comparison is not strictly reliable, and as Mr. Post has a few minor items of expense, insurance for example, that are not included in the above, the exact cost would be a trifle greater than here shown. Depreciation would only be apparent to a small extent in the above figures" (24 October 1898, file 980014c, Dow Papers).

43. Maintenance charges were included in expenses "chargeable to manufacture." Amounts charged to "equipment" were strictly betterment and addition charges and were not included in the cost of product. The record gives no indication of how these distinctions were made during this period. However, at least after H. E. Hackenberg became secretary (in 1900), the company followed a "conservative" policy of charging to current manufacture everything but new plant and equipment. For further discussion of this, and the related question of depreciation policy, see Levenstein (1991, chap. 5).

high quality of the bleach, rather than the continued high cost of bleach or the declining selling price.[44]

In April 1900, after the departure of Cooper and Helman from the Midland and the installation of a former Dow employee as general manager, Midland began producing a weekly report similar to that at the Dow Company (fig. 3.6). It provided information on both physical consumption of inputs (e.g., "potash used," "fuel used"), output (e.g., "pounds potassium bromide made"), inventories ("pounds potassium bromide in stock"), shipments ("pounds potassium bromide shipped"), and the division of the week's expenditures between operations ("chargeable to manufacture") and betterments and additions. It also included data on the operation and efficiency of the brine wells. Two measures of efficiency, one technical and one financial, were included. They were "pounds bromide per 1000 lbs. brine" and "apparent cost per pound."[45]

This was the first time that Midland's report systematically distinguished between expenditures on contemporaneous production and expenditures on plant and equipment. This reflected a change in the investment posture of the company. While during Helman's tenure all profits were distributed to stockholders, after Dow became president, the company accepted, at least in principle (it did not remain independent long enough to establish any practice), the notion that a portion of income would be retained and reinvested. In fact, the lack of any depreciation charges during Helman's tenure suggests the possibility that, in addition to consuming the profits of the company, the shareholders were also consuming its capital.

It was also at this juncture that monthly financial reports, including an income statement, were produced for the first time (fig. 3.7). Helman had produced his balance sheet statements only on an annual, and occasionally semiannual, basis. Hackenberg, the new treasurer, had prepared a printed form for the new report, insuring greater regularity in the items included and in its general organization. These changes probably reflect Hackenberg's greater familiarity with professional accounting procedures. That is to say, the demand for this change appears not to have been managerial, but rather to have arisen from a desire to have the account books follow convention.[46] However, particularly after the merger of the Midland and Dow companies, monthly income figures were used for both monitoring for effort and long-term planning.

44. See letters from H. H. Dow to J. H. Osborn, 29 November 1898, file 980013c, and 1 February 1899, file 990009c, Dow Papers.

45. An amount was entered for the latter item only three times during the twenty-five weeks that the form was produced. Problems measuring gaseous bromine apparently created difficulties in measuring output accurately on a weekly basis. Because estimates of the amount of gaseous bromine contained in the "bromine towers" were necessary to calculate average cost, the form refers to that measure as "*apparent* cost per pound."

46. The firm increased its capitalization from $100,000 to $300,000 following these changes in the accounting system. Correspondence indicates that management felt that having more standardized accounting procedures would facilitate its access to capital markets.

# The Midland Chemical Co.

Factory Report No *4*

Week ending *Apr 29*       190 *0*

Potash used *lbs* ........................................ *8182*

Fuel used *cds* ........................................ *102*

Pay roll chargeable to manufacture ..... *126.18*

Pay roll chargeable to betterment
                    and addition ................ *.0*

All other expenditure chargeable
                 to manufacture ........ *7.0.57*

All other expenditures chargeable
          to betterment and addition ..... *22.29*

Pounds potassium bromide ~~made~~ *barreled* *8969*

Pounds potassium bromide in stock .... *30207*

Pounds potassium bromide shipped .......... *0*

Hours run ........................................ *138*

Average load ................ amperes ...... *337*

Average brine pumped—

    Well No. 1 ... pounds per minute ...... *88*

    Well No. 2 ....    "        "      ...... *152*

    Well No. 3 ....    "             ...... *155*

Pounds bromide per 1000 lbs. brine ...... *1.28*

Apparent cost per pound ................ *.08/2¢*

Remarks ........................................

........................................

*James Graves*       Manager.

Fig. 3.6   General manager James Graves's weekly report,
Midland Chemical Company, 1900

Fig. 3.7   Monthly financial statement, Midland Chemical Company, 1898–1900

Thus we observe that, with the adoption of a more innovative strategic posture by the Midland and Dow companies, demands for new forms of information, designed to fill new functions, were created. The first systematic production of data on the internal operations of the firm focused on monitoring processes and monitoring production workers for effort. Those data were then used, sometimes in a modified form (i.e., input costs were aggregated to produce a measure of average cost), for monitoring plant management for effort and ability and, by plant management, for short-term planning.

### 3.5.4  Stage 4: Information in the Multiproduct Firm

The systematic production and use of data in management accelerated after the merger of the Midland and Dow companies. The new firm was substantially larger (capitalized at over a million dollars). Immediately following the merger it increased its capacity considerably by constructing a second bleach plant, a much improved new bromide plant, and a new electric power plant. It also began experimenting with the addition of a third product, sulphur chloride. While Dow was somewhat notorious for his "hands on" approach to management of the growing firm, the increasing number of reports and growing references to the data included in both minutes of daily meetings of plant management and correspondence with Cleveland indicate the new uses made of such information.

After the merger in 1900, the company faced, for the first time, the difficulties in measuring cost in a multiproduct firm. Its initial response was to change little in how bromides and bleach costs were calculated. Where joint costs had to be divided, it relied on the firm's own history as its guide. As the number of products of the firm increased, this response became inadequate, and new methods were adopted. The firm also began to produce more disaggregated measures of cost that reported average input costs for particular inputs (e.g., lime cost per pound of bleach, packaging cost per pound of bleach, etc.) that were product-specific.

The information system continued and increased the production of physical measures of quality and efficiency. These measures were produced primarily for use by plant management to monitor processes and make short-term planning decisions, but summary data (i.e., more aggregated data) were also provided to the firm's board of directors on a regular basis, allowing them to monitor effort and ability on the part of plant management.

The Midland Chemical Company's practice of monthly financial statements was adopted. More detailed monthly income statements for each chemical were also produced. The system of monthly reports was adapted, in steps, to provide management, particularly at the level of the board of directors, with data that would allow it to allocate capital resources among the various products on which research was conducted at Midland (i.e., to aid in long-term planning).

### 3.5.4.1   The Weekly Report: Timeliness Trade-offs

A new weekly report, introduced immediately following the merger, simply combined the two reports of the original firms (figs. 3.5 and 3.6). This continued to include both financial and technical data and was distributed to members of the board of directors as well as Dow and Graves at the Midland plant. However, partly because the production of financial data occurred with a lengthier delay, and partly because financial and technical data were made accessible to different members of plant management, several modifications were shortly made in the regular report forms.

In October 1900, a new "preliminary" report form was introduced, in response to complaints, mostly from the treasurer Charles Post, that the lengthier weekly report was not being produced promptly (fig. 3.8).[47] The new report was printed on one-inch-by-three-inch card stock.[48] It reported only net pounds of bleach made and "Lbs. [bleach] per Ampere day" (a measure of technical efficiency) for both plants A and C (the bleach plants) and net pounds bromide barreled and "averaged Lbs Brine pumped per minute" (also a measure of technical efficiency) for plant B (the bromide plant). Several copies were made each week and sent to members of the board of directors. These physical measures of output and efficiency, regularly used by plant management in monitoring the production process, were available essentially instantaneously. Monetary data were available only with a delay.

### 3.5.4.2   Monthly Cost and Efficiency Reports

The firm continued to produce the data that had previously been included in the general manager's weekly report. It was now divided among several differ-

---

47. Post wrote to Dow, "Can you arrange to have the weekly reports sent in more regularly? I have frequent inquiries from the stockholders here, and it will be a great favor to me if the report for the previous week could be here as early as Wednesday. As you know, they are sometimes a week or more late, and if I could say to those inquiring that the report will be in on Wednesday, it would be a great convenience to us all" (27 April 1900, file 000012c, Dow Papers). Dow responded, "We can arrange to send you the output for each week on the following Monday morning, and by increasing our office force we could get a complete report out by Wednesday, but in that case there would not be enough work to keep them busy the balance of the week. As it is now our office force is of such size that we can get the reports of one week out of the way before the reports of the next one come in, but are not able to do much better than that. Under the present arrangement you see it would be impossible to promise the reports before Saturday afternoon, and they will not reach you until Monday morning" (30 April 1900, file 000012c). Post wrote back, "Your letter in regard to statement received yesterday. If [sic] course, it is not contemplated that you should increase the office force at present, but I was not aware that that would be necessary in order to get the statement in the following week, as you have sometimes sent them more promptly than you have been doing recently. However, if you could send me a short statement, giving the production for the week, amount sold, and price received, that would answer every purpose until your clerk would have time to make a complete statement" (2 May 1900, file 000012c). See file 010070 for samples of the new report. See file 000005 for the first nine weeks of the new report series.

48. The first nine weeks of the report were typed on half-size sheets of paper. See file 000005, Dow Papers.

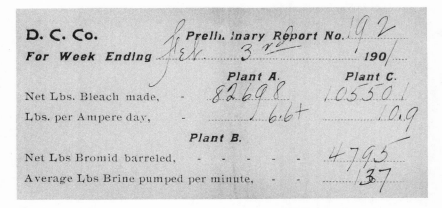

**Fig. 3.8    Preliminary weekly report, Dow Chemical Company, 1900–?**

| Factory Report Plant B | | | | | | | | Fiscal Year Ending May 31, 1905 | | | | | |
|---|---|---|---|---|---|---|---|---|---|---|---|---|---|
| | June | July | Aug | Sept | Oct | Nov | Dec | Jan | Feb | Mch | Apr | May | Jkl |
| Lbs Bromine Mfd | 3825 | 7788 | 7001 | 4820 | 2127 | 9381 | 2295 | 728 | 155 | 7 | | 54 | 38167 |
| Lbs Acid Used | 4855 | 6849 | 8155 | 5568 | 3955 | 9290 | 3480 | 1330 | — | | 2665 | | 46147 |
| % Acid | 127½ | 87¾ | 116⅘ | 116⅘ | 186⅔⁄₁₀ | 111⁷⁄₁₀₀ | 132¾⁄₁₀₀ | 182⁹⁵⁄₁₀₀ | | | | | |
| | | | | | | | | | | | | | |
| Lbs NH₄Br Mfd | — | — | 66 | 479 | 0 | 417½ | 2518½ | 1420 | 263 | 904 | 2416 | 2904 | 11284 |
| Ammonia in NH₄Br | — | — | | 383 | | 333 | 2012 | 1136 | 211 | 723 | 1933 | 1694 | 8425 |
| Ammonia Used | — | — | 366 | 281 | 380 | 2605 | 1451 | 613 | 380 | 2294 | 2118 | 10507 |
| Excess of Ammonia Used | — | — | 2 | | 47 | 593 | 315 | 402 | 265 | 361 | 424 | 1801 |
| Excess of Ammonia % | — | — | 6⁄₁₀ | | 14¹¹⁄₁₀ | 29⁴⁷⁄₁₀₀ | 27⁷²⁄₁₀₀ | 190⅚⁄₁₀₀ | | 18⁴⁷⁄₁₀ | 11⁴⁵⁄₁₀ | 21³⁸⁄₁₀₀ |

**Fig. 3.9    Monthly factory report, Dow Chemical Company, 1902?–1914?**

ent monthly reports, each of which had a somewhat different focus and audience. The monthly "factory report" (fig. 3.9) is one of several reports that were regularly produced, primarily for use by plant managers, that focused on technical and quality considerations. The report shown here gives technical data on the Midland bromide plant's production of liquid bromine and ammonium bromide, two of the newer products of the firm. Quality control became increasingly important as Dow Chemical integrated forward and was faced with a more competitive environment. The purity of Dow bromides increased from about 80 percent at the time of the merger to 99 percent in 1903. This gave it access to the European market, which had a very restrictive pharmacopoeia. It also allowed it to support an increase in the U.S. pharmacopoeia, which it could satisfy and its less diligent domestic competitors could not.

Average cost measures were included in several different reports, including the monthly financial statements (fig. 3.10), the "statement of monthly earn-

Form 2. 1909

THE DOW CHEMICAL COMPANY.

DETAILED STATEMENT OF EARNINGS AND EXPENSES FOR *February* 1908

| SALES. | ~~Bleaching Powder.~~ | | Bromid Potassium. | | TOTAL. |
|---|---|---|---|---|---|
| *Gross Sales* | 383013 | | | | |
| Less Discount and Allowance, | 10545 | | | | |
| Total Net Sales, | 372468 | | | | |
| Increase or Decrease* in Merchandise, | 64943 | | | | |
| Total Earnings, | 437411 | | | | |
| EXPENSES. | | Av. per 100 lbs. | | Av per lb. | |
| 1. Maintenance of Bldgs. & Grounds, | * * | | | | |
| 2. Maintenance of ~~Tools & Mach's.~~ *$CCl_4$ Eqpt.* | 11038 | | | | |
| 3. Maintenance of ~~Power Plant.~~ *$CHCl_3$ Eqpt.* | 10150 | | | | |
| 4. Maintenance of Traps, | | | | | |
| 5. | | | | | |
| 6. Maintenance of D Tanks. | | | | | |
| 7. Maintenance of Absorbers, | | | | | |
| 8. Maintenance of Bromid Plant, | | | | | |
| 9. " *in General* | 4249 | | | | |
| 10. | | | | | |
| 11. | | | | | |
| Total Maintenance. | | | | | |
| 12. Superintendence, | | | | | |
| 13. Fuel, | | | | | |
| 14. Engineers and Firemen, | | | | | |
| 15. Misc. Factory Expense, | 7081 | | | | |
| Total Operating, | | | | | |
| 16. ~~Bleaching Powder,~~ *$CCl_4$ Mfg Ex* | 29163 | | | | |
| 17. ~~Bromid Potassium,~~ *$CHCl_3$ " "* | 267431 | | | | |
| 18. | | | | | |
| 19. | | | | | |
| 20. | | | | | |
| 21. | | | | | |
| Total Manufacturing, | | | | | |
| Total Factory Expense, | | | | | |
| % to Total Earnings, | | | | | |
| Gross Factory Profit, | | | | | |
| Selling Expense, | | | | | |
| 25. Salaries & Expenses of Sales Office, | 3525 | | | | |
| 26. Commissions, | | | | | |
| 27. Advertising, | | | | | |
| Total Selling Expenses, | | | | | |
| % to Total Earnings, | | | | | |
| General Expense, | | | | | |
| 28. Salaries of Officers and Clerks, | 18500 | | | | |
| 29. Office Supplies and Expenses, | 944 | | | | |
| 30. Legal, | | | | | |
| 31. Insurance, | 3873 | | | | |
| 32. Miscellaneous, | | | | | |
| Total General Expense, | | | | | |
| % to Total Earnings, | | | | | |
| Total Expenses, | | | | | |
| % to Total Earnings, | | | | | |
| TAXES. | 1403 | | | | |
| Total Expenses and Taxes, | 357357 | | | | |
| % to Total Earnings, | | | | | |
| NET EARNINGS. | 80054 | | | | |
| ~~% to Total Earnings.~~ *Less Interest* | 11419 | | | | |
| Decrease in red. | 68635 | | | | |

**Fig. 3.10 Detailed statement of earning sand expenses, Dow Chemical Company, 1900?–1907?**

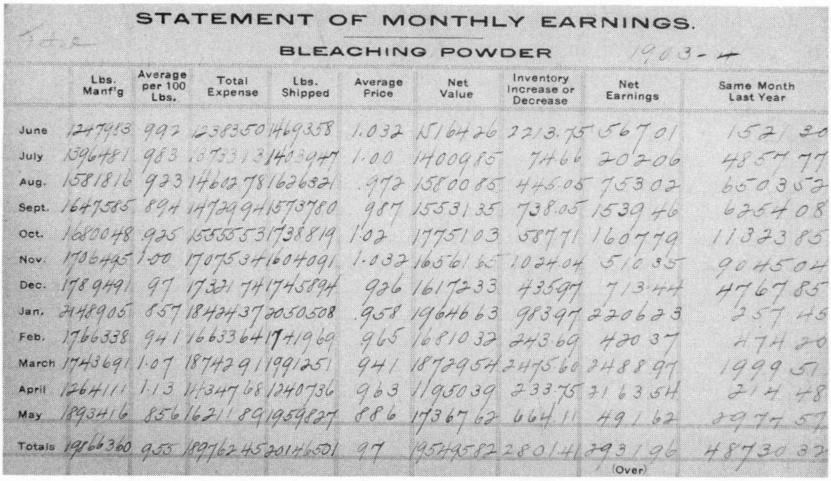

STATEMENT OF MONTHLY EARNINGS.

BLEACHING POWDER 1903-4

| | Lbs. Manf'g | Average per 100 Lbs. | Total Expense | Lbs. Shipped | Average Price | Net Value | Inventory Increase or Decrease | Net Earnings | Same Month Last Year |
|---|---|---|---|---|---|---|---|---|---|
| June | 1247983 | 992 | 1238350 | 1469358 | 1.032 | 1516426 | 2213.75 | 56701 | 152130 |
| July | 1396481 | 983 | 1373313 | 1403947 | 1.00 | 1400985 | 7466 | 20206 | 485777 |
| Aug. | 1581816 | 923 | 1460278 | 1626321 | .972 | 1580085 | 445.05 | 75302 | 650352 |
| Sept. | 1647585 | 894 | 1472994 | 1573780 | 987 | 1553135 | 738.05 | 153946 | 625408 |
| Oct. | 1680048 | 925 | 1555553 | 1738819 | 1.02 | 1775103 | 58771 | 160779 | 1132385 |
| Nov. | 1706495 | 1.00 | 1707534 | 1604091 | 1.032 | 1656165 | 1024.04 | 51635 | 904504 |
| Dec. | 1789491 | 97 | 1732174 | 1745894 | 926 | 1617233 | 43597 | 713.44 | 476785 |
| Jan. | 2148905 | 857 | 1842437 | 2050508 | .958 | 1964663 | 98397 | 220623 | 25745 |
| Feb. | 1766338 | 941 | 1663364 | 1741969 | .965 | 1681032 | 243.69 | 42037 | 47420 |
| March | 1743691 | 1.07 | 1874291 | 1991251 | 941 | 1872954 | 2475.60 | 248897 | 199951 |
| April | 1264111 | 1.13 | 1434768 | 1240736 | 963 | 1195039 | 233.75 | 316354 | 21448 |
| May | 1893416 | 856 | 1621189 | 1959827 | 886 | 1736762 | 664.11 | 49162 | 89775 |
| Totals | 19866360 | 955 | 18976245 | 20146501 | 97 | 19549582 | 280141 | 293196 | 4873032 |

(Over)

**Fig. 3.11 Statement of monthly earnings, Dow Chemical Company, 1902–10**

ings" prepared for each product (fig. 3.11), and detailed (i.e., disaggregated) cost reports for each product.[49] The primary use of the average cost measure was still to give the stockholders in Cleveland a simple way of monitoring the effort and ability of management in Midland and comparing that performance over time. It was not used regularly by plant management to identify inefficiencies (i.e., to monitor processes), or in other ways that would directly inform short-term planning decisions about operations.

This is partly because cost data were not produced in as timely a fashion as other nonfinancial measures of production efficiency. Hence, pounds per ampere day could be reported on the preliminary report, as it was calculated regularly for in-plant use, while average costs took longer to compute. When average costs were computed on a weekly basis, the weekly reports frequently fell behind. Even after monthly reports were introduced, it was not uncommon for the reports to be late. For example, a report comparing the efficiency of the Mount Pleasant and Midland bromide plants stated, "Owing to extra work in Mr. Bennett's department the monthly production statements and balance sheets for bromine and carbonate are several months behind. . . . Mr. Bennett hopes to have his statements brought down to date within two or three weeks, and we should then be able to finally check the logic of the above reasoning" (Statement on Bromine Losses, 28 September 1905, file 050034x, Dow Papers).

49. The form reproduced in figure 3.10 was originally designed for use by the Dow Chemical Company but later modified for use by a second Midland Chemical Company, whose primary products were chloroform and carbon tetrachloride. Only forms that have been so modified are still in existence. Hence the handwritten changes in some of the items on the form.

For these and other reasons, monetary measures played a secondary role in both short-term planning and monitoring processes at the plant. In 1908 Herbert Dow compared the relative usefulness of bookkeeping and "factory efficiency methods" for informing plant-level planning and sided heavily with the latter.

> Successful manufacture, as I see it, consists in having all the operations run right practically all the while, and in order that this may be so it is necessary that when one step goes wrong it shall be detected and remedied immediately and to do so requires a means of control that is continually at work. For example, we analyze the brine in our bromide plant every half hour to make sure that the current and brine are proportionate to each other so that the maximum output is obtained. For example, there are probably a thousand places where the cost of Bleach might be increased. It would be absolutely impossible to devise a book-keeping system that would detect where the error was, and a system that would subdivide bleach charges so that in case the cost were too high it could be located a little closer than it can at present, would undoubtedly be some advantage but the advantage would be so slight that in actual commercial work it would not be worth while. (To H. E. Hackenberg, 31 August 1908, file 080015x, Dow Papers)

Another reason these measures of cost per pound were not used in short-term planning is that the data were not given to managers of individual plants. The only plant management that had access to these data were Dow; Graves, the general superintendent; and Bennett, the bookkeeper and assistant treasurer. Despite recognizing the benefits that might arise from giving these managers this information, it was decided that the risk of competitors obtaining this information was too great to permit its wider dissemination.[50]

This measure was used to monitor the effort (and therefore provide incentives to) of plant managers. Plant managers were aware of this and of the general method used to calculate costs. This appears to have been sufficient to influence their behavior without their observing the numbers produced by the information system. In at least one case a bromide plant manager specifically asked that he be given data on the costs of his plant, and that they be systematically compared with those of the other bromide plant.[51] In another case a plant superintendent asked that the charges for power consumption to his plant be reduced and charged to another plant, because he was not receiving power at the rate desired.[52]

50. See letters from H. E. Hackenberg to H. H. Dow, 25 May 1905, file 050014x; A. E. Convers to H. H. Dow, 22 May 1905, file 050011c; H. H. Dow to A. E. Convers, 24 May 1905, file 050011x; A. E. Convers to H. H. Dow, 31 May 1905, file 050011x; and H. H. Dow to A. E. Convers, 2 June 1905, file 050011x, Dow Papers.
51. See letter from Shepherd, superintendent of the Mount Pleasant bromide plant, to H. H. Dow, 21 March 1907, file 070052c, Dow Papers.
52. See letter from C. W. Jones, superintendent of the bromide plant, to H. H. Dow, 26 September 1912: "For the past few weeks the extraction of B plant [the Midland bromide plant] has not averaged quite 90%. At least another 5% might have been extracted had we gotten the desired

The use of this measure as a monitor for Herbert Dow was sufficient under ordinary circumstances. However, when the firm's finances reached crisis proportions in 1903, due to a fall in the price of bleach simultaneous with large expansion by the Dow Company, the board of directors demanded much more timely and more disaggregated information that would allow them to directly intervene in decisions that had previously been left to Dow.

Thus in August 1903 the executive committee of the board of directors requested the production of a weekly report on the firm's cash position.[53] The report, which continued to be produced for at least two years, included cash received and disbursed, cash on hand (or overdraft), sales of bleach and bromides, accounts receivable, and accounts payable.

The board was also given, from January 1902 to September 1903, a breakdown of cost per pound for bleach into all of the component accounts to which current expenses were charged. This allowed them to monitor Herbert Dow's decisions on a more detailed basis. These data were produced before and after this period, but only for the information of Dow and Graves.[54]

Thus, during this period the quantity and types of information systematically collected about internal operations continued to increase. In general, though there were exceptions, management relied on nonmonetary data for monitoring processes and making short-term planning decisions. Monetary measures were more frequently used for monitoring people for effort; the board of directors usually relied on highly aggregated measures to monitor Herbert Dow. More disaggregated monetary measures were used to monitor managers farther down in the firm hierarchy. Finally, as discussed below, as

---

current, as we used to get. We have been getting a good supply of brine, but have not gotten sufficient current to handle it. The trouble seems to be due to favoring the caustic and chlorine plants. Since the maintenance of wells and cost of pumping brine is charged up to the Bromide plant, we are paying something that we are not permitted to use. We request that if it is not deemed expedient to give B plant the desired current, that a charge be made against the caustic and chlorine plants in favor of B plant, proportionate to the amount of loss we are forced to suffer; that is, a certain percent of the cost of maintenance of wells and pumping of brine be charged to caustic and chlorine plants" (file 120008x, Dow Papers). This is the first indication that I have seen of the costs measured by the accounting system being an issue of tension between the managers of the different areas.

53. See letter from H. E. Hackenberg to H. H. Dow, 5 August 1903, informing him that the executive committee would like to review all bills before payment and requesting that he send them "weekly all the information that you can give them of any kind relating to the business of the company. I have written Mr. Bennett to prepare a statement such as is contemplated" (file 030028c, Dow Papers). The only existing copy of this report is dated 11 March 1905, file 050045x.

54. See letter from Bennett, the bookkeeper, to Hackenberg, the secretary of the company, discussing the audit report by Haskins and Sells, 11 July 1905: "The information contained in Exhibit B. schedule No. 1 has practically been compiled in this same form in our office here for the past several years for the benefit of the General Manager and the Superintendent, who, of course, wish to know the cost of all raw materials etc. I believe that the President and Secretary both stated that such details should not be laid before them except as they cared to investigate the records from time to time in this office. I am forwarding these records as they may be some help if a new classification is desired" (file 050061x, Dow Papers).

the firm became more multiproduct, new informational forms were developed to aid in long-term planning.

### 3.5.4.3    Measuring Profits by Product

The most significant change in the accounting system following the merger was the production of data that allowed the board of directors to compare the profitability of its products. The computation of average profit for each product seems to have played an important role in shaping thinking about the relative profitability of different products and the allocation of capital to the production of various products (i.e., long-term planning). Changes were made in the method of calculating average profits for each product in 1905 and 1909. Each of the changes was designed to recognize the increasing multiproductness of the firm.

At no point during this period do we see the regular compilation of rates of profit on different lines of product that Chandler (1977) and Johnson (1975) have argued are the culmination of the development of accounting in the multiproduct firm.

The new monthly financial statement (balance sheet and income statements) also included a report entitled "Detailed Statement of Earnings and Expenses" (fig. 3.10). In this report, the firms expenditures were divided between bleach and bromides. Product expenditures were then reported as a percentage of gross earnings. Net earnings (i.e., profits) for each product are reported. Similar data were included, along with nonmonetary data, on the "Statement of Monthly Earnings" prepared for each product (fig. 3.11). The latter report shows manufacturing profit, while the former gives profits net of sales and general expense.

The production of these measures required that the firm divide the expenses of the firm between these two products. As might be expected, the division chosen reflected the historical evolution of the company. The maintenance of wells, for example, which had been the property of the Midland Chemical Company, was charged entirely to bromides. When the companies were separate, the Midland had provided debrominated brine to the bleach company at no cost, and even after the merger the capacity of the bromide plant did not constrain the capacity of the bleach plant (i.e., debrominated brine was not scarce), so bromides were charged with the entire cost of producing the raw brine. On the other hand, the maintenance of the electric power plant, built by the Dow Chemical Company, was charged primarily to the cost of bleach, though an estimated charge, based on the estimated output of the bromide plant, was charged to the cost of bromides, and credited to bleach. Note that both these charges were maintenance charges. The firm did not include any allocated fixed or depreciation costs in its cost of product, even when it was advised to do so by outside auditors.[55]

---

55. See Levenstein (1991, chap. 5) for a more detailed discussion of the Haskins and Sells report and the response of Dow management to it.

The use of these historically based divisions became problematic, however, as the number of products of the firm increased. These procedures were changed as a result of the recommendations of the 1905 audit by Haskins and Sells.[56] It had previously been the practice of the company to produce measures of product cost for bleach and bromides, as described above, on a regular basis. By 1905, however, these were not the only products of the company. The company sold electricity and water to the City of Midland and to other Midland firms. More importantly, an increasingly larger fraction of its output of chlorine was not consumed as bleach. Instead chlorine itself was sold to other firms that had built plants adjacent to the Dow Chemical Company for that purpose. These included the Midland (II) Chemical Company, which manufactured chloroform and carbon tetrachloride, and the Merck Company.[57] The Dow Company would itself use chlorine to produce a wide range of products over the next ten years. The accounting system at Dow treated the income from these various sales of power and chlorine as credits to the cost of producing bleach. No attempt was made to determine the cost incurred or profit earned on these transactions. While this allowed the firm to avoid the inherent arbitrariness involved in the allocation of joint costs, it also made it more difficult to evaluate the profitability of new products as they were introduced.

The Haskins and Sells 1905 report recommended creating separate accounts to credit receipts for sale of chlorine, electricity, water, and so forth, rather than simply crediting them to the cost of bleach.

> Certain accounts affecting the cost of product were found to be credited with the amount received for sale of electric current and other services. The materials and supplies inventory accounts were also found credited with the selling price of materials sold at a profit. These accounts were adjusted to eliminate the credit representing such element of profit, and the amounts for sale of electric current and water service from the operating plant are stated in Exhibit "B" as sales. (20 June 1905, p. 4, file 050061x, Dow Papers)

When this change was made, it led to problems in interpreting the cost of bleach figures that were produced later, as, absent these credits, bleach appeared more expensive.[58] The total profits earned by the company in the joint production of bleach and power were, of course, unchanged.

Haskins and Sells also recommended creating separate accounts to which

---

56. 20 June 1905, file 050061x, Dow Papers.

57. The Midland (II) Chemical Company was formed in 1902 by Herbert Dow, A. W. Smith, and W. O. Quayle. After several years of less than successful operation, its entire facilities were leased to the Dow Chemical Company in 1908. The Midland (II) Company was purchased by the Dow Company in 1914.

58. See letters from H. H. Dow to A. E. Convers, 31 October 1905, file 050012c; C. A. Post to H. H. Dow, 1 November 1905, file 050021x; H. H. Dow to C. A. Post, 3 November 1905, file 050021x; C. A. Post to H. H. Dow, 6 November 1905, file 050021x; and H. H. Dow to C. A. Post, 14 November 1905, file 050021x, Dow Papers.

to charge the cost of producing water and power sold to the city, and so forth, so that an estimate of the profit on these transactions could be made: "It is suggested that the maintenance of properties not employed in manufacturing be charged to separate maintenance accounts from those applicable to cost of production, so that the cost of maintaining such properties can be applied against the rental received therefrom" (20 June 1905, p. 5, file 050061x, Dow Papers). While this change led to confusion and difficulty in the short run, it highlighted the increasing profits that the firm was earning from chlorine consumed in other forms besides bleach.

Bennett's initial response to this proposal to set up separate accounts for each product varied depending on the importance of the product in the overall strategy of the Dow Chemical Company.

> I believe our method of handling the credit of sales with possibly the exception of the sales of Chlorin gas while probably not correct from a strict accounting standpoint has been correct inasmuch as the business is conducted only for the manufacture of Bleaching Powder and Bromides, and these credits have only been used to obtain the correct cost of Bleaching Powder and Bromides, and the profit contained in these credits is small in comparison to the total amount. (Letter from E. W. Bennett to H. E. Hackenberg, 11 July 1905, file 050061x, Dow Papers)

Despite Bennett's reservations, the existing records indicate that the company did decide to treat all items sold symmetrically, showing a separate profit for each item (fig. 3.12). The problem of allocating joint costs was not easily solved, however. Herbert Dow wrote to A. E. Convers, H. E. Hackenberg, and C. A. Post explaining the new method of computation of costs, and the difficulties arising therefrom.

> So far we have been unable to find a satisfactory system for separating the cost of chlorine sold Mr. Quayle and electric light sold the city. On this account, the cost was charged in with the Bleaching Powder, and the total receipts from Chlorine and electricity therefore stand, at the present time, entirely as profit. This system, of course, is just as bad as the old one, in which the profits stood as a credit to expense, but it is now in such shape that by another month we can probably show it as an independent item of profit. (31 October 1905, file 050012x, Dow Papers)

The problem was solved for the time being, but arose repeatedly as new products were added.[59] These difficulties were exacerbated when the company in-

59. Three years later Herbert Dow was still writing to Cleveland to explain the difficulties in dividing up joint costs among the increasing number of products.

What has brought this matter up is a more or less exhaustive investigation of last month's run of the benzoate plant. In carrying this work out we find there is no one here who has a sufficient combination of chemical and book-keeping knowledge to be sure that the results obtained represent the actual conditions, (and if we wished to be extremely particular, we might say that strictly accurate accounting in this case is an absolute impossibility). In the benzoate plant there are a number of steps in the process and these steps are not so clear cut and well defined that

FORM 2

**THE DOW CHEMICAL COMPANY.**

INCOME ACCOUNT.

| | Month of July 190 7 | | | From Beginning of Fiscal Year | | |
|---|---|---|---|---|---|---|
| | NET SHIPMENTS BILLED | COST OF SHIPMENTS BILLED | APPARENT PROFIT | NET SHIPMENTS BILLED | COST OF SHIPMENTS BILLED | APPARENT PROFIT |
| Bleaching Powder, | 2185654 | 2204572 | 18918 | 4719077 | 4424510 | 294567 |
| Bromids, | 1674108 | 1219406 | 454702 | 3057513 | 1977207 | 1080308 |
| Sodium Benzoate, | 171847 | 113225 | 58622 | 751588 | 611403 | 140185 |
| Chlorin, | 114684 | 69478 | 45206 | 241277 | 146178 | 95099 |
| Bromozone, | | 380 | 380 | 19115 | 5968 | 13147 |
| Waste Brine, | | | | | | |
| Power and Current, | 28726 | 9295 | 11431 | 63670 | 25345 | 38325 |
| | 400 | | 400 | 8 | | 8 |
| Total, | 4175419 | 3616356 | 559063 | 8853042 | 7190611 | 1662431 |

**LESS SELLING & GEN'L EXPENSES.**

**SELLING EXPENSES.**

| | | | | | | |
|---|---|---|---|---|---|---|
| Salaries and Expenses of Salesmen, | | | 285 | | | 53834 |
| Commissions, | | | | | | |
| Salaries—Sales Department, | | | 12034 | | | 24068 |
| Incidentals, | | | 12093 | | | 15231 |
| Total Selling Expenses, | | | 52627 | | | 93133 |

**GENERAL EXPENSES.**

| | | | | | | |
|---|---|---|---|---|---|---|
| Salaries and Expenses of Officers, | | | 67253 | | | 131973 |
| Salaries of Clerks and Attendants, | | | 25734 | | | 51468 |
| Printing and Stationery, | | | 771 ✓ | | | 5725 |
| Telephone and Telegraph, | | | 5419 ✓ | | | 5957 |
| Exchange and Collection Fees, | | | 197 ✓ | | | 409 |
| Credit Service and Collection Costs, | | | | | | |
| Legal Expenses, | | | | | | 19060 |
| Alterations and Repairs to Office F. & F. | | | 679 ✓ | | | 3716 |
| Incidentals, | | | 7364 | | | 17146 |
| Total General Expenses, | | | 107417 | | | 231054 |
| Total Selling and General Expenses | | | 160044 | | | 324187 |
| Gross Income from Operations | | | 399019 | | | 1338244 |

**CREDITS TO INCOME.**

| | | | | | | |
|---|---|---|---|---|---|---|
| Cash Discounts—Received, | | | 9219 | | | 21829 |
| Interest          " | | | 46112 | | | 93108 |
| Income Unclassified, | | | 2167 | | | 4584 |
| Proceeds from Sale of Scrap, Cinders, Etc. | | | 20503 | | | 66109 |
| Rental for Dwellings and other Property, | | | 171 | | | 3591 |
| Suspense, | | | | | | |
| Total Credits to Income, | | | 77830 | | | 182039 |
| Gross Income, | | | 476849 | | | 1520283 |

**CHARGES AGAINST INCOME.**

| | | | | | | |
|---|---|---|---|---|---|---|
| Cash Discount Paid, | | | 24832 | | | 54103 |
| Interest on Notes and Accounts, | | | 57892 | | | 108032 |
| Gratuities and Donations, | | | | | | 500 |
| Accounts Written Off, | | | 29780 | | | 29780 |
| Suspense, | | | 67211 | | | 134406 |
| | | | 25 | | | 2960 |
| Total Charges against Income, | | | 182215 | | | 379281 |
| Net Apparent Profit for Month, | | | 294634 | | | 1141002 |

**Fig. 3.12   Monthly financial statement, income account, Dow Chemical Company, 1907–13**

troduced a new electrolytic cell in 1913 that jointly produced chlorine and caustic soda.[60] They were apparently outweighed by the information made available for an increasing number of products. The importance of this decision to calculate separately the cost of chlorine and other chlorine products is highlighted by the company's decision, in 1913, to withdraw from the bleach business and use all of its chlorine output to make higher-value products.[61]

Further changes in the costing system were made in 1909. The content of the changes in 1909 is not as clear from the record, but the purpose is. To a meeting of plant management on 30 July 1909, "Bennett stated briefly reasons for the change in system being necessary, principally because of the sale of a more extended line of products, which line is growing. The old system was not satisfactorily adaptable to even the present business, whereas present system has already shown our old idea as to cost of chlorine wrong. Present system is adaptable to increased line of manufacture" (Minutes Book of daily plant meetings).

Simultaneous with these changes a new set of monthly reports was introduced that highlighted the net earnings and price-cost margin (the difference between "Av. Price Received" and measures of "Average Cost") of each product (fig. 3.13). These reports were discussed at monthly meetings of the board of directors and were used to evaluate the success of both new and old product lines. The use of price-cost margins and net income, compared only informally to expected incremental investment, to inform long-term planning capital allocation decisions, continued throughout the period under study.

## 3.6    Conclusion

From 1892 to 1898 the Midland Chemical Company kept a very sparse set of records that did not much resemble standard accounting practice. The fi-

---

they can be isolated one from the other without introducing complications that would not seem advisable.

For example, Plant E is shut down. The benzoate plant derives steam from Plant E, as does one water works. During the time that Plant E is shut down nearly a full crew of firemen is employed and a big boiler and more or less big pipe kept hot with attendant losses. If it were not for the benzoate plant we would probably shut down plant E and get our water supply entirely from the other station. We are not sure of this fact, however, as the forcing of the pumps at the other station might not be satisfactory in every respect. During frosty weather it would be necessary to keep a boiler in Plant E running. Under these circumstances should the benzoate plant be charged an extra price for steam during the time that Plant E is not running?

If so, the rule would apply in a number of other cases and some of them are much more involved and complicated than this case. (H. H. Dow to H. E. Hackenberg, 31 August 1908, file 080015x, Dow Papers)

This suggests that, contrary to traditional accounting history, and similarly to Johnson and Kaplan's (1987) argument, firms in this period had a clearer notion of avoidable and incremental costs than did the accountants of the day.

60. Chlorine-caustic cells, though of a different design, had been in use at Niagara Falls since 1897 (Trescott 1981).

61. They continued to produce bleach for several years, however, selling to their established customers.

```
                    BLEACHING POWDER
                    MONTH OF APRIL 1912.
                    ----------
```

COMPARISON:

|  | April 1912 | March 1912 | April 1911 |
|---|---|---|---|
| Net Earnings | 1,329.56 | 1,507.10 | 2,563.49 |
| Lbs. Shipped | 1,995,446 | 1,909,181 | 1,537,630 |
| Av.Price Received | 1.246 | 1.25 | 1.25 |
| Av. Total Cost | 1.31 | 1.17 | 1.40 |
| Lbs. Finished | 2,050,554 | 1,842,505 | 1,460,493 |
| Av. Factory Cost | 1.19 | 1.08 | 1.35 |

Selling price normal.

Average factory cost abnormally high, partly due to high cost of lime. This was probably due to enormous stock of lime on hand in process, preventing securing of a correct inventory of the lime.

Package cost also high.

High total chlorine content in Bleaching Powder also increased the cost of chlorine per 100 lbs. of Bleach.

Auditor.

May 11th, 1912.

**Fig. 3.13    Monthly product report, Dow Chemical Company, 1910–13?**

nancial reports of the company were produced annually, or sometimes semiannually, but certainly not with enough frequency to be used as aids in management. That the irregular arrangement of these accounts prevented them from being used even as an aid to potential stockholders is indicated by Hackenberg's having them rewritten prior to an increase in capitalization and subsequent merger with the Dow Chemical Company.

I presume that I now have all the bills and books, etc. of the Company from its organization, and while I have not had time to more than casually look through the books, a system of accounts has evidently been employed at variance with anything in my experience of fifteen years, and I think it quite important to get the expert at work to write up a new set from the beginning, as soon as possible, especially in view of our intention to increase the Capital Stock to $300,000.00. (Letter from H. E. Hackenberg to H. S. Cooper, 18 January 1899, file 990047x, Dow Papers)

With Hackenberg's arrival in 1898, the accounts were kept with greater care and in a fashion comprehensible to others. Perhaps more importantly for our purposes, he instituted the production of monthly financial reports. This practice was adopted at the Dow Chemical Company when he became its secretary in 1900. These reports were used both by Herbert Dow and the board of directors to monitor effort by plant management.

Meanwhile, Herbert Dow, first at the Dow Process Company and then at the Dow Chemical Company, was experimenting with the use of reporting procedures such as daily job cards and weekly reports on factory efficiency, measured both in terms of physical consumption of inputs and their dollar cost. The former provided information that was used to monitor employee effort and make short-term planning decisions regarding plant operations.

After the merger of the Dow and Midland Chemical companies, the information system continued to be adapted to provide very frequent technical measures of quality and production efficiency, for use in monitoring processes and short-term planning, somewhat less frequent monetary measures, primarily used to monitor people for effort, and measures, even less frequent but still quite regular, of net profit on an increasing number of products, used somewhat informally to make long-term planning decisions.

While many factors influenced the firm's decisions regarding the collection and calculation of cost data, including the recommendations of professional auditors, the most important determinants were changes in firm strategy and the organization of the markets in which the firms' products were distributed. The firm's accounting records evolved during this period from a fairly haphazard affair, used rarely in the management of the firm, to a complex system that produced daily, weekly, and monthly reports used actively by both plant management and the board of directors to monitor plant managers and make long-term capital allocation decisions. As the firm evolved from one that produced only one product and sold it in cartelized market to one that produced many joint products sold in increasingly competitive markets, the demands on the information system changed. The modifications of the information system instituted by management seem to have responded well, if not always smoothly, to these new demands. Some of these modifications reflect movement toward modern standard accounting procedures, and some are quite distinct.

# References

Arnold, H. L. 1899. *The complete cost keeper.* New York: Engineering Magazine Press.

Baiman, Stanley. 1982. Agency research in managerial accounting: A survey. *Journal of Accounting Literature* 1(Spring):154–213.

Campbell, Murray, and Harrison Hatton. 1951. *Herbert H. Dow: Pioneer in creative chemistry.* New York: Appleton-Century-Crofts.

Chandler, Alfred D., Jr. 1962. *Strategy and structure.* Cambridge: MIT Press.

———. 1977. *The visible hand: The managerial revolution in American business.* Cambridge: Harvard University Press.

Chatfield, Michael. 1977. *A history of accounting thought.* Huntington, NY: R. E. Krieger Publishing Co.

Demski, Joel S., and David M. Kreps. 1982. Models in managerial accounting. *Journal of Accounting Research,* Supp. 20:117–60.

Dow, Herbert H. Papers. Post Street Archives, Midland, MI.

Garner, S. Paul. 1976. *Evolution of cost accounting to 1925.* Tuscaloosa: University of Alabama Press.

Greif, Avner. 1989. Reputation and coalitions in medieval trade: Maghribi traders. *Journal of Economic History* 59:857–82.

Jacoby, Sanford. 1985. *Employing bureaucracy: Managers, unions, and the transformation of work in American industry, 1900–1945.* New York: Columbia University Press.

Johnson, H. Thomas. 1975. Management accounting in an early integrated industrial: E. I. du Pont de Nemours Powder Company, 1903–1912. *Business History Review* 49:184–204.

Johnson, H. Thomas, and Robert S. Kaplan. 1987. *Relevance lost: The rise and fall of management accounting.* Boston: Harvard Business School Press.

Kistler, Linda H., Clairmont P. Carter, and Brackston Hinchey. 1984. Planning and control in the nineteenth century ice trade. *Accounting Historians Journal* 11:19–30.

Lazonick, William. 1988. Theory, history, and the capitalist enterprise: Lending *The economic institutions of capitalism* a visible hand. Manuscript. New York.

———. 1990. *Business organization and the myth of the market economy.* Cambridge: Cambridge University Press.

Levenstein, Margaret. 1989. The feasibility and stability of collusion: A study of the pre–World War I bromine industry. Manuscript. Lansing, MI.

———. 1991. Information systems and internal organization: A study of the Dow Chemical Company, 1890–1914. Ph.D. diss., Yale University, New Haven.

Littleton, Ananias Charles. 1933. *Accounting evolution to 1900.* New York: Russell and Russell.

Loveday, Amos J. 1980. Technology, cost accounting, and management in the cut nail industry of the upper Ohio valley, 1865–1890. *Business and Economic History* 9:41–50.

Lubar, Steven. 1984. Managerial structure and technological style: The Lowell mills, 1821–1880. *Business and Economic History* 13:20–30.

McGaw, Judith A. 1985. Accounting for innovation: Technological change and business practice in the Berkshire County paper industry. *Technology and Culture* 26:703–25.

Metcalfe, Henry. 1885. *The cost of manufactures.* New York: J. Wiley and Sons.

Previts, Gary John, and Barbara DuBois Merino. 1979. *A history of accounting in America.* New York: John Wiley and Sons.

ten Have, O. 1976. *The history of accountancy.* Palo Alto, CA: Bay Books.

Trescott, Martha M. 1981. *The rise of the American electrochemicals industry, 1880–1910: Studies in the American technological environment.* Westport, CT: Greenwood Press.

Tyson, Thomas. 1988. The nature and function of cost keeping in a late nineteenth century small business. *Journal of Accounting History* 15:29–44.

Whitehead, Don. 1968. *The Dow story.* New York: McGraw-Hill Book Co.

Yates, Dorothy Langdon. 1987. *Salt of the earth: A history of Midland County, Michigan.* Midland, MI: Midland County Historical Society.

Yates, JoAnne. 1989. *Control through communication: The rise of system in American management.* Baltimore: Johns Hopkins University Press.

## Comment    Barry Supple

Margaret Levenstein's paper raises a number of issues the importance of which is relevant to both company biography (in this case the early history of Dow Chemical) and more general themes (notably the symbiotic relation between accounting systems and management control on the one hand and markets and management strategies on the other).

The presentation of my comments on her paper may be helped if it is introduced by my own summary of what I take to be its highlights—which, at the least, will expose the degree to which I have grasped, or (it may well be) misunderstood, Levenstein's argument.

The core of the paper is the contrast between two types of information systems, although occasionally the phrase has a rather grandiose ring, dealing as we are with a fairly primitive institution, rather threadbare archives, and sketchy pieces of paper.

In any event, the "systems" under discussion are identified with two firms, whose histories were closely interwoven and ultimately identified by merger.

The original firm, the Midland Chemical Company, founded in 1892, is seen by Levenstein as a noninnovative enterprise, dominated by the aspirations of its nontechnical owners, who restricted the activities and ambitions of its striving and ambitious founder, Herbert Dow. The firm's investors were apparently content with a "mercantile" system of accounts, that is, broad reports by the general manager on his cash situation and the overall cash flow of the firm. By the same token, there was little systematized information available that would have been relevant to the monitoring of plant management and performance (product costs and quality, efficiency, and profitability).

In the paper these lackadaisical procedures are related to the participation of Midland in a cartel (where sales were assured but limited) and to the resulting absence of any very strong incentive to control costs. This seems persua-

Barry Supple is professor of economic history at the University of Cambridge and Master of St. Catharine's College.

sive as far as it goes, although it seems to me that it would also have been helpful if the paper had provided some critical appraisal of the implications of the scale of operations involved; after all, a Mickey Mouse business may not need any very elaborate communication networks, and in these years Midland was hardly a giant among enterprises. But, whatever the relevance of grandiose concepts, the board's attitude and constraints ultimately led to the resignation of the founder, Dow.

Second, and by way of contrast, Levenstein discusses the case of the Dow Chemical Company (founded by Dow after he left Midland). Dow Chemical, she argues, provided a different context for information systems, since it first of all pursued a much more vigorous policy of product and process innovation and diversification, and subsequently exemplified a more aggressive attitude to market expansion and competition.

Although the direction of the functional relationship is not always clear, these strategies were associated with the gradual extension of Dow's system of information flows. This involved the use of daily time cards to keep track of labor (and then to analyze costs over time) and the compilation of weekly reports enumerating the cost of different plant activities and measuring technical efficiency and product quality.

Meanwhile, in 1898 Herbert Dow had gained control of Midland, which (not surprisingly) adopted the practice of weekly financial and technical reports. Further, Midland's treasurer, H. E. Hackenberg, introduced a system of monthly financial reports.

In 1900 the two firms merged, with Hackenberg as secretary. Now the monthly reports he had devised at Midland were adopted at the new corporation, and reporting systems were amalgamated and developed, being used primarily to monitor plant activity.

At this point we encounter the other stem of Levenstein's argument: the adducing of statistical information was extended from the sphere of financial reporting for the benefit of shareholders interested primarily in final performance. Now it was also adapted to the management and plant needs of a multiproduct firm—including the need to measure the profitability of different products, albeit not with the regularity and overriding investment implications to which Chandler has drawn our attention.

At the same time, however, Levenstein makes the point that much of the financial/cost reporting was still for the benefit of the board of directors, whereas more "technical" reporting (that is, reports on physical efficiency, throughput, and quality) evolved as a tool for (plant) management—a logical and perhaps necessary step at a time when quality control was becoming more important competitively. She quotes Dow himself on the superiority of "factory efficiency methods" over financial bookkeeping, and points to the secrecy surrounding unit cost data (with intermediate management being denied access to it)—both points that seem to bear out Thomas Johnson's thesis (in chap. 2 in this volume).

In practice, however (and again exemplifying some of Johnson's general themes), problems and pitfalls emerged because of the conceptual and practical difficulties of allocating joint costs between different products, and receipts between different accounts. Levenstein makes the point that until 1905 internal accounting was confused in its treatment of the firm's multiple products, and she illustrates this at two levels.

First, the division of costs between bleach and bromides was a function of the historical organization of the company (with the result that the cost of producing some products and the pattern of costs as a whole were unknown or neglected). Second, when the firm diversified into the production and sale of electricity, water, and chlorine, income was credited to the cost of producing bleach, and "no attempt was made to determine the cost incurred or profit earned on these transactions." Consequently, the firm found it difficult to evaluate the profitability of new products.

I have gone into this point at length, because it seems to me to need more explication in terms of the main themes of the paper. Given that these procedures seem to reflect inadequate information systems, how does that square with the paper's other implied argument, that Dow Chemical's systems exemplified a sensitive response to the pressures of a multiproduct firm operating in a more competitive market? What, in the end, determines the quality of the information system adopted? Is there scope for innovation in such a system, and would we expect competition to produce the best possible system at any one time?

These questions are the more pertinent in view of the fact that from 1905 on, as a result of the auditors' report, receipts from the sale of the new products (chlorine, electricity, water) were credited to separate accounts, rather than to the cost of the bleach with which their production had been associated. Curiously, however, Levenstein makes the point that "this change . . . led to problems in interpreting the cost of bleach figures that were produced later," since they made it seem more expensive. Yet, on the surface, the procedure seems more rational and managerially helpful than the preceding system: allocating incomes and (because of an associated recommendation) costs more nearly where they originated. For in this way the profitability of different operations was more easily measured, although the "jointness" of production means that conceptual precision could not be perfect.

In any event, it would have been helpful to have been told a little more about these innovations in information systems—or, since the records are obviously imperfect, to have been provided with a more extensive discussion of possibilities.

What might have been the respective role of accountants and managers? How much of a handicap was the confusing of accounts and products when it came to attributing costs and incomes? How far is the intervention of the auditors (which appears to have achieved an improvement in accounting and information) consistent with Johnson's theory that the objectives and directives of auditors did not always produce the best information basis for management?

In many respects Levenstein's conclusions (implicit and explicit) seem inescapable: subtle physical measures are obviously more useful devices than cash flow data for assessing the performance of different production processes; a firm that does not need (or does not think it needs) to worry about competition and has a generous profit margin will be that much less concerned with close monitoring of its technical efficiency and product costs; multiple products and/or competitive markets and/or an ambition to expand aggressively will (like hanging) concentrate a man's mind wonderfully; accurate cost accounting is better management practice than imperfect cost accounting; a knowledge of the structure of costs and the performance of productive agents is a better basis for business enterprise than a simple knowledge of a single financial outcome for a multiplicity of activities; and the needs and concepts of auditors and accounts concerned with final outcomes are not necessarily the same as those of managers, although on this last point I sense some confusion in that in this instance the professionals' intervention appears to have been a step toward better and more relevant information.

Leaving this last point aside, however, what is still not entirely clear from the material in Levenstein's paper is the extent to which accounting and information flows were "functional" in the sense of arising more or less directly and inescapably from the managerial needs of the business. Obviously, they were not purely so; first, because some of them appear to have been imposed by accountants whose perspective was different from that of managers; second, because innovation and diffusion depended on the outlook and abilities of individual managers; and third, because it is inconceivable that at any one point in time the content and flow of management information are as perfect as they might be—that is, it is obviously possible to envisage an as yet undevised or unapplied improvement, in which case business could perform at a level superior to the current one, and information (or any other) systems that might be generated by current "needs" are not being so produced.

And yet, this paper does on the whole give the impression that what happened was predetermined—the product of need—in the sense that there was a close fit between information and the market situation and strategy that it served.

I appreciate that this is a little unfair to Levenstein in that she does not claim that Midland performed optimally with the data it generated (i.e., it is possible to envisage a more efficient and profitable use of resources facilitated by better information, so that the spatchcock system used imposed its own obvious handicaps in terms of opportunities forgone).

Nevertheless, the tone of the argument is set by Levenstein's somewhat strained references to the relationship between changes in markets and firm strategy, shifts in the demand for information, and the evolution of information systems, and by her claim that, in modifying the information system, management responded well to the new demands of the competitive sale of joint products.

The potential vulnerability of the general argument is exposed by the paper's conclusion, which does little more than highlight the principal narrative facts and associate them with some not particularly subtle concepts (distinctions between information used to monitor employee effort, to make short-term planning decisions, to monitor processes, etc.) and some analytical generalizations about the presumed role of strategy and markets in shaping information systems. The trouble, of course, is that we are here dealing with such a simple level of business organization and such a restrained degree of development that there seems to be a disconcerting contrast between the simplicity of the material and the apparent sophistication of the analysis.

Part of the problem is that so many of the potentially broader implications of the argument are left to be deduced by each reader from the paper itself. Indeed, it is precisely because there is so little apparent assessment of how far these events were representative, or of what might have been alternatives to them, that what happened at Midland and Dow Chemical have the air of functional inevitability.

And yet economists as well as historians should resist this conclusion. In saying this I do not mean to regress to the banalities of old-fashioned business history, seeking explanations and rationale in the unpredictability of individual effort and heroic enterprise. But the essence of the problem can be summarized in a number of questions that are only partially dealt with in Levenstein's paper: How far is organizational innovation a logical (and apparently inevitable) outcome of business needs? Why are information systems improved? In what sense are they "needed" at particular points in time? Why are they not "improved" even more at particular points in time?

Nor do I think that we should be too preoccupied with modernity. Reading about Dow's enthusiasm for "factory efficiency methods," I was reminded of the Boulton and Watt engine manufactory, one hundred years before, where processes were subdivided and measured, where machine speeds were studied and costed, where the average time and expense involved in making each part were calculated. In the evolution of information systems, as in so much of human activity, progress is not linear. More than this, when dealing with exiguous material, commonsense is often a better guide than excessively grand conceptualizations.

# 4

# Investing in Information:

## Supply and Demand Forces in the Use of Information in American Firms, 1850–1920

JoAnne Yates

In chapter 1 in this volume, Daniel M. G. Raff and Peter Temin point out that, contrary to the assumptions of much economic theory of prior decades, "information is costly and hard to find." That fact has significant implications for how information is used in decision making within firms. The period from 1850 to 1920 was one of firm growth and evolution. During it, many American firms first recognized the value of and invested in systematic internal information; of necessity, they also came to recognize its costs.[1] This paper focuses on the interaction over time of supply and demand factors affecting investment in and use of internal information.

Section 4.1 briefly explores the growing demand for internal information during this period. Section 4.2 looks at supply factors affecting the use of internal information. It describes the growth of information technologies, including mechanical and bureaucratic devices and systems, that were adopted to lower the costs of handling internal information. By lowering the cost of collecting, transmitting, analyzing, storing, retrieving, and disseminating internal information to those making and implementing decisions, these technologies made it economic for firms to acquire and use more information.

The longest section (4.3) shows how these supply and demand factors interacted over time in a single company, the Scovill Manufacturing Company. This case study reveals that changes in the availability and flows of informa-

JoAnne Yates is associate professor of management communication at the Sloan School of Management, Massachusetts Institute of Technology.

The author would like to thank Peter Temin for his extensive and helpful comments on multiple drafts of this paper. She also benefited from the comments of other participants in the NBER Preconference and Conference on Microeconomic History, especially those of Bengt Holmstrom, the commentator for this paper, and Naomi Lamoreaux.

1. I have discussed this development at length in Yates (1989). Much of the historical detail in this paper is drawn from that book or from materials gathered for the book, though it is framed and interpreted differently for this paper.

tion occurred unevenly, affected by factors such as managerial needs, financial and human investments in the existing system, and costs of changing the system. Section 4.4 draws some conclusions from this case study and suggests some parallels for contemporary firms.

## 4.1    Information Demand: Growth, Structural Evolution, and Systematic Management

In the small, single-function American firms that predominated before the mid–nineteenth century, market prices and availability were the main sources of information used in decision making by owner/managers (Johnson and Kaplan 1987; Chandler 1977). Account books and correspondence documented external, market transactions; virtually no information was recorded or collected about internal operations, which were managed by the direct oral supervision of the owner/manager(s).

The early nineteenth-century textile factories deviated from this norm. In these factories, where multiple functions were combined in the same facility and where ownership was separated from management, factory owners created the first, relatively primitive cost accounting systems. These information systems, according to Johnson and Kaplan (1987), allowed owners to monitor the costs and profits of their operations to assure that internal, managerial coordination of multiple functions was as efficient as that provided by the market when the functions were separate.

In subsequent decades, the railroads and the telegraph companies appeared, expanding markets for other goods while growing themselves. As these firms grew, expanded their geographical range, and lengthened their hierarchies, their managers faced and gradually responded to new demands for internal information. In the 1840s, the need to assure safety and honesty in dispersed firms led to initial innovations in internal information gathering and dissemination in railroads (e.g., Salsbury 1967). Regular, if still relatively limited, flows of information up the hierarchy documented monetary transactions. Written rule books and instructions documented rules and regulations concerning railroad operations and disseminated them down the hierarchy. Beginning in the 1850s, many growing railroads encountered crises of profitability when growth led to diseconomies of scale and the competitive environment prevented passing costs directly on to customers (Chandler 1977). Major eastern railroads such as the New York and Erie Railroad and the Pennsylvania Railroad instituted extensive systems of data collection and analysis—involving major innovations in financial, cost, and capital accounting—during the 1850s and subsequent decades. They developed a system of records and reports to draw information up the hierarchy for monitoring, assessing, and comparing performance within and among their divisions.

Growth alone was not necessarily enough to create a demand for extensive internal operating information. During the same period, the Illinois Central

Railroad, for example, grew quite large (at one point it was the longest railroad in the country), but it had less competition than many eastern lines, and its profits were bolstered by supplementary revenues from the sale of land granted to it by Congress. It was buffered from the most serious consequences of operating inefficiencies and dominated by managers who believed that personal leadership and exhortation, rather than systematic collection and monitoring of information, would elicit efficient operations. Thus its management made only the minimal investments in its internal information system necessary to guarantee safety and honesty and to prevent cash flow crises. Only in 1887 did its new president Stuyvesant Fish, a financier who believed in monitoring financial and operating data in much greater detail, begin to overcome internal resistance to change, aided by new reporting requirements imposed by the Interstate Commerce Commission and decreased profitability resulting from increased competition (Yates 1989, chaps. 4 and 5).

In the mid– and late nineteenth century many manufacturing firms adopted new production technologies, expanded to serve the larger markets created by the railroads and telegraph, and took on multiple functions. At this point, they encountered their own crises of profitability. Confronted by the inefficiency and chaos that resulted from growth and vertical integration without changes in managerial methods, they began to grapple with methods of improving efficiency. Their managers began to demand systematic internal information for use in achieving efficient coordination. In developing internal information systems, manufacturing firms did not, for the most part, depend on the advances already made by the railroads; faced with similar problems, they rediscovered many of the same principles.

Their search for more efficient operating procedures was shaped by an emerging ideology. The systematic management philosophy emerged in the fledgling management literature during the final decades of the nineteenth century.[2] Writers in this tradition noted the breakdown in horizontal and vertical coordination that resulted from expansion of the hierarchy in both directions. To improve efficiency, they advocated systematizing (that is, standardizing) and documenting all operations from the shop floor to the managerial office, and establishing flows of written information up and down the hierarchy to coordinate them. Operating policies and results were documented to reduce dependence on the specific individual, whether worker or manager, and to create an organizational memory. Information was systematically recorded and drawn up the hierarchy from the shop floor to higher levels of

---

2. Discussions of this movement may be found in Litterer (1961a, 1961b, 1963) and Jelinek (1980). The broad but amorphous systematic management movement should not be confused with the more narrowly focused scientific management movement, which emerged around the turn of the century as one element of that broader movement. While Frederick Taylor and his followers focused on improving efficiency on the shop floor, the broader movement was concerned with systematizing operations at all levels from the top to the bottom of the firm. For discussion of the relationship of these two movements, see Nelson (1974).

management. At each level, the information was analyzed and used in monitoring and evaluating lower levels as well as in making decisions about operations. The downward flow was made up of written orders, instructions, and policies—the results of decisions based on the upward flows—communicated down the hierarchy to those implementing policy.

In the period from 1880 to 1920, growing manufacturing firms gradually adopted many of the uses of internal information advocated by systematizers, as proponents of the philosophy were often called. They came to depend on extensive vertical flows of written information to coordinate operations. This philosophy, then, spurred demand for internal information in firms.

Growth and increased organizational complexity alone did not account for the large increase in demand for such flows of information. Growth and complexity created a demand for better coordination, but not necessarily for this method of coordination. For example, Masahiko Aoki has recently pointed out that methods of coordination less dependent on vertical flows of written information were adopted in Japanese firms (Aoki 1990). In those firms, horizontal and often oral coordination and exchange of information played a much more important role than in American firms (though not displacing all vertical coordination). Aoki argues that economic efficiency alone does not account for the differences between western and Japanese patterns of coordination, and that historical and cultural factors may have shaped the patterns. One such factor was the emergence of the ideology of systematic management in American firms during the decades surrounding the turn of the twentieth century. This philosophy, which saw no benefit in building consensus, would have been less congenial to Japanese social norms and traditions.

## 4.2  Information Supply: Changes in Information Technology

This increased demand for internal information might have been curtailed by its high cost, except for some changes on the supply side of the equation. Changes in information technology adopted by American firms between 1840 and 1920 reduced the cost of using internal information. During that period a variety of technologies were adopted for collecting, transmitting, storing, retrieving, analyzing, and disseminating the increasing amount of information being collected. Some of these improvements were mechanical or electrical devices that fit a traditional definition of technology (e.g., typewriter, adding machine, telegraph), while others were bureaucratic techniques with only limited links to physical devices (e.g., forms, indexing systems, graphic representations). They were adopted in an attempt to control the rising costs of handling the increasing amounts of information being collected. Supplementing this cost-control motive was an added element of ideology—in this case, it might be called fad—driving adoption.[3] These technologies came to be seen

3. I am indebted to Naomi Lamoreaux for bringing to my attention the possibility of an ideological component on the supply, as well as the demand, side of the information equation.

as visible symbols of the modern management techniques fostered by the systematic management philosophy. Whatever the specific motive for adoption, these technologies generally influenced the economic trade-offs concerning the use of information, reducing costs and thus increasing the supply of internal information available at a given cost.

### 4.2.1   Recording and Compiling Information

The actual recording and compiling of operating information occupied increasing amounts of managerial and clerical time as demand for such information increased. Soon the costs of the task became an obvious target for reduction. Both mechanical devices (the typewriter) and clerical techniques (preprinted forms) were adopted to reduce the time and thus cost of recording and transcribing information.

The typewriter lowered the costs of all written documentation, whether recording or disseminating information. Handwriting was a slow and thus expensive method of producing documents. Over the previous two centuries there had been many attempts to mechanize the production of documents, but until the last quarter of the nineteenth century none was commercially successful because none was able to reduce the speed of this activity below that of handwriting (Bliven 1954; Current 1954). The first successful mass-produced typewriters emerged from the Remington Factory in 1874. They were not initially aimed toward the general business market, but toward court reporters, authors, and other specialized niche users. But even before touch typing was developed, typewriters operated by experienced typists could produce around seventy-five words per minute, in comparison to about twenty-five words per minute for pen and paper, a fact that quickly attracted business.

The typewriter was also instrumental in lowering costs in other ways. Before the typewriter, documents were sometimes produced in final form by clerks and sometimes by higher-paid managers or even owners. Because touch typing was a specialized skill that required training, its introduction made more strict the allocation of document production to lower-priced clerical labor. That clerical labor became increasingly female in the 1890s and the early twentieth century, further lowering its cost. Female clerks were paid, on average, less than male clerks, and the mechanization and feminization of the occupation lowered the wage for all clerks in comparison to wages of manufacturing workers (Weiss 1978; Rotella 1981; Davies 1982; Goldin 1990).

In the 1880s and 1890s growing firms adopted the typewriter just in time to decrease the rising costs of their increased written communication (both internal and external). In some cases the adoption of the typewriter was either accelerated or slowed by the status the device quickly acquired as a symbol of modern business methods. At Du Pont, for example, the older, more conservative generation was initially reluctant to adopt it, and had to be convinced of its effects on costs before investing in it. The younger, more progressive du Ponts, on the other hand, adopted such modern devices immediately, even before their management methods had increased written documentation to the point where such devices were essential (Yates 1989, 210–19). Whatever the motivation, typewriters clearly reduced the costs of all types of written documentation.

Another technology, this time clerical rather than mechanical, specifically reduced the time and thus cost of recording and compiling standardized data on a routine basis: forms. In the early nineteenth century, information about financial transactions was recorded in ruled, double entry accounting books. Most other documents were written out in full on blank paper. As routine reporting or operating information began to increase around midcentury, daily, weekly, and monthly reports proliferated. Since the typewriter had not yet entered the picture, both the explanations and the figures had to be laboriously written out by hand for each report. Moreover, the person writing such reports could easily omit or alter some category of information, lessening the value of the record for comparative analysis. And because the figures were typically embedded in text, anyone attempting to compile sets of information at higher levels had to search for the key figures.

Printed forms (later, often typed and duplicated) with spaces for entering specific information were adopted in the latter part of the nineteenth century to make "clerical work easier than would be possible if the blank sheet of paper were used," as one systematizer later explained (Leffingwell 1927, 470). These standard forms provided all of the information that did not vary from one reporting period to the next, leaving room for the varying information to be filled in (by hand or with a typewriter) for each report. They both reduced the time spent in recording information and encouraged consistency and "system" in the data recorded. Moreover, because the same information was always in the same place on forms, they made it easier to extract the data for compilation and analysis at higher levels.

Tables further simplified extraction of data. Frequently the reports started out with figures embedded within text. Sometimes before reports were turned into preprinted forms and sometimes after, tabular formats were often adopted, reducing the amount of text and thus facilitating the recording of data and its later extraction. Around the turn of the century, the tab function was developed for typewriters, further speeding up the recording of tabular data (Leffingwell 1926).

The managerial publications that emerged at the turn of the century were full of articles recommending forms for collecting and compiling data. Many of these articles suggested specific sets of forms for specific purposes (e.g., "System for Factory Purchases," 1903). Others gave general guidelines for designing forms that would be as efficient as possible for those filling them out and those extracting data from them at higher levels for further compilation (e.g., Barnum 1925). By 1925, a book on designing forms had been published (Clarke 1925). For their ability to promote consistency in data while increasing clerical efficiency, forms came to be seen as almost synonymous with "system," one of the primary values promulgated by the systematic management movement. Thus they acquired a popularity in their own right, perhaps even beyond their efficiency value, as a symbol of modern, systematic management methods.

Together, the typewriter and forms reduced the costs of recording and compiling information, thus allowing firms to record increasing amounts of it before cost became prohibitive.

### 4.2.2  Transmitting Information

The major development in transmitting recorded information, the telegraph, appeared early in the period under discussion.[4] It increased the supply of information by radically increasing the speed of transmission, not by reducing the cost of transmitting a certain number of words. The telegraph made it possible to use time-sensitive internal information that previously could not be transmitted fast enough to be of any value in decision making.[5] In addition, it facilitated rapid routine flows of information where speed was worth the extra cost.

Before the telegraph was introduced to the United States in 1844, information could travel only as fast as a person could travel, by boat, stagecoach, or other conveyance. While a firm's manufacturing facilities were usually located in a single area, owners or sales agents might be some distance away. Information could be exchanged only as fast as the mails could travel. Thus agents in hot competition with rival firms might promise goods by a certain date without knowing whether the order could be delivered on time, or cut prices to negotiate sales, making contracts without the direct input of firm management because a delay could lose them the sale. Such interactions were a frequent source of friction between firms and their agents throughout the nineteenth century (e.g., Broehl 1984, 187–91; Yates 1989, 207, 219–21). With the telegraph, information about such negotiations could often be exchanged within the necessary time frame. Thus firms could exert more central authority over agents by insisting that no unauthorized price cuts be taken or that rush orders be confirmed with headquarters.

Firms did not necessarily take full advantage of the new transmission capability offered by the telegraph. In 1856, after Du Pont finally installed a private telegraph line to connect it to the Wilmington telegraph office several miles away, the firm immediately began using it on an ad hoc basis to confirm orders and to arrange rapid delivery of powder. It did not, however, use the telegraph to rein in its sales agents disbursed around the country. Even near

---

4. The telephone, which appeared in the 1870s, facilitated oral communication and coordination but did not seem to curb the rapid growth of recorded information. Since my focus here is on that recorded information, I will not discuss the telephone.

5. The telegraph's influence on markets has been discussed in DuBoff (1980, 1983) and in Yates (1986), and will not be considered here. The telegraph had an interesting influence on the flow of internal information in railroads, especially as it was used in railroad dispatching. Since this use is so specialized, however, I will omit it from the following discussion.

the end of the century, after the sales function was rearranged and a few principal agents were given salaries and put in charge of commission-based subagents with contracts requiring them to follow company pricing as communicated by letters and telegrams, friction continued over price cutting by agents in the field.[6] Even with the telegraph, Du Pont was unable or unwilling to control its agents.

At about the same time, however, Repauno Chemical Company, partly owned (and later to be wholly absorbed) by Du Pont, was exerting much more control over its agents. E. S. Rice, Du Pont's Chicago agent, belittled Repauno's Chicago agent by noting that he "is unable to make necessary prices, and in fact under his instructions can not meet competition without first communicating with the home office," a policy that would have been unworkable before the telegraph.[7] In fact, however, in the early twentieth century Rice's own methods were to be revealed as inefficient and ineffective, and Repauno's methods, which took full advantage of the additional control offered by the telegraph, were to become the model for all of Du Pont.

Initially, urgent but ad hoc exchanges of information such as these about the pricing and delivery of particular orders were the principal internal uses of the telegraph. Its high per-word cost—in the 1850s, the first ten words of a message between New York and Chicago cost $1.55, while most prepaid letters cost only $0.03 (U.S. Bureau of the Census 1975)—made it unattractive for more routine uses. While the price difference did not narrow, by the 1880s some growing firms with special needs saw the value of telegraphic communication for more routine communication. The integrated meat-packing firms that emerged in that decade, Swift and Armour, paid about $200,000 per year for telegraphic communication to coordinate the processing and transportation of beef via refrigerator cars (Chandler 1977, 396). Without such rapid routine communication, many cars of beef would have spoiled when they were stranded between the midwestern slaughterhouses and eastern distribution points or when they arrived at inappropriate distribution points. Slower modes of communication were virtually worthless in coordinating flows of perishable products, and telegraphic communication was well worth its high cost. Moreover, in cases where the telegraph was used heavily for internal communication, costs could be reduced by use of telegraphic cipher codes, which also helped firms maintain secrecy over public telegraph lines.

The telegraph thus facilitated high-speed internal transmission of information, allowing much closer coordination over distances in cases where owners

6. See correspondence from E. S. Rice, Du Pont's Chicago agent, to Du Pont headquarters, in accession 500, series 1, part 1, series B, vols. 307–10, Hagley Museum and Library, Wilmington, DE. See Yates (1989, chap. 7) for more details of Du Pont's and Repauno's relations with their agents.

7. E. S. Rice to Du Pont headquarters, 30 August 1888, accession 500, series 1, part 1, series B, vol. 309. The analysis revealing Rice's high unit cost is discussed in Chandler and Salsbury (1971, 628 n. 90).

or managers recognized that the value of the communication exceeded its cost.

### 4.2.3  Storing and Retrieving Information

To be useful in decision making, information had to be stored in such a way that it was readily retrievable when it was needed. For comparisons of one period's operating results to those of previous periods, for example, the latter had to be available and accessible. To analyze the profitability of various customer accounts, managers had to have access to correspondence and records concerning that customer's orders. Moreover, if documentation of systems and policies was to be a useful replacement for reliance solely on individuals, that documentation had to be available for consultation both by those governed by the policy and by those monitoring and determining policy. As the amount of operating information being gathered and of policies and procedures being documented increased around the turn of the twentieth century, accessible storage became increasingly problematic. An interlocking set of devices and clerical systems for vertical filing of documents emerged at the end of the nineteenth century and was widely adopted as a way of increasing accessible storage. Soon after came vertical files of structured data cards. These innovations in storage technology increased the supply of information available to those making and implementing decisions (Yates 1982).

In the late nineteenth century, most companies stored documents and correspondence in a combination of bound volumes, pigeonhole desks or cabinets, and letter boxes. Both traditional accounts of external transactions and copies of outgoing correspondence (whether to external parties or to other company sites) were recorded in large bound volumes. Accounts were recorded directly into the volumes, initially by hand and later using special posting machines related to typewriters. Internal and outgoing correspondence and other documents freshly written or typed in special copying ink were "press-copied" into bound volumes. This process involved dampening and compressing the original between tissue-paper pages of a large volume (while other pages were protected from the dampness by inserted pieces of oil cloth). The dampness and pressure on the copying ink transferred a reverse image of the document onto the side of the tissue page facing the original. That image showed through to the other side of the thin paper, where it could be seen correctly. This form of copying and storage fixed items in the chronological order of creation.

Incoming correspondence and internal reports, on the other hand, were folded into packets and annotated on the outside with date, correspondent, and sometimes subject, then stored in pigeonholes. Locating a particular item in pigeonholes typically required pulling out and unfolding many documents.

In the late nineteenth century, as the volume of correspondence and internal documents increased in growing firms, letter boxes that stored documents flat often replaced pigeonhole storage. It was easier to find a particular document in a given letter box than in a pigeonhole desk or cabinet, since the documents were no longer folded; yet the boxes were usually stored on edge on shelves (like bound volumes), and the user still had to pull down, open, and rifle through them to locate a given document. Then papers on top of the desired document had to be lifted out in order to remove it. A further development, cabinets with drawers of flat files, eliminated the first step but did not improve the others. Moreover, incoming and internal documents were separated from outgoing correspondence, which was still press-copied into bound volumes. Thus someone trying to trace an ongoing exchange of information had to consult multiple storage devices.

To eliminate this problem of bound volumes, copying had to be separated from storage. Two methods for copying documents onto loose sheets rather than into bound books, both adaptations of existing technology, emerged towards the end of the century. The rolling press copier simply press-copied documents onto a continuous role of tissue paper, which was then cut into pieces of appropriate lengths (Wigent, Housel, and Gilman 1916). Carbon paper had been available since quite early in the nineteenth century, but for a long time it could only be used with a stylus or pencil, not with the sharp quill or steel pens that would tear the paper or be blunted when pressed down hard enough to make a carbon copy (Proudfoot 1972). It was immediately clear that carbon paper could be used with the typewriter, which entered businesses in significant numbers in the 1880s and 1890s. Both rolling copiers and carbon paper produced the loose copies necessary to free firms from bound chronological storage of outgoing correspondence. Carbon paper proved to be the cheaper and more convenient method and was clearly more widespread in business by early in the twentieth century, according to a government study undertaken in 1912 (President's Commission on Economy and Efficiency 1912).

With loose copies of outgoing documents available, a critical step in the evolution of storage and retrieval systems could occur: the combining of all documents on a single subject, whether outgoing, incoming, or internal, into a single storage system accessible by subject. While this reorganization of information could have occurred within the existing box files, it generally awaited the introduction of vertical filing to the business world in 1893 (Chaffee 1938, 4). This method of storage involved both a device and a bureaucratic system. As a device, vertical filing consisted of the now-familiar manila folders, dividers, and cabinets of the correct size for storing them in an upright position. As a bureaucratic system, vertical filing was introduced as a method of combining all documents on a single subject, regardless of origin, into a single, centralized storage system and organizing them by subject or some other indexing scheme suitable to the needs of those using them.

Many books and articles were published on filing systems and various methods for organizing and indexing them (e.g., Wigent, Housel, and Gilman 1916; Hudders 1916). Proponents of vertical filing noted its advantages over the old systems (press books plus letter boxes or flat files) both in efficiency of use—a folder with all the relevant information on some subject could easily be located and lifted out—and efficiency of space (e.g., Hoskins Office Outfitters 1912; Hudders 1916). They also argued the virtues of various indexing and organizing systems, from alphabetical to decimal.

The shift from a predominantly chronological system that separated documents by origin to one that combined all related documents with access based on subject or some other functional scheme clearly made information more accessible for those making or implementing decisions. In effect, this change increased the supply of internal information. (There is even some evidence that the vertical files, which quickly became decentralized in spite of expert recommendations to maintain centralized files, encouraged the generation of increased internal documentation. Presumably managers had more incentive to document facts and opinions when they knew that the documents would be accessible in the future.) In addition to their direct value in lowering the cost of retrieving information, filing systems, like forms, came to be seen as symbols of the modern, systematic methods of management. Thus, symbolic reasons reinforced efficiency reasons in firms' decisions to adopt this information storage technology.

A variant of vertical filing, the vertical card file, was soon adopted in many firms to create a more compact database of sales or production statistics, or even of a firm's central accounts (Clark 1916; Morse 1900; Leffingwell 1926, 1927). Initially, these card files simply used forms (often tabular ones) pre-printed onto stiff cards. Cards were organized by a single scheme (e.g., a customer's name), and other information could be extracted from each card once it was located. Soon devices were added to card files to aid in the rapid retrieval of data by multiple categories. Metal tabs painted different colors were clipped to the top or bottom of the cards in designated positions to aid a clerk in locating and retrieving all cards with a particular characteristic. In some cases, punched holes or notches were used in conjunction with special drawers and rods to extract cards with certain characteristics. As one advocate of such card storage and retrieval systems noted, "The need for extensive cross-indexing which would otherwise be necessary for close and analytical utilization of the data, is by this method successfully eliminated in nearly every case" (Schlink 1918, 136).

These systems were essentially databases storing structured data that could be extracted along multiple dimensions. They greatly increased the supply of structured data readily available for analysis, thus presumably increasing its use. For example, the extensive tabbed card file maintained by Du Pont's Sales Record Division was used in 1913 to respond to twenty-three thousand routine inquiries within the headquarters Sales Department, as well as to many special requests from the field.[8] The data it provided aided in following

8. This information is based on an untitled and undated document (ca. 1914) describing and justifying the Sales Record Division's role in the department. It is in the Du Pont records (accession 500, group II, series 3, file 127) housed in the Hagley Museum and Library.

up on trade and in monitoring sales personnel. Improved storage and access made information easier and less expensive to use.

### 4.2.4  Analyzing Information

In the late nineteenth and early twentieth centuries, a variety of adding machines, calculating machines, and statistical tabulating machines were introduced to speed data manipulation and calculations. Some of these were specialized bookkeeping machines developed for use in accounting departments to post entries and calculate running totals. But as the systematic management philosophy encouraged the widespread use of information throughout firms, neither extensive calculations nor the office machines that facilitated them were limited to accounting departments any more.

Tabulating machines were the most powerful technological systems (each of them was actually composed of several devices) for analyzing data. They both sorted data into categories (even more rapidly than card files) and performed calculations. The electromechanical Hollerith tabulator was initially developed to process the data collected for the 1890 U.S. Census. The devices making it up were used for various functions: punching holes in the cards to record the data in encoded form, sorting the cards by categories, and counting and/or calculating as desired. Other tabulating devices, including the mechanical Powers machine, followed the Hollerith. One systematizer noted the value of such machinery in reducing the time and cost necessary for performing large computations: "Wherever the classifying and analyzing of statistics or the compiling of reports is part of the daily routine of any business enterprise, there the tabulating machine can be of invaluable service . . . because it will serve more economically and with greater speed and accuracy than a large clerical force" (Leffingwell 1926, 176). Calculators and tabulators helped firms use more information more quickly and less expensively than ever before, increasing their effective supply of internal information. As with the personal computer today, such machines may also have had a symbolic or fad value beyond their contribution to efficiency.

### 4.2.5  Disseminating Information

The increasing amount of information flowing up and down firms created two types of problems in dissemination. The data being recorded, analyzed, and passed up the hierarchy created what would now be described as information overload for top decision-makers. Fewer and fewer people were getting more and more information at the top levels of the hierarchy. Ways of presenting information for easier understanding were needed. Downward flows of information, on the other hand, posed a problem of getting notices of policies and procedures to increasing numbers of people at the bottom levels of the hierarchy, preferably in a form that could be consulted in the future. Presentational techniques and duplicating methods and devices were adopted to address these two problems.

Reading and absorbing even the most relevant of the enormous amount of available information was increasingly difficult for middle and top management. The tabular forms developed to ease compilation of data also made information somewhat easier for its recipients to use than did prose documents with embedded figures. Still, extracting trends and comparisons from tables took time and study, and as the amount of available information increased, decision-makers often did not have time to study all of it. Around the turn of the century, graphs and charts emerged as an important managerial tool for dealing with this problem. Such techniques may be considered a bureaucratic information technology for disseminating information in a form more efficient for its recipients to absorb.

While graphic representations of data had existed for at least a century by then, only in the late nineteenth and early twentieth centuries did they begin to be used to display managerial data (Funkhouser 1937; Yates 1985). Introduced into firms by engineers-turned-managers, graphs gained popularity in the early twentieth century as a modern way to assure that the information gathered and analyzed at some cost to the company would be used to aid in managing it. William Henry Leffingwell, an early twentieth-century expert in office systems and machinery, summarized the prevailing view: "There is . . . no doubt that a graphical chart, correctly made, shows tendencies much quicker and impresses the mind more accurately and emphatically than do figures" (1927). An earlier systematizer noted that the executive "must have reports of his costs, his sales, his profits or his loses, but he must have them in such forms that he can interpret them instantly and draw conclusions for future guidance. . . . In a modern organization the executive obtains this information through a system of graphic records, a simplified summary of countless departmental statistics and itemized reports" (Parsons 1909, 214–15). Because they were not able to get through all of the reports and documents sent to them, around 1920 Du Pont's Executive Committee went so far as to have a comprehensive set of graphs developed around the firm's return on investment formula, and to have a room specially equipped to display them to the committee for decision making (Yates 1985).

Disseminating the increasing number of notices, bulletins, and other statements of policies and procedures flowing down the hierarchy required another type of information technology: some method of duplicating documents in numbers ranging from half a dozen (e.g., for notices to department heads) to hundreds or even thousands (e.g., to all employees). Press copying made one or at most two (relatively dim) copies. Initially, there were only two alternatives for creating multiple copies: writing or typing a notice repeatedly, or having it printed. Both were costly and time-consuming processes. While railroads, with wide hierarchies and critical safety issues, depended heavily on expensive printing for such downward flows of information, manufacturing firms were reluctant to incur that expense. In the late nineteenth century, rapid and inexpensive methods of creating small and large numbers of document copies became available and were rapidly adopted by firms to aid in disseminating information to employees (Yates 1982).

Carbon paper and the typewriter provided a solution for small numbers of copies. In addition to providing the loose copies demanded by vertical filing, carbon paper used with fine onionskin paper by a strong typist could make up to ten copies at one typing. Thus in the 1880s, as firms adopted the typewriter, carbon paper became a way for them to create small numbers of copies. This method was convenient, rapid, and inexpensive for downward communications at the upper, narrow part of the hierarchy, or in small units. It could also be used to reach a larger population by having each department head or foreman circulate a single copy around a group. When used this way, however, the individual employees did not keep a copy, thus making later reference more difficult. A method was still needed for creating larger numbers of copies.

Two such copying methods emerged in the last quarter of the century. The hectograph and related methods used a gelatin bed to transfer an original, which was typed or written in aniline dye, onto up to one hundred copies (Proudfoot 1972, 34–36). This process was the predecessor of the more convenient spirit duplicating method that was introduced in the 1920s and was still common as late as the 1970s. Duplicating methods based on the stencil principle passed ink through holes in a stencil master to make hundreds and even thousands of copies from a single master. Thomas Edison first introduced the stencil technology to America, initially with his electric pen and later with the Edison mimeograph marketed by the A. B. Dick Company (Proudfoot 1972). Like the typewriter (with which the stencil process was soon coupled), stencil duplicating was not originally marketed for use within firms; it was advertised as a way to disseminate information outside of firms, as with advertising circulars, price lists, and musical scores.[9] Large firms such as the railroads and telegraph companies, however, were quick to see the value of this technology to their internal communication, and soon stencil advertisements listed internal circulars and notices among the items the devices could be used to duplicate.

By the end of the nineteenth century, duplicating technologies were widely used for quick and inexpensive dissemination of large numbers of notices or other mass distribution items within firms. These devices ensured that those at lower levels received their own copies of such notices so they could refer to them in the future. Such copies also helped fill the vertical filing systems that quickly proliferated throughout firms.

9. The target market is revealed in contemporary advertisements, such as an advertising circular "Edison's Electrical Pen and Duplicating Press," 1876, in the Edison National Historic Site in Menlo Park, NJ, and in catalogues issued by retail businesses carrying such equipment, such as "Catalogue of Telegraph Instruments and Supplies," Western Electric Company, 1883, Trade Catalogues, Hagley Museum and Library.

### 4.2.6   Information Technology and Information Supply

The information devices and techniques used by mid-nineteenth-century businesses to handle information would have been hard pressed to handle the volume of internal information that firms used by the early twentieth century. In response to the growing demand for internal information, mechanical and clerical technologies emerged and were widely adopted to aid in every phase of information handling, from collecting and compiling it to disseminating it. To some extent, the mechanical and bureaucratic technologies of information came to be seen as external symbols of modern, systematic management, giving the supply side, as well as the demand side, an additional ideological component.

In some cases, the techniques or devices already existed in some form, but were only widely adopted when the need emerged. Carbon paper and graphic presentation of data, for example, fall in this category. In other cases, technologies were created or significantly developed in direct response to the market demand created by business information needs. In the 1920s Leffingwell argued that what he terms the "office appliance industry" of mechanical devices such as the typewriter, adding machine, duplicator, and tabulator resulted from the new demand for uniform, systematic methods of management:

> When business method was individual and self-centered and business aims narrow and secretive, there was little incentive for inventive genius to burn the midnight oil in the search for business machinery. The demand for mechanical office appliances did not exist because there was no similarity of method. But as similarity of method spread through the exchange of ideas, the possibilities for mass production attracted some of the keenest minds in the country, who turned to making machines and devices that would simplify the mass of problems crowded into the business man's day. As a result, an immense industry has been created—an industry which produces office machines and devices for the entire world. (1926, 18)

Thus demand factors were significant in spurring increases in the supply (and decreases in the cost) of information technologies, which in turn increased the affordable supply of information within the firms. These reinforcing tendencies were further enhanced as the technologies themselves came to be seen as evidence of modern management techniques, and thus were adopted for ideological as well as efficiency reasons.

By increasing the supply of affordable information, these information technologies played an important enabling role in the development of large firms, especially vertically integrated ones that needed to coordinate multiple functions. I would argue that without these techniques and devices, the supply of information available to firms at reasonable prices would not have kept pace with the increasing demand as firms grew, took on additional functions, and systematized their management.[10] Thus growth and vertical integration might have been limited, or new managerial methods for internal coordination, methods less dependent on vertical, paper-based information flows, might have been developed.

## 4.3    Scovill: A Case Study of the Evolution of an Information System

In any given firm, the internal information system evolved unevenly, the product of continual interplay between supply and demand factors. Changes in information technology often involved significant investment in money and time, as well as shifts in power within the firm. While some changes were incremental, others involved real discontinuities in procedures and capabilities. This section demonstrates that process in the Scovill Manufacturing Company.[11]

The case discussion is organized primarily as a narrative, to preserve the complexities and interactions over time. I will periodically step back into a more analytic mode, but the narrative structure is essential to the point. The theoretical and analytic approaches characteristic of economics generally assume the actors' motives and often see a sequence of events as a single event. The narrative structure used below tries to capture the unfolding of events in time and to understand the actual motives of actors whenever possible. It examines the complex interactions between supply and demand, including the influences of factors such as ideology and power, in a single company's use of internal information. While the specifics of this case are not generalizable, it provides a view of the types of factors and dynamics that may be present in many firms and that economists must understand to make sense of firms' uses of internal information.

### 4.3.1    The Early Years: No Systematic Internal Information

Founded in Waterbury, Connecticut, in 1802 as a manufacturer of brass buttons, Scovill was initially a family partnership, and then several interlocking partnerships, each of which produced a product line. By 1850, when it was incorporated, there were three such partnerships manufacturing buttons, hinges, and photographic plates, as well as semifinished brass products. The

10. The supply side of the information equation may have reinforced the demand differences between Japanese and American management methods. The nature of the Japanese written characters precluded a Japanese typewriter that could produce text faster than it could be produced by hand. Thus even if the demand for extensive written communication had been high in Japan, the slow speed and high cost of producing records and documents might have prohibited the level of use that developed in American firms.

11. A more detailed discussion of Scovill is in Yates (1989, chap. 6), one of three case studies in the book. The surviving Scovill records that serve as a basis for the story reside in Baker Library of the Harvard University Graduate School of Business Administration. Scovill has survived and thrived in recent years as a diversified Fortune 500 firm.

newly consolidated and incorporated firm, which had a work force of over 150 people, thus had multiple product lines requiring several different processes. The rolling, casting, and different finishing "rooms" were essentially separate departments, run by skilled workers who reported directly to the owners. Nevertheless, at this time and for another two decades, Scovill collected virtually no internal operating information for use in decision making, depending solely on accounts of external transactions and oral interactions with the skilled workers.

Scovill lagged behind the contemporaneous textile factories discussed above in its use of systematic internal information for coordination. The internalization of multiple products and processes left it without pricing information once provided by the market. Nevertheless, the firm as a whole, though it faced competition in its various markets, was a successful and growing concern.

One fairly unsystematic source of internal information for Scovill was its correspondence with sales agents and later store employees. Until 1846, when Scovill established its own store with salaried employees in New York, sales were handled principally by commission agents (Marburg 1952). Relations with the sales agents and initially with the store were relatively unstandardized, with no systematic flows of information except for the rendering of semiannual accounts of transactions in traditional form. Otherwise, correspondence was ad hoc and situation-specific.

Minor developments in correspondence between the New York store and Waterbury headquarters reflect changes in the cost of transmission and duplication. In 1845 and 1851, postal rates dropped significantly, lowering Scovill's cost for letters to New York from 12.5 cents per sheet to 3 cents for most letters (U.S. Bureau of the Census 1975). The change from hand copying to press copying of letters (sometime before 1854) reduced the time and thus cost of copying the increased number of letters into bound volumes. In a change that probably reflects both increased business and decreased costs, the number of letters exchanged had increased significantly by the mid-1850s, while the length of each letter had decreased. Still, except for the traditional semiannual accounts, the flow of information continued to be unsystematic.

Predictably, a major source of friction evident in the correspondence was a tendency for agents to cut prices to meet the competition. As an agent stated his case in one such dispute with the owners in Waterbury, "I am bound to comply with your instructions but I do presume you do not wish me to adhere to a stipulated price when your competitors are selling for less."[12] Since letters took from a day to a week (depending on weather) to travel from Waterbury to

---

12. Taylor to Scovill, 16 March 1829, case 13, Scovill Collection 2, Baker Library, Harvard University Graduate School of Business Administration. Hereafter materials from this collection will be inserted parenthetically in the text, in this form: Scovill 2/13, 16 March 1829.

New York, requiring approval from headquarters for any changes in price would have lost many sales. This situation continued until after the telegraph came to Waterbury in 1849. The telegraph reduced, though it did not entirely eliminate, this friction.

Although the firm gradually came to use the telegraph fairly frequently,[13] it was used almost exclusively to exchange price and timing information about specific, urgent orders. Thus it enabled the firm to improve service to distant customers. Because of the high cost it was not used for less time-sensitive communication, which continued to take place in correspondence.

### 4.3.2 The Late Nineteenth Century: Initial Progress in Using Internal Information

The first major change in Scovill's use of internal information came in the 1870s at the hands of C. P. Goss, company secretary, and M. L. Sperry, company treasurer. These two men, who were hired as bookkeepers in the 1860s, established a managerial dynasty that governed the firm longer than the Scovill family did. They instituted "a system of bookkeeping from which the profits of the various sections of the business—mill, . . . button, burner, aluminum departments, and so on—could be discovered" (Bishop ca. 1950, 73). Various record-keeping forms and a monthly statement were created as part of the system.[14] On the basis of these records, the main office recorded into bound volumes monthly and yearly figures for sales, production, labor, and interdepartmental transfers of materials for each department, as well as sales by sales office. The information provided by this bookkeeping system did not allow costing of the different specific products produced by each department (e.g., the many types of buttons made by the Button Department), but it at least gave Sperry, Goss, and the president a picture of overall results of each department.

Why was this primitive cost accounting system introduced at this time, rather than at the point of incorporation in 1850 when several functions had been combined in a single firm, theoretically creating a need for internal information to supplement market signals? The addition of the firm's first layer of general management under the top executive may be significant in the actual timing. Before Goss and Sperry rose to secretary and treasurer, the owners were aided only by skilled workmen and bookkeepers. The two men represented a significant new layer of management that had to be vertically coordinated. By inventing or, more likely, adapting a cost accounting system already used elsewhere, they improved their ability to serve as the link be-

---

13. By 1877, one in ten communications in the press book of outgoing correspondence (Scovill 1/461) was a telegram.

14. These forms have not survived to the present, but they survived past 1945, when they were noted by a company historian in a historical list of forms (which has survived in the Scovill Collection in Baker Library), and were used by Bishop in preparing his manuscript. Only one of the bound volumes has survived (Scovill 1/242, 1881–87).

tween the president, on the one hand, and foremen and workers, on the other. While Johnson and Kaplan (1987) have identified the internalizing of multiple functions in a single firm as the main factor responsible for the rise of cost accounting, Scovill's history suggests that the introduction of a layer of general management under the owners (a factor also present in the textile mills) was significant as well. This conclusion is in agreement with Chandler's (1977) emphasis on the growth of middle management as a key innovation in the development of the firm.

The new system remained the principal source of systematic internal information for the next few decades. It survived from the 1870s, when the firm numbered just over three hundred employees and assets were about $1 million, into the early twentieth century, when the firm employed well over a thousand and assets were about $3 million (see tables 4.1 and 4.2), virtually unchanged (Bishop ca. 1950).

No corresponding downward flow of recorded information was instituted

Table 4.1    Growth in Employment at Scovill

| Year | Approx. Number of Employees |
|------|------------------------------|
| 1850 | 157 |
| 1874 | 314 |
| 1880 | ~400 |
| 1887 | ~1,000 |
| 1892 | 1,157 |
| 1914 | ~4,000 |
| 1916 | ~12,000 |

Source: All figures are from Bishop (ca. 1950), 200, 205–6, except that for 1880, which is from penciled notation in case 253, Scovill Collection 2, Baker Library, Harvard University Graduate School of Business Administration.

Table 4.2    Growth at Scovill in the Late Nineteenth Century

| Year | Net Earnings | Assets | Year | Net Earnings | Assets |
|------|--------------|--------|------|--------------|--------|
| 1880 | $ 80,133 | $1,225,743 | 1891 | 117,502 | 1,628,227 |
| 1881 | 136,141 | 1,308,841 | 1892 | 149,026 | 1,722,060 |
| 1882 | 76,473 | 1,519,395 | 1893 | 94,066 | 1,686,475 |
| 1883 | 62,505 | 1,621,621 | 1894 | 84,975 | 1,724,408 |
| 1884 | 36,696 | 1,547,413 | 1895 | 198,567 | 1,945,496 |
| 1885 | 81,238 | 1,571,330 | 1896 | 62,027 | 1,816,572 |
| 1886 | 101,476 | 1,639,342 | 1897 | 254,745 | 1,905,208 |
| 1887 | 93,280 | 1,617,765 | 1898 | 338,745 | 2,058,286 |
| 1888 | 338,745 | 1,671,508 | 1899 | 427,958 | 2,322,483 |
| 1889 | 209,629 | 1,614,152 | 1900 | 242,649 | 3,081,492 |
| 1890 | 76,767 | 1,657,297 | | | |

Source: Cases 253 and 254, Scovill Collection 2, Baker Library, Harvard University Graduate School of Business Administration.

within Scovill's plant during this period, in spite of the growth in work force. In fact in 1887, when the firm already employed about one thousand, Sperry explicitly stated his opposition to written policies:

> We have never had any shop rules printed. There is a general understanding that ten hours constitute a day's work and that the hands are expected to do a day's work if they get a day's pay. Each department is under the direction of a foreman, in whom we trust and who sees that the hands are industrious and attend to their business. If they do not do it, he sends them off and gets others. . . . We do not think printed rules amount to anything unless there is somebody around constantly to enforce them and if such a person is around printed forms can be dispensed with. (Bishop ca. 1950, 205)

An internal telephone system was installed early in the 1880s to allow oral exchanges between the office and foremen at various mill and shop facilities, but the foreman retained informal and direct control over the workers.

In the last two decades of the century, correspondence with Scovill employees outside of Waterbury continued to provide relatively unsystematic information. By the 1880s Scovill had stores in Boston and Chicago as well as New York. The firm's correspondence with all parties, including customers and suppliers as well as its own stores, was increasing rapidly. Early in the decade, Scovill filled five 1,000-page press books per year. From 1883 through 1885 this total climbed to six, seven, and then eight volumes per year, then leaped to ten volumes in 1886. For the rest of the decade and into the next, the number hovered around nine to ten volumes each year.[15]

In 1888, after the big increase in correspondence, Scovill adopted the typewriter (Scovill 1/315, 1888). The timing suggests that the acquisition was motivated by need more than by fad and that it was a response to, rather than a cause of, the increase. This time-saving device, along with the hiring of a female typist by 1889 and a second one by 1893 (Bishop ca. 1950, 460), relieved the increasing burden of document production on Goss, Sperry, and other office personnel. The new recording technology and division of labor lowered the costs of document production, thus enabling the firm to continue expanding its correspondence without incurring excessive costs. The flow of information from its stores, however, continued to be unsystematic.

### 4.3.3  John Goss and the Systematic Expansion of Internal Information

The next major set of changes in Scovill's acquisition and handling of internal information came when the second generation of Goss management introduced the philosophy and techniques of the systematic management movement into the firm to cope with growth. When the company president under whom C. P. Goss amd M. L. Sperry had worked for three decades died in 1900, they served consecutively as presidents of the firm. In the years be-

---

15. Since most letters were one page long, the shift from handwriting to typing did not radically alter the capacity of a single press volume.

tween the turn of the century and World War I, the firm grew to four thousand employees, the managerial hierarchy expanded, and a series of different departmental forms were adopted. Early in the period C. P. Goss's son, John, became first superintendent of the Burner Department and later general superintendent of manufacturing. During that time this proponent of the period's managerial trends created an extensive internal information system at Scovill.

In his 1905 "Report Made to the General Manager on Timekeeping in the Departments" (Scovill 2/34, "Notices, 1905–1907," 22 February 1905), John Goss revealed his sympathy with the systematic management philosophy. He noted that potentially costly inconsistencies in payroll timekeeping—one area of data collection—had emerged across departments over time. The problem arose, he asserted, because "the responsibility unchecked rests entirely upon the department superintendents and their subordinates to systematize or leave unsystematized those details which are vital to the payroll scheme." He urged "those in authority over all the departments to get together with the data and decide upon a plan which shall be simple and at the same time applicable to all alike." Thus he wished to take some authority from the department superintendents, including himself, and draw it up to a higher level of management by centralizing and standardizing information collection. To prevent any misunderstandings or deviations, he recommended establishing a set of regulations, to be disseminated downward by printing them in each payroll book. His analysis of the problem and recommendations for solving it suggest that his belief in systematic management transcended his own local interests.

Over the next decade, he and other Scovill executives instituted many systems for collecting and analyzing internal information. For example, he stated in one document, "It is desirable to get systematized as soon as possible the method of receiving goods on our various orders from outside sources of supply, so that we may be sure of getting a reasonable report from the proper source of information upon the quality of each lot of material that arrives" (Scovill 2/34, "Orders and Instructions," 20 July 1909). Such a process was systematized by creating forms or tickets on which information about the material was recorded. This information had immediate value to those using the material next. It could also be analyzed later to aid in the choice of suppliers, as well as to track the inputs into particular orders and to reduce waste. This was one of many such systems put in place.

In 1907 John Goss developed a new set of monthly cost analysis sheets for the Burner Department (Scovill 2/333). After demonstrating the usefulness of his new methods on a small scale, he extended them to the rest of manufacturing as he rose to general superintendent of manufacturing in 1910. Tabular forms were used for recording monthly costs for each room of each department, with the costs categorized into maintenance and repairs, supplies, direct and indirect labor, and interdepartmental transfers. Each of these categories was further subdivided to provide greater analytic detail. Monthly summary sheets for the whole department were compiled from these sheets. Finally, from these the office prepared yearly analyses, including totals, overhead figures, and the ratios of each of the other types of costs to direct labor costs. The yearly summary also included a column for the previous year's figures, for comparison. The yearly summary report for 1907 left blank the column for the previous year's figures, since the old Sperry and Goss system did not provide the information necessary to make direct comparisons.

A brief history of Scovill's system of accounts, written decades later by a company historian, labels this set of changes the "formalization of cost factors in a series of analytical records, the results of which could be reported to the main office executives and there used in decisions. . . . This seems to have been developed into a well articulated 'cost office' in or soon after 1910."[16] By 1916 this system of cost accounts was so extensive that employees were issued bound, printed books, each about one inch thick, describing the system and explaining the forms and criteria for charging costs to different accounts. This documentation of the system explained its role as follows: "The price at which goods are sold is based on their cost; they are not sold at less than cost, but at cost plus a profit. Since no manufacturing business could exist long without making profits, it becomes evident that the success of any business depends to a great extent on the accuracy of its cost system. The system of accounts is, now-a-days, closely interwoven with the cost system and has become of equal importance" (Scovill 2/236, 1916).

So important a change had both costs and benefits to the firm. In addition to the costs of devising the scheme and creating new forms, there were costs for disseminating instructions on how to use them and costs for monitoring their use. Still, the new system had clear benefits, as well. While the old Sperry and Goss system allowed the firm to compute an approximation of the overall profits of each room or department, the updated system focused on the cost structure of each unit's operations and eventually the costs of specific products. As implemented in 1910, it allowed management to monitor the relative contributions of different types of costs and to see at a glance the ratio of each category and subcategory to direct labor cost. Such amounts and ratios could be compared from room to room and over time. It also provided figures on the supplies and labor wasted on spoiled work, allowing them to address quality issues. As the system was further articulated, it provided more and more detail on specific costs. Whether all of this detail was worth its costs or whether John Goss and Scovill were at some point simply following the dictates of systematizers cannot readily be determined.

The cost accounts and other new data collection and analysis systems being introduced by John Goss and others brought more and more information to executives. At the same time that they were introducing such systems, they

16. E. H. Davis, "System of Accounts," a typed document inserted in a 1916 instruction book for the accounting system (Scovill 2/236). Internal evidence suggests that the summary was written in the 1940s.

began to adopt graphic techniques of presenting some of the new data being generated. To make cost comparisons between the Burner Department in 1907 and its successor Manufacturing Department in 1908 easier to comprehend, Goss had the data from the sheets graphed for easy comparison (Scovill 2/ 328). A few years later, cost data was being graphed as a time series. Clearly extra clerical time was required to make such graphs. The cost was outweighed for Goss by some combination of the time savings, the improvement in understanding for the executives, and the symbolic value of using graphs.

At the same time that Goss was establishing an upward flow of internal information, he also established a downward flow to standardize and document policies, rules, and orders. In the late nineteenth century, C. P. Goss and Sperry had initiated the first upward flow, but they rejected on principle a corresponding downward one. By the early twentieth century, the work force was still larger, and additional levels had been added to the hierarchy. Still, a change in ideology as much as size probably drove the introduction of written downward communication at exactly this time.

Sometime before 1905, John Goss began issuing to his workers and foremen in the Burner Department a variety of written announcements, notices, and specific orders, generally aimed at systematizing their procedures.[17] As he rose to the position of general superintendent, he continued to issue them to a wider audience, including department heads, and also to diffuse this practice throughout the organization. By at least 1908, C. P. Goss was also issuing occasional notices, and by the second decade of the century, notices, instructions, and manuals were being issued at all levels of the organization (Scovill 2/34, "Orders and Instructions," 1905–14). The idiosyncratic methods of individual foremen, superintendents, and other lower and middle managers were curbed by the increasing systematization of procedures at every level.[18]

Consistent methods for handling such internal communication had not yet been devised; individual notices were produced, disseminated, and stored in a variety of ways. Rather than copying them in the press books used for outgoing correspondence, John Goss had them typed with multiple carbon copies. He kept the original and one copy in his own box file.[19] Another copy (or several copies, when he became superintendent of manufacturing) was rubber-stamped with a list of rooms in the affected department. This copy was circulated from foreman to foreman, each one checking off or initialing the appropriate room name. Such a system guaranteed that all foremen saw the

17. The earliest surviving written order (in Scovill 2/34, "Notices") is dated 28 January 1905, but it is designated Superintendent's Order no. 137, suggesting that Goss had been issuing such orders for many months.
18. The content of these notices and their role in systematizing procedures are discussed in detail in Yates (1989, 172–76).
19. The originals and copies in the folder labeled "Notices, 1905–1907" (Scovill 2/34) have two holes punched at the top, indicating that they were stored in a Shannon file, a box file with an arched wire that held papers in place through the punched holes. The carbon copy in each case is stamped "File."

notice, but not that they had ready access to it for future reference.[20] Goss was to note later that each foreman had his own way of doing things and wanted to change his methods as little as possible (Davis ca. 1968, 13). Thus the system was clearly suboptimal because it depended on the foremen's easily distorted memory of the notice instead of the notice itself. Nevertheless, it was not until sometime in the second decade of the century that the firm adopted duplicating technology. The delay may have been linked to another problem, the lack of a system for local storage of documents. That problem was soon to be addressed comprehensively.

### 4.3.4    Investing in Storage and Retrieval: Vertical Filing

By the second decade of the twentieth century, Scovill's information storage and retrieval system was under increasing pressure from internal and external sources (Yates 1982). New categories of documentation were being generated within the Waterbury facilities, as part of the upward and downward flows of recorded information John Goss initiated. These had no obvious storage place in the system of press books and letter boxes used for correspondence. This internally generated information was stored haphazardly and inconsistently, if at all.

Waterbury's rapidly growing correspondence with the external world, including its own stores, posed additional problems. Shortly after the turn of the century, Waterbury established a separate series of press books for its correspondence with the New York store (Scovill 1/510–58), presumably to make this internal correspondence easier to find, as well as to reduce the volume of the main series. In the first decade of the century, this new series filled two to three press books a year. By the second decade, however, this series alone exceeded in yearly volume that of Scovill's entire correspondence in the late nineteenth century. In 1911, headquarters started using the more convenient carbon copies and rolling press copies instead of copying directly into press books. For the first three years after the change, however, they bound these loose copies into chronological volumes functionally equivalent to the press books, generating twelve and thirteen volumes a year in 1912 and 1913. While neither the main press book series nor the letter boxes of incoming correspondence have survived from the early twentieth century, probably because of their enormous bulk, they no doubt increased correspondingly.

The enormous growth of this correspondence had consequences for storage and retrieval. Storage space alone clearly posed a problem, but retrieval was potentially more problematic. Consulting all of the correspondence with and about a single customer or transaction (e.g., to resolve a dispute, assess a request for credit, etc.) required searching many press books and letter boxes.

---

20. One foreman, E. G. Main, had each notice retyped in his office and stored the typed copy on his own Shannon file. This system gave him access to the notices, but at a high cost in retyping them.

The chronologically organized press books of external correspondence were indexed by correspondent but not by subject. Unless the precise dates of the desired letters were known, the indexes and then the press copies of several volumes (each covering a month or less) might have to be consulted. In addition, the searcher would have to consult the box files of incoming correspondence and the separate press books and box files for correspondence with the New York store about that customer. Clearly, retrieval was more time-consuming in the early twentieth century than it had been in the late nineteenth.

There is some evidence that by 1913 more significant problems of storage and retrieval had begun to appear, though their frequency and severity are hard to judge. A letter from Waterbury to the New York store admitted defeat in one attempt to retrieve a requested piece of information: "Replying to yours of the 24th regarding terms to Jos. L. Porter & Co., we are sorry that our record for 1908 is quite as inaccessible as yours seem to be, and, unless you consider the matter of enough importance, you will let the matter pass" (Scovill 1/558, 26 December 1913). Accessibility had become a limiting factor in consulting some recorded information. This incident may have been an isolated one, or it may represent a recurrent event indicating that Scovill's correspondence was exceeding the firm's ability to handle it with its existing storage system.

Even before this incident, Scovill had begun looking into new storage and retrieval systems, though it is not clear whether they were driven primarily by the inefficiencies and accessibility problems of the current system or by a desire to adopt the most modern office methods for symbolic reasons. Redesigning the firm's entire storage and retrieval system required both purchasing equipment and changing procedures, and this investment was considered carefully in advance. In late 1912, an investigation of filing practices at another brass company resulted in a report on "Vertical Letter Filing; as practiced by the Bridgeport Brass Co." (Scovill 2/26, 12 December 1912). This report described the organization, principles, equipment, and procedures used at that firm in minute detail, indicating the importance Scovill itself put on these matters as it explored the options for its own use. The report noted, for example, Bridgeport's total dependence on carbon, rather than rolling press, copies; its methods for combining all correspondence to, from, and about a customer in a single place under that customer's name; its use of subdivisions by subject headings "where they control the correspondent, as in the case of their own agents or stores"; and its method of moving old correspondence, in vertical file transfer cases, into a fireproof vault every six months.

Establishing a similar system at Scovill required a considerable investment. Scovill had to obtain new equipment, including such items as file cases, folders, dividers, and tabs. In addition, it had to abandon its previous investment in letter presses and rolling press copiers, as well as any inventory of letter press paper and letter boxes. Finally, and perhaps most significantly, it had to abandon the human investment in the old, familiar procedures and invest in new procedures, including overcoming any resistance to them. One year after the Bridgeport Brass report, and only one week after the letter confessing inability to locate a desired piece of information, Scovill announced the new system.

Headquarters timed the introduction of the new system to take effect at the beginning of 1914, stating in its correspondence with the New York store, "On January 1st we shall start a new system of filing our letters and we shall use the vertical system of filing" (Scovill 1/558, 27 December 1913). It gave the New York store careful directions about its letters to Waterbury, requiring that they limit each letter to one subject, usually a particular customer, and that they provide that customer's name at the top of the sheet as a subject indicator to aid in filing it. The change increased standardization at the expense of store autonomy, and thus encountered some resistance. A follow-up letter a few days later noted the store's failure to follow the new rules in some letters and stated, "We are changing our system of filing, and we must INSIST that you pay particular attention to this matter" (Scovill 1/558, 31 December 1913). This reminder seems to have elicited better compliance.

The firm was thus committed to making the new files an effective storage and retrieval system allowing them ready access to stored information. After the initial investment, the system clearly increased the supply of accessible internal correspondence by reducing the cost of searching for it. Moreover, the carefully planned centralized correspondence file was soon supplemented by unplanned decentralized files in the offices of managers down to the level of foremen.[21] These local repositories of information soon included copies of downward notices (the adoption of stencil duplicating technology in the second decade of the century now allowed each foreman to keep a copy of each notice) and of upward reports of the sort introduced by John Goss.

Repositories of readily retrievable information were now available at all levels of management. A foreman or superintendent could consult downward directives (or be referred to them by a higher-level manager) to determine standard operating procedures. The general superintendent and other superintendents and managers could consult cost summaries and other types of reports to analyze performance over time and to compare performance among units. The new filing system provided an accessible organizational memory that reduced the incremental cost of future reference to information.

The unplanned proliferation of decentralized files also seems to have stimulated increased documentation of lateral exchanges (Yates 1982; 1989, 184–86). While many upward and downward communications have survived from before the advent of the vertical filing system, there is no surviving lateral

21. A set of files for two foremen and for E. H. Davis, the statistician, have survived from this period (Scovill 1/26).

correspondence within the Waterbury facilities from that period. The surviving post-1914 set of files from a single foreman, however, is dominated by lateral messages. The new filing system was responsible for the survival of these documents, and probably for their numbers, as well.

Many of these lateral memos were clearly written for documentation more than for conveying new information—they were intended to create a record that each party could keep on file. Many started out "confirming our discussion" or "confirming our telephone conversations." A series of communications between the foreman of the Casting Shop and someone of comparable level in the Research Department, for example, documents the high level of tension between the two departments about power and authority issues. One message from the foreman of the Casting Shop begins by quoting a previous message from the Research Department about suspending certain weekly reports and analyses. It continues as follows:

> I would like to go down on record as saying that if at any time I wish to have any part of the program, which has been agreed upon by the Research Committee and myself, suspended I will notify the Research Committee. This to my mind is a serious subject and unless you feel that it is impossible for you to give us the required information, in so far as analyses are concerned, I will expect that the program agreed upon by the Research Committee and myself, be adopted and not the program outlined in your letters of above dates. (Scovill 2/26, 25 March 1918)

Managers had very little incentive to document lateral exchanges of position if they were not available to both parties for future reference. Before vertical files, there was no consistent way to store them to guarantee their availability in the future. After the proliferation of files throughout the organization, each party could keep copies in a local set of files, and thus had more incentive to create them.

### 4.3.5   E. H. Davis and the Postwar Rationalization of the Information System

With the new filing system, all the essential elements of Scovill's information system were in place. In the next few years, the firm grew rapidly in response to the demands and opportunities of World War I (see table 4.3 for some financial measures of the firm's growth during this period). The information system grew increasingly vast and complex. By 1919, over two hundred different routine reports (each of them issued at intervals ranging from weekly to yearly) drew information in a variety of forms into the general superintendent's office. Because the various reports had emerged at different times over the preceding fifteen-year period and responded to a variety of needs, some of which had changed over time, the reporting system itself needed to be systematized. In 1918 the Research Department, which had been

Table 4.3          Growth at Scovill in the Early Twentieth Century

| Year | Net Earnings | Dividends | Assets |
|------|-------------|-----------|--------|
| 1900 | $   242,649 | $   200,378 | $  3,081,492 |
| 1901 | 200,000 | 199,088 | 3,368,376 |
| 1902 | 492,999 | 199,168 | 3,368,376 |
| 1903 | 331,123 | 211,430 | 4,621,494 |
| 1904 | 413,700 | 255,116 | 4,718,145 |
| 1905 | 392,647 | 324,210 | 5,159,167 |
| 1906 | 595,575 | 290,162 | 6,266,330 |
| 1907 | 767,286 | 323,064 | 6,366,026 |
| 1908 | 469,229 | 324,106 | 6,324,836 |
| 1909 | 497,864 | 324,112 | 6,772,851 |
| 1910 | 517,082 | 324,112 | 7,257,228 |
| 1911 | 501,344 | 324,112 | 8,128,503 |
| 1912 | 709,854 | 377,694 | 8,213,958 |
| 1913 | 402,624 | 400,000 | 8,086,591 |
| 1914 | 456,995 | 400,000 | 8,351,659 |
| 1915 | 5,974,362 | 900,000 | 17,520,561 |
| 1916 | 13,403,462 | 5,550,000 | 28,001,237 |
| 1917 | 9,204,884 | 6,500,000 | 33,528,791 |
| 1918 | 2,130,903 | 2,425,000 | 27,970,944 |
| 1919 | 2,156,025 | 1,000,000 | 30,260,896 |
| 1920 | 983,967 | 1,000,000 | 30,722,660 |
| 1921 | 937,764 | 1,507,782 | 28,702,416 |
| 1922 | 989,408 | 1,000,000 | 28,771,904 |
| 1923 | 3,167,761 | 2,062,500 | 35,020,027 |

*Sources:* Figures from 1900 to 1910, plus assets for 1911 and 1912, come from case 254, Scovill Collection 2, Baker Library, Harvard University Graduate School of Business Administration. Subsequent figures come from Moody's (1916, 1919, 1924, 1931).

created shortly before the war, hired E. H. Davis to establish a Statistics Office. In doing so, Scovill was investing further resources in its internal information system.

In his attempt to improve statistical analysis of data for decision making, Davis was forced to begin by exploring and assessing the entire upward flow of information in the firm. In an initial report mapping out the task before him, Davis described the development of the existing information system:

In this plant as in all plants, notation is made locally covering productive progress. In the beginning certain basic records—such as memoranda, job tickets, etc.—were essential for the consistent performance of the work itself. From this, gradually, more permanent records were organized— either as files in which the working records were preserved or in the form of summarized rescripts [i.e., reports] from them—and thus a sort of numerical history was developed as a background in the more important production offices. Subsequently they became the basis for comparative estimates, contract making, etc. (Scovill 2/34, 13 August 1918)

His preliminary tasks, as he stated them in this report, did not involve analyzing the statistics but rather improving the quality and consistency of the data to be analyzed by addressing shortcomings in the information-gathering system. His initial goals were as follows:

X. A general survey of the existing statistical or record situation in the plant as a whole through a study of printed forms now in use.
Y. Repair work in department record systems, by filling gaps, remedying present deficiencies and inaccuracies, etc.
Z. Standardization of department records.
W. Anticipating and providing for changes of record necessitated by future changes in the work of production departments.

Davis intended to achieve these goals gradually, first gathering and investigating all data collection forms and making his office "a clearing house of reference as to *what* current records actually exist, and *where* they are available." He would then make inquiries into the appropriateness of records of various departments. "Eventually," he continued, "this office may become the regular depository of carbon copies of many such reports or records, as they are made; and thus a general body of statistical data covering the entire plant will be accumulated, by a sort of evolution rather than by radical change effective by executive order." John Goss, as a rising member of a managerial dynasty, had initially recommended and later instituted increasing numbers of executive orders effecting radical changes in the information system in the early years of the century, overcoming opposition when necessary. Davis was a newcomer with neither familial ties nor line position to give him authority. Moreover, by the time of his arrival, substantial material and human investment had already been made in the elements of the current system. What was possible and necessary, he decided, was an incremental approach to rationalizing it.

His first steps in this process, described in a follow-up progress report three months later, involved gathering records and reports from throughout the firm (Scovill 2/34, 8 November 1918). He saw the data as falling into six areas: "Production Statistics," "Process Statistics," "Inventory of Stores Statistics," "Industrial or Employment Statistics," "Financial or Monetary Statistics," and "General and Economic Statistics." Cost accounting was (and continued to be) handled by a separate organization, the Cost Office (Scovill 2/34, 16 May 1919). The records and reports Davis gathered revealed many inconsistencies, but in accordance with his incremental plan he did not attempt an immediate revision of the reporting system. Instead, in some cases he established an "intermediate step": "The receipt of original reports is now, in many cases, followed by a consistent tabulation of the information, and then by charting the results."

This strategy, while avoiding conflict with line managers, had costs. In the following passage from a memo concerning production reports for the Wire Mill, Davis revealed both the inconsistencies in reported information in the firm and the difficulties and costs of dealing with them:

> Comparing these reports with the production reports now being made by the Statistics Office for the Rolling Mill and for screws and rivets, I note the following differences in arrangement:
>
> 1st. The Wire Mill report, being weekly, does not permit of exact summary for even months. The report does not give the items per day, so that a reference to the Office books will be necessary to determine a 31-day month total. This was done, I recall, several months ago when a special production report was called for by Mr. John Goss.
>
> 2nd. The items are given in total, without analysis into orders and shipments for manufacturing departments and orders and shipments for outside customers.
>
> 3rd. No record is kept and no figures are given respecting undershipments or overshipment on orders. Mr. Roper's opinion is that there is an average overshipment not in excess of 10%, but probably in excess of 5%.
>
> Should it be desired to present a monthly production report from this Mill on the same basis as the others I have mentioned, it would be necessary either to make a periodical survey of the books in Mr. Roper's Office or else to establish a duplicate set of bookkeeping similar to that which the Statistics Office is now doing for the Rolling Mill and, in a lesser measure, for screws and rivets. Unless this should be desired by the officers who now receive Mr. Roper's report, I should advise leaving the matter alone, for the time being at least. The present work of the sort which we are doing occupies the whole time of one clerk, or about one-fifth of our present clerical force.
>
> The general question of production reports, their form, content and analytical detail, is one which I think may properly be raised for consideration at some appropriate time. The question might be raised in regard to each one of the departments, with the possible exception of the Manufacturing Department. For this, the question will have to do more with certain types of product than with the entire output of the department. Such a conference would, I suppose, be properly one of the various officers to whom such reports are of interest. My connection with the matter would only arise later, after it had been decided just what should be done.
>
> The uniformity and comparability of reports of this sort are as important as their completeness and almost as important as their accuracy. (Scovill 2/ 34, 16 May 1919)

While Davis explained that certain types of analysis were made difficult or impossible by the inconsistencies between these production reports and those of two other segments of the firm, he also stated that the clerical cost of having the Statistics Office compile such a report on the basis of existing information was, at this point, prohibitive. The obvious solution was to revise the whole system of records and reports at the source to make them uniform and comparable. While Davis saw such a radical revision of the reporting system as an issue "which I think may properly be raised for consideration at some appropriate time," he recognized that any such change would challenge the power of the Wire Mill management to determine what information was collected. That decision, he stated, must be made by the "various officers to whom such reports are of interest." Changing the system required considerable investment in power to overcome vested interests. Thus he was forced to move slowly, taking on only as much as he could handle at any given time.

To help him in the statistical work his office undertook, Davis turned to devices that would, after an initial investment, reduce the costs of analysis. Scovill's Cost Office already had a Hollerith machine for tabulating large amounts of data (Scovill 2/34, 12 November 1918). Nevertheless, Davis immediately requested a Powers tabulator and files to hold the punched cards, justifying his need as follows: "The Powers Machine will open up a large field of statistical investigation and presentation. A certain amount of preliminary experimentation is necessary in handling data susceptible of treatment in any one of several ways. This machine will make possible a series of provisional experiments now prohibitive on account of the time and labor required, and will facilitate actual operation along the lines eventually adopted" (Scovill 2/34, 8 November 1918). The symbolic appeal of such a modern piece of machinery was probably significant and may have contributed to the early timing of this request. The need for more analytic capacity, however, seems to have been real. One example illustrates why extensive manipulation of data without the aid of a tabulator such as the Powers machine was prohibitive: the hospital accident report, one of several that Davis took over from the Cost Office, had used 17,000 Hollerith punch cards in 1917 alone. The clerical work required to manipulate that much data without a tabulator, even with the help of calculating machines for the actual calculations, would have been prohibitively time-consuming and expensive. Thus he saw the value of investing in the most versatile labor-saving machinery to reduce the cost and increase the supply of quantitative analysis in the future. An office inventory taken three years later reveals that Davis also had a Monroe Comptometer, a Burroughs Electric (Adding or Calculating) Machine, and a Millionaire Calculator (Scovill 2/34, 18 August 1921).

Davis knew that his job was not done when he completed his statistical analysis; he also invested in techniques and devices for disseminating data. One of his first steps was to standardize the format (including scale, type of chart, form of data, etc.) of graphic reports issued by his office.[22] The standards both supported the integrity of the data and decreased the cost of rou-

22. A note (presumably written by Davis) on the back of his file copy of his first report, noted the need to establish these standards. Within two months, he issued a "Scale Selection Chart and Plotting Guide" establishing standards for the size of paper and the scale to be used on cumulative charts, given their expected or actual total accumulation (Scovill 2/34, 12 October [1918]).

tinely creating such charts. A publication on "Graphs in the Presentation of Business Statistics and Reports" from a series entitled "Modern Business," found in Davis's files, laid out many of the principles he followed, and may have been his inspiration:

> The form of statistical or graphic reports made in any business house should be carefully worked out and standardized, so that reports may be compiled from month to month as a matter of clerical routine rather than as a matter of special investigation. By thus standardizing the reports the data likely to be required can be on hand promptly when needed by the executives and can be compiled at small cost, since such compilation is a matter of routine and likewise is apt to be more free from error than a special investigation, which also requires expert work.[23]

Davis used graphs frequently in presenting his analyses in subsequent years, for everything from daily graphic analyses of metal mixtures used in casting (Scovill 2/34, 25 February 1919) to a major study comparing the firm's statistics from 1914 and 1920.[24] By standardizing graphic methods, he reduced the cost of using graphs to making information more accessible to those using it, as well as following another popular trend.

Davis also acquired an electrical device to aid him in presenting his graphs and other forms of information to decision-makers. In outlining his progress three months after his original report, he included the category "Publicity of Results," under which he noted that "a reflecting lantern has been ordered, and on its receipt and installation in a suitable room we shall be ready for illustrative conferences" (Scovill 2/34, 8 November 1918). This early equivalent of an overhead projector would enable him to present and comment on his data to company executives, further increasing the supply of information to decision-makers. The fact that he ordered this piece of equipment so early, before he had made much progress on standardizing the content of the various routine reports, suggests that in this matter, like that of the analytic machinery, he was motivated by a desire to keep up with modern trends in office equipment as well as to disseminate information efficiently.

While Davis's main goal in all his actions was to increase the flow of meaningful statistical analysis to executives, his efforts had the side effect of reducing the amount of unnecessary information reaching the general superintendent's office. In attempting to make his office a "clearing house of reference," Davis first compiled lists of all the reports that were supposed to be sent to the general superintendent's office, then began filing copies of all these reports in his own office. To make sure his "database" was complete, he compared his lists with what he received and queried any discrepancies.

23. "Graphs in the Presentation of Business Statistics and Reports," Modern Business, report no. 84, found in Davis files (Scovill 2/34). The report was apparently issued by some subscription service. Internal evidence suggests that it came out between 1915 and 1918.

24. A description of the 1914/20 comparative study, which has not itself survived, remains (Scovill 2/34, 28 July 1939).

This process led Davis to uncover a number of reports that had once been mandated during John Goss's push to increase reporting of internal information, but that no longer served a very useful purpose to him. Many of them had been silently eliminated already, but never officially removed from the books. In one such instance, for example, Goss made the following determination about a report:

> With reference to the weekly fire inspection report and the report of indicator post gate shut-offs made by Mr. Barker of the Plant Protection Department, I do not think it necessary to send these reports to me in the future unless to draw attention to some peculiar or abnormal condition. I shall depend upon you to keep the inspections going, but the clerical work of making out the reports can be saved. If there are any other similar reports which you think can be cut out please give me an expression of your opinion with reference to the same. (Scovill 2/34, 8 March 1920)

In general, Davis's investigations combined with postwar pressure to cut costs as earnings fell (see table 4.3) led Goss to question the value of specific reports. His belief in a basic tenet of systematic management, the value of information in measuring and improving internal efficiency, had initially driven a vast proliferation of reports to pull information into his office. Now, however, he weighed the value of the information more carefully against its costs, as he stated in another such instance: "I am giving up certain reports that do not seem to me worth while to continue further in view of the labor required to compile them" (Scovill 2/24, 25 April 1921). The net impact of this reassessment of the internal information system may be approximated by looking at Davis's lists. While the 1919 list of reports to the general superintendent contained 200 reports, that figure had dropped to about 150 in 1920, and to about 50 by 1921 and 1922. While some may still have been compiled and used at lower levels, evidence suggests that many were eliminated.

## 4.4  Conclusion: Uneven Acquisition and Use of Internal Information in Firms

This paper has explored some aspects of the supply and demand for information within firms during the late nineteenth and early twentieth centuries, when most firms first established extensive internal information systems. The case study highlights some important interactions among technical, organizational, and financial factors in acquiring and using information during that period. This historical case also seems to have some suggestive parallels in today's firms.

### 4.4.1  Investing in Information in Yesterday's Firms

In Scovill and many other manufacturing firms in the late nineteenth and early twentieth centuries, information demand was being driven by growing firm size and complexity, coupled with the ideology of systematic management. At the same time, developments in office methods and devices—which often became symbolically associated with the systematic management ideology—decreased the cost of handling information, thus enabling firms to increase their supply of information at a given cost. Without these technological developments, even discounting for their symbolic appeal, the cost of acquiring the amount of information desired for the systematic management of a large multifunctional firm would probably have been prohibitive. Such firms might not have evolved in the same way without the supporting changes in information technology. Other forms of coordination might have replaced vertical coordination by flows of written information, or firms might have remained smaller and less functionally complex.

The case study of Scovill shows the ways in which supply and demand forces interacted in real firms, and the unevenness of changes in the acquisition and use of information. Investments in Scovill's information system did not necessarily take place at the point when we might expect the demand first to be felt. For example, cost accounting was not introduced at the point when the multiple processes and products initially coordinated by the market through separate (though interlocking) partnerships were internalized into a single, incorporated firm. Only twenty years later was a cost system introduced, initiated by a new layer of management. Similarly, the desire to appear modern and systematic may in some cases have led to an increase in the supply of information before it was needed. For example, E. H. Davis purchased devices for the analysis and dissemination of statistical information before he had solved the more basic issues concerning what types of information should be collected.

In addition, the information system did not immediately respond to reduced or modified demand for certain types of information. E. H. Davis discovered many reports that John Goss judged no longer worth the clerical time to compile, but that were not completely eliminated until Davis drew attention to them in his review of the reporting system. He also discovered that some reports did not provide information in the form that would be most valuable to the firm's executives in monitoring and comparing its own production across units. Since these reports were entrenched among middle managers who used them on the departmental or unit level, changing them to another form required writing off the local investment in the existing form, challenging the power balance within the managerial hierarchy, and overcoming inevitable resistance. The units did not want to give up familiar procedures to provide better information for the firm as a whole. In addition, improved comparability across units may have been perceived as a threat to those with weaker records. Somehow both local and firm-level perspectives needed to be taken into account, requiring an evolutionary, rather than revolutionary, approach to change.

By 1920, when my study ends, Davis was just beginning to get the existing reports under control. Over time, he must have been just about as successful as those in similar firms, since Scovill continued to grow and its rank by asset within its SIC code did not vary much from 1917 (seventh with $33.5 million) to 1930 (eighth with $48.2 million) to 1948 (sixth with $72.1 million; Chandler 1990, appendices A.1, A.2, and A.3).

### 4.4.2 Parallels in Today's Firms

Today, rapid changes in information technology continue to reduce the cost of acquiring, analyzing, and presenting a unit of information, at the same time that increasingly global markets, demands for customization, and rapid changes in all types of products and technologies augment the demand for information. Changes in the supply of information are particularly salient, with computer and telecommunications technologies evolving at an extremely rapid rate.

While the declines in cost per unit of information processed have been and continue to be dramatic, at 30–40 percent per year for components such as logic devices and random access memory, the expected improvements in productivity, especially in white-collar occupations, have not always materialized (Jonscher 1988; Yates and Benjamin 1991). The preceding historical analysis suggests at least two general explanations for these facts, one focusing on the stage of the information-handling process facilitated by various technologies, and the other focusing on complex interactions between organizational and technological change over time.

Modern information technologies have radically improved the speed and reduced the cost of collecting (e.g., computerized capturing of data from manufacturing processes), transmitting (e.g., via computer and phone lines or satellite transmission), storing and retrieving (e.g., standard and relational databases), and analyzing (e.g., mainframes, parallel processing systems, personal computers) information. There have also been improvements in the physical aspects of dissemination (e.g., rapid electronic dissemination to any number of recipients via electronic mail or fax). These stages of information handling have also, at least in theory, become more integrated, allowing information to flow from one to the next without pause or reentry of data. Compatibility problems, however, continue to make the benefits of integration elusive, and sometimes undercut the benefits of improvements in the separate stages of information handling.

Still, these changes have greatly increased the amount of information available within firms. As we saw in the historical case, increases in the amount of information available to executives brought a mounting burden of information overload. Corresponding changes in the nature of the analysis and in the presentational aspects of dissemination are needed to make increasing amounts of information yield their potential value to the firm. Such improvements may be gained in part through further advances in computer technology (e.g., expert systems and enhanced graphic capabilities linked to standard business applications) and in part through more intelligent use of existing ones.

This first explanation also suggests the need for the second one, which focuses on organizational and technical change over time. In modern firms, as in Scovill, new technological capabilities are adopted at uneven intervals, not continuously and incrementally. Investment decisions interact with issues of information needs, ideology, and organizational power. As each element of an organization's information system is established, it becomes entrenched locally by virtue of the human and nonhuman capital invested in it. Further change may thus be resisted until a crisis point is reached. In periods of rapid change, today as in the early twentieth century, new systems may be introduced on top of or beside each other, with additions made almost haphazardly, sometimes for reasons of ideology rather than of efficiency or economy (e.g., when a firm buys new technology because one executive believes that computerization is necessary to keep pace with other firms, but no one has a clear vision of what need it will fulfill). Often, entrenched systems remain in place, as well. In some cases unanticipated organizational consequences may result in barriers to full implementation, or to modifications in the main results or capabilities of the system.

Many firms today are in a situation similar to that faced by Scovill when it hired E. H. Davis. They have adopted a patchwork of information technology responding to perceived or actual needs, but have not yet stepped back to take an integrated look at the system as a whole. Thus some information may be collected and processed (however cheaply) that is not worth the cost of executive time to consider. Conversely, some valuable information may not be available because of inconsistencies in the information systems of different organizational units. All of these factors could undercut the expected productivity gains, at least in the short term.

Judging by an earlier period of rapid change in information needs and information supply, mismatches between the supply and demand for information may develop at any given time because of the complexity of organizational and technical issues involved. This paper suggests that incorporating the cost and scarcity of information into economic models requires understanding the process by which information, especially internal information, is acquired and used within firms. Acquiring information involves making large and often long-lasting investments in capital, human and nonhuman. The decisions to make these investments are shaped by many organizational and technological factors, as are their consequences. The assumption that firms can buy information in increments of any size and that they will do so at the moment when its value exceeds its theoretical cost is appealing but may not reflect the unfolding dynamics of information acquisition and use within firms.

# References

Aoki, Masahiko. 1990. Toward an economic model of the Japanese firm. *Journal of Economic Literature* 28(March):1–27.

Barnum, C. L. 1925. The layout and arrangement of printed forms. *Office Manager* 1(April):74.

Bishop, Philip W. Ca. 1950. History of Scovill Manufacturing Company. Manuscript. Baker Library, Harvard University Graduate School of Business Administration, Scovill Collection 2, case 59.

Bliven, Bruce, Jr. 1954. *The wonderful writing machine.* New York: Random House.

Broehl, Wayne G., Jr. 1984. *John Deere's company: A history of Deere and Company and its times.* Doubleday and Co.

Chaffee, Allen. 1938. *How to file business papers and records.* New York: McGraw-Hill.

Chandler, Alfred D., Jr. 1977. *The visible hand: The managerial revolution in American business.* Cambridge: Harvard University Press.

———. 1990. *Scale and scope: The dynamics of industrial capitalism.* Cambridge: Harvard University Press.

Chandler, Alfred D., Jr., and Stephen Salsbury. 1971. *Pierre S. du Pont and the making of the modern corporation.* New York: Harper and Row.

Clark, E. A. 1916. How we keep costs in our 75-man plant. *Factory* 17(October):405–8.

Clarke, Wallace. 1925. *Shop and office forms: Their design and use.* New York: McGraw-Hill.

Current, Richard N. 1954. *The typewriter and the men who made it.* Champaign: University of Illinois Press.

Davies, Margery. 1982. *Women's place is at the typewriter.* Philadelphia: Temple University Press.

Davis, E. H. Ca. 1968. Recollections of Scovill and Waterbury, 1916–1968. Informal, typed memoir. Baker Library, Harvard University Graduate School of Business Administration, Scovill Collection 2, case 59.

DuBoff, Richard B. 1980. Business demand and the development of the telegraph in the United States, 1844–1860. *Business History Review* 54(Winter):459–79.

———. 1983. The telegraph and the structure of markets in the United States, 1845–1890. In *Research in Economic History* 8:253–77. Greenwich, CT: JAI Press.

Funkhouser, Howard Gray. 1937. Historical development of the graphical representation of statistical data. *Osiris* 3(November):281–342.

Goldin, Claudia. 1990. *Understanding the gender gap: An economic history of American women.* New York: Oxford University Press.

Hoskins Office Outfitters. Ca. 1912. Trade catalogue. Philadelphia. Hagley Museum and Library, Wilmington, DE.

Hudders, E. R. 1916. *Indexing and filing: A manual of standard practice.* New York: Ronald Press Co.

Jelinek, Marian. 1980. Toward systematic management: Alexander Hamilton Church. *Business History Review* 54(Spring):63–79.

Johnson, H. Thomas, and Robert S. Kaplan. 1987. *Relevance lost: The rise and fall of management accounting.* Boston: Harvard Business School Press.

Jonscher, Charles. 1988. An economic study of the information technology revolution. Management in the 1990s Working Paper 88-053. Cambridge: MIT Sloan School of Management.

Leffingwell, William Henry, ed. 1926. *The office appliance manual.* National Association of Office Appliance Manufacturers.

————. 1927. *Office management: Principles and practice*. New York: A. W. Shaw Co.

Litterer, Joseph. 1961a. Alexander Hamilton Church and the development of modern management. *Business History Review* 35(Summer):211–25.

————. 1961b. Systematic management: The search for order and integration. *Business History Review* 35(Winter):461–76.

————. 1963. Systematic management: Design for organizational recoupling in American manufacturing firms. *Business History Review* 37(Winter):369–91.

Marburg, Theodore F. 1952. Commission agents in the button and brass trade a century ago. *Bulletin of the Business Historical Society* 16(February):8–18.

Moody, John. 1916, 1919, 1924, 1931. *Moody's analysis of investment and security rating book*. New York.

Morse, F. C. 1900. Keeping accounts without books. *System* 1(September): no page numbers.

Nelson, Daniel. 1974. Scientific management, systematic management, and labor, 1880–1915. *Business History Review* 48(Winter):479–500.

Parsons, Carl. 1909. *Business administration*. New York: System Co.

President's Commission on Economy and Efficiency. 1912. Memorandum of conclusions reached by the commission concerning the principles that should govern in the matter of handling and filing correspondence and preparing and mailing communication. . . . Circular 21. National Archives, Washington, DC.

Proudfoot, W. B. 1972. *The origin of stencil duplicating*. London: Hutchinson and Co.

Rotella, Elyce J. 1981. The transformation of the American office: Changes in employment and technology. *Journal of Economic History* 41(March):51–57.

Salsbury, Stephen. 1967. *The state, the investor, and the railroad: Boston and Albany, 1825–1867*. Cambridge: Harvard University Press.

Schlink, F. J. 1918. Getting the most out of index cards. *Industrial Management* 55(February):135–38.

System for factory purchases. 1903. *System* 3(January): no page numbers.

U.S. Bureau of the Census. 1975. *Historical statistics of the United States: Colonial times to 1970. Part 2*. Washington, DC: Government Printing Office.

Weiss, Janice Harriet. 1978. Education for clerical work: A history of commercial education in the United States since 1850. Ed.D. diss., Harvard School of Education.

Wigent, William D., Burton D. Housel, and E. Harry Gilman. 1916. *Modern filing: A textbook on office systems*. Rochester, NY: Yawman and Erbe Manufacturing Co.

Yates, JoAnne. 1982. From press book and pigeonhole to vertical filing: Revolution in storage and access systems for correspondence. *Journal of Business Communication* 19(Summer):5–26.

————. 1985. Graphs as a managerial tool: A case study of Du Pont's use of graphs in the early twentieth century. *Journal of Business Communication* 22(Spring):5–33.

————. 1986. The telegraph's effect on nineteenth century markets and firms. *Business and Economic History*, 2d series 15:149–63.

————. 1989. *Control through communication: The rise of system in American management*. Baltimore: Johns Hopkins University Press.

Yates, JoAnne, and Robert I. Benjamin. 1991. The past and present as a window on the future. In *The corporation of the 1990s*, ed. Michael Scott Morton, 61–92. New York: Oxford University Press.

# Comment    Bengt R. Holmstrom

Yates's paper is an admirable piece of investigation, rich in fascinating details about the early developments of modern information technology. It begins with a very informative, general summary of the evolution of this technology around the turn of the century and follows it up with a case study of the Scovill firm, one of three case studies described in Yates's excellent book on this same topic. My discussion cannot do justice to the great effort and care that has gone into this enterprise. My limited objective is to comment on potential connections between this work and modern organization theory. I share Daniel Raff's and Peter Temin's optimism that there is scope for more interaction between business historians and organization theorists. I am particularly convinced that historical accounts can and should have more influence on the development of organization theory. Of course, I would hope that the reverse exchange is of benefit too, though I must leave this to the better judgment of historians, since I do not have a real perspective on their scientific mandate. To test the case, I will offer an alternative, theoretical lens through which one could view Yates's topic. I hope it will go a little distance towards convincing doubting historians (and apparently there are many, judging from this morning's heated debate) that there is some export value in organization theory.

But first a few words about the import value (from my perspective) of business history.

For some time already, microeconomists have been busy developing a better understanding of the economic role of organizations. It is fair to say that we have had measurable success. We have identified trade-offs that appear central for explaining organizational variety, and we have learned to model them reasonably well. In fact, the ability to model has developed so fast that the bottleneck no longer is in the methods of theory, but rather in our limited knowledge of the complexion of organizations. It is an understatement to say that we are behind in testing our theories. The truth is that we are in desperate need of facts. Without empirical guidance, we no longer know in what direction we should proceed.

Business history can obviously help quench some of our thirst for facts. Empirical work on organizations is unlikely any time soon to become a sophisticated econometric exercise. By its very nature, facts about organizations are not easily captured in simple numerical tables to which regressions can be applied in any meaningful sense. The initial kind of empirical work I am envisioning, therefore, is very much in the spirit of the historical accounts I have witnessed at this conference.

Indeed, most of the information about organizations that we presently draw on is anecdotal. It is collected from the popular press, from trade journals,

Bengt R. Holmstrom is the Edwin J. Beinecke Professor of Management Studies at the School of Organization and Management, Yale University.

and from case studies. But there are obvious drawbacks in relying on contemporary evidence. Besides being poorly organized, such evidence has not passed the test of time. Observing today's events does not allow us to separate fads from lasting organizational improvements. Take for instance the recent wave of leveraged buy-outs. In my view, there is no way of telling yet whether these should be considered successes. They could prove failures, and we could be over with them in a hurry. To interpret them as optimal organizational responses, before more evidence is gathered, or to proclaim an eclipse of the corporation, as some have done, is certainly premature.

I am afraid that we often make the mistake of placing too much weight on recent developments. We behave like the market analysts, who find reason in every turn of events. And reason is easy to find, given the arsenal of explanations that modern theories possess. To maintain discipline, a more systematic approach is called for. This is where historical studies can play a major role. History, with its long-term perspective, naturally filters out aberrations, leaving in clearer view the organizational characteristics that account for survival. Also, by scanning a larger landscape in one sweep, a historical study circumvents some of the selection biases present in monitoring everyday developments. The temptation to focus on organizational features that match one's own theories, while overlooking the ones that do not, may be the most serious empirical problem for organization theory. Under the historical lens, tailored theories cannot escape scrutiny as easily.

Historical studies have a second advantage over contemporary studies. A look at the formative years of business enterprise is a look at simpler organizational forms, operating in simpler environments. I think the recent accounts of medieval trading arrangements are illustrative. They seem to point unambiguously to the presence of incentive problems. Apparently, fear of mismanagement and fraud shaped ancient agency relationships. By contrast, attempts to understand modern executive and management contracts are hampered by complications such as tax effects. By the same logic, studies of primitive societies, some of them contemporary, have provided clearer evidence that risk-sharing and incentive problems impact the design of cooperative organization, because the setting is much purer than today's complex economy.

Finally, I should stress the importance of having history remind us that organizations evolve all the time. Modern organization theory is largely premised on the notion that the institutions we observe are driven by the demands for transaction efficiency. Of course, optimizing models can in principle take dynamics into account, but in practice they rarely do. Static models that attempt to explain firm boundaries or their internal structure overlook the constant change in their shape and scope. A theory of the life cycle of a typical firm remains to be developed. The need for such a theory is well underscored by tales such as Yates's description of Scovill.

Let me now turn to Yates's paper. The paper has two major themes. One is to argue that information technology and organizational change are closely linked. The other is to point out that the interaction between the two does not take place as smoothly as theory would lead one to believe. Rather it is discontinuous and often triggered by crises or by coincident changes in the executive office. For this reason, Yates notes, new methods at Scovill are adopted sometimes later, sometimes earlier than implied by marginal calculus. That seems quite believable, though the paper does not really present any hard evidence. In fact, there is surprisingly little reference to financial data. Linking performance figures to the changes that took place would have been quite desirable.

The emphasis on idiosyncratic details (or seemingly so) is in keeping with the traditions of historical analysis. To some extent at least, historians are out to unearth and preserve the "raw data." This has much to commend itself. Sifting through the details can provide ideas for new theories. Also, for students of management, for instance, the organizational and technological dynamics described in the paper hold important lessons about the role power, personalities, and past policies play in the day-to-day affairs of running a business.

Yet I am less convinced that many of the details are important in trying to identify what accounts for the ultimate success of organizations. I am reminded of a case I taught recently, which recollects the Japanese entry into the U.S. motorcycle market. From a distance, the case reads like a textbook instance of a producer exploiting economies of scale in a large home market to enter profitably a smaller market dominated by less efficient firms. In a few bold moves, the small firms are all but driven out. Yet when one reads the detailed history of the case, a very different story emerges. It turns out that the Japanese did not have much of a strategy at all, and what there was of it was completely flawed. Only by accident, it seems, did they hit on a winning combination. But what difference does this make? The fact remains that, whether chosen by serendipity or by conscious calculation, the strategy proved successful. And the reason it did so had a lot more to do with the economic logic of the situation than with its idiosyncratic path. I submit that the moral of this story may often carry over to the historical study of organizational change.

Yates's other theme, that innovations in information technology interact closely, if not in lockstep, with organizational developments, is of particular interest to modern organization theory, as this theory almost exclusively derives its predictions from the assumption that information is costly to communicate and process. In a general way, Yates's account confirms this basic premise. She points to evidence that coordination needs created a demand for centralized information processing, and she also indicates that there were concerns about misappropriation of financial assets and hence a need to control operations more tightly. But perhaps the data would have allowed more significant contact with recent theory. Let me illustrate it with one example.

The theoretical work closest to Yates's study is the work by Milgrom and

Roberts on modern manufacturing.[1] They develop a model that attempts to explain the recent move away from mass production to flexible production. The roots of the theory can be traced to Jay Galbraith, a sociologist, who articulated the view that firm organization is largely conditioned by uncertainty.[2] Firms respond to uncertainty either by reducing it or by adapting to it. Uncertainty can be reduced by controlling the environment (as the American automobile industry is claimed to have done) or via improved internal communication (as in Scovill's case). Adaptation can be accomplished by maintaining more slack (e.g., by raising inventory levels) or by decentralizing authority (which Scovill also tried).

The notable aspect of Galbraith's theory is that it makes significant reference to market structure and technology. It makes clear that one cannot look at information systems and organizational design in isolation. This is so, not only because production and demand functions condition what can be done internally, but because the list of instruments for coping with uncertainty include technological and product choices as well. According to this theory, we should be asking questions such as, How well could Scovill control the demand side? What did its production technology look like? What technological options did it have? Can one detect any systematic changes in inventory management in conjunction with shifts in information systems? Did the firm make to order at any point? Yates does refer to production technology and market conditions, but rarely and rather disconnectedly from the rest of her story. They should be given more serious attention, because they exhibit important complementarities with organizational variables.

The significance of complementarities is well developed in Milgrom's and Robert's work. They note that complementarities induce convexities in the objective function of firms: marginal adjustment in a single instrument (e.g., information acquisition) is often suboptimal, because other instruments (e.g., incentives and control variables) complement it. When changes eventually occur, they tend to be discrete and involve the full range of instruments, organizational as well as technological. The shift from mass production to flexible production illustrates this principle. That it was triggered by reductions in the cost of data processing and flexible technology seems accepted. The key insight is that these factors reinforce each other in a way that causes the shift to take place in one big move, rather than insidiously (in any given firm).

Put differently, Milgrom's and Robert's theory tells us that organizational, informational, and technological attributes of the firm tend to appear in clusters. Flexible manufacturing technology, low levels of inventory, low investment in demand information, multiskilled labor, all go together because they complement each other. By the same logic, a firm with mass-production tech-

1. Paul Milgrom and John Roberts, "The Economics of Modern Manufacturing: Technology, Strategy, and Organization," *American Economic Review* 80(1990):511–28.
2. Jay Galbraith, *Designing Complex Organizations* (Reading, MA: Addison-Wesley Publishing Company, 1973).

nology is likely to choose the opposite attributes. What we do not see is a random mix of these attributes. This is a significant prediction.

One of the virtues of focusing on comovements in firm attributes is that such a theory is not rendered useless when there are multiple equilibria. By this I mean that the theory is not predictively empty as soon as it must admit that there can be several possible outcomes. To take an example, much has been made of the differences between Japanese firms and U.S. firms. Many have asked, How can this be consistent with a single theory of optimization? And most have concluded that culture must play a significant part. That may well be the case. An alternative interpretation is that we are witnessing two different equilibria of the same system (indeed, at some level this is almost a tautological statement). But whichever interpretation one gives to the history of events, it need not change the conclusion that firm attributes should cluster in particular ways. If Milgrom and Roberts are correct, the flexible manufacturing firms in the United States should soon exhibit patterns of operation and organization significantly similar to their Japanese counterparts.

Studying the firm as a cluster of attributes is reminiscent of modern business cycle theory, which concedes that it cannot predict business cycles but still is capable of explaining comovements within the cycle.

This leads me to end on an optimistic note. Historians like to stress idiosyncrasies and path dependence. We are where we are, in part because of historical accident. What I have said above implies that path dependence and other noneconomic factors need not conflict with organization theory nor make its optimizing premise irrelevant. Even if economic theory cannot single out the path of development, it can say a lot about comovements along the path. Thus, there is a road we can travel together.

# 5 Information Problems and Banks' Specialization in Short-Term Commercial Lending:
## New England in the Nineteenth Century

### Naomi R. Lamoreaux

In their relations with the external world, banks face two basic kinds of information problems: ascertaining the creditworthiness of those to whom they loan their funds, and convincing those from whom they obtain funds of their own creditworthiness. This essay uses the historical experience of banks in nineteenth-century New England to explore the interaction between these two kinds of information problems and the policies bankers adopted in granting loans. I argue that as credit markets grew increasingly large and impersonal over the course of the century, bankers found it more and more difficult to evaluate the financial standing of potential borrowers and also to inform depositors and investors about their own performance. These new difficulties forced banks to alter the way in which they conducted their business and, as a consequence, the role they played in the larger economy. Whereas in the early part of the century, banks had loaned funds for a variety of purposes, including investments in fixed capital, by the end of the century they mainly specialized in the business of short-term commercial and brokers' loans, leaving loans for

Naomi R. Lamoreaux is associate professor of history at Brown University and a research associate of the National Bureau of Economic Research.

The author has greatly benefited from the comments and suggestions of Charles Calomiris, Timothy Guinnane, Michael J. Haupert, Thomas K. McCraw, Peter Temin, participants in the NBER Conference on Microeconomic History, and members of the economic history seminars of the University of Michigan, Northwestern University, and the University of Illinois. She thanks also her research assistant Andrew Morris and the many helpful archivists and employees she encountered at the National Archives, the Harvard Business School's Baker Library, the Rhode Island Historical Society, the Fleet National Bank, Shawmut Bank, and the Bank of Boston. She is grateful to the National Endowment for the Humanities, the American Council of Learned Societies, and the John Simon Guggenheim Foundation for the financial support that enabled her to take leave from teaching to pursue this research. This article is part of a study of banking in industrial New England (eastern Massachusetts, Rhode Island, southern New Hampshire, and southern Maine—Connecticut is excluded from consideration by reason of its orientation to New York) and hence retains the geographical focus of the larger project.

**161**

long-term purposes to other types of intermediaries. Although banks continued to support capital formation by granting credit to brokers on the collateral of stocks and bonds, they no longer had any direct relationship with the firms that issued the securities. As a result, as banking operations became more specialized, banks lost their ability to monitor and influence the businesses upon whose prosperity the value of their portfolios depended.

## 5.1   Insider Lending by Early-Nineteenth-Century Banks

In order to analyze this process of transformation, one must understand how banks functioned in the first half of the nineteenth century. Compared to their modern counterparts, the operations of early banks were very simple, and bank management usually consisted of only a few salaried employees. The largest institutions might be staffed by a cashier, several tellers and clerks, and perhaps a bookkeeper; the smallest might employ only a cashier. But regardless of size and number of employees, the real locus of power in an early-nineteenth-century bank was its board of directors, one of whose members served as president. Committees of directors supervised the day-to-day business of the bank, often involving themselves in minute operational details. More important, the directors were responsible for determining the bank's lending policy: they decided how much money the bank could afford to loan and which borrowers were deserving of funds.[1]

If one examines the lending policies pursued by these directors, one discovers that early banks differed from modern institutions in a very striking way: the bulk of their loans went to directors or to other insiders. For example, at the Pawtuxet Bank (chartered in Warwick, Rhode Island, in 1814), a list of notes discounted from the early 1840s shows that fully 53 percent (by value) belonged to James Rhodes, the partnership J. Rhodes and Sons, or various manufacturing enterprises associated with the partnership of C. and W. Rhodes. James Rhodes was both president and a director of the bank until his death in 1841, and his brothers, Christopher and William (the principals of C. and W. Rhodes), also served from time to time as directors, with Christopher succeeding to the presidency upon James's death. Other members of the bank's board of directors absorbed an additional 16 percent of the loans.[2] Similarly, at the Wakefield (Rhode Island) Bank, chartered in 1834, the obligations of two local manufacturers, Samuel Rodman (a director) and Isaac P. Hazard (a kinsman of Rodman and several other directors), accounted for 54

---

1. This generalization is based on my reading of the records that are extant for a number of early banks in Massachusetts and Rhode Island (see also Redlich 1947, 18–20).
2. These totals probably understate the proportion of notes discounted for the benefit of insiders, because they are based on information about promisors only. The names of endorsers were not included in the records (Directors' and Stockholders' Minute Book, 1815–85, Pawtuxet Bank, Rhode Island Historical Society Manuscript Collections, Rhode Island Historical Society Library, Providence.

percent of the discounts outstanding as of 1 March 1845. Notes involving members of the three interrelated families that controlled the bank (the Rodmans, Hazards, and Robinsons) accounted altogether for 84 percent of the bank's total loans.[3]

Investigating the situation in late 1836, Rhode Island's banking commissioners found that insider lending was a widespread phenomenon. "At two of the [Providence] banks lately visited," they reported, "one half of the whole amount respectively loaned by them, was discounted for the accommodation of the directors, and of copartnerships of which they were members. At a third, three-fifths of the aggregate loans went into similar hands." Indeed, as a result of their investigation the commissioners were forced to conclude that the practice of insider lending had become so pervasive that banks were "to a considerable extent mere engines to supply the directors with money."[4]

New Hampshire's bank commissioners arrived at similar conclusions (Smith 1967, 233–34), as did their counterparts in neighboring Massachusetts. In 1838, for instance, the Massachusetts state legislature passed a law offering special privileges to any bank that would restrict its loans to directors to 30 percent of its capital stock, unless shareholders expressly authorized higher limits. Of the state's nearly 120 banks only 29 (including only 2 in Boston) accepted this condition. As for the rest, upon examining their books the commissioners noted, "The liabilities of the directors in most of the Banks, which have not accepted the Act, are above the limits established by the law" (Massachusetts, General Court 1839, 13–14). Nor were regulators alone in this assessment; bankers themselves admitted that directors frequently turned to their own institutions for loans. Indeed, Boston banker Thomas E. Cary attempted to justify the practice in 1845: "It would certainly be advisable that bank directors should be men of property, retired from business, who never wish to borrow money. But this cannot be. Such men can but rarely be induced to trouble themselves with engagements of this nature, and the duty of lending from the bank is left to be performed, in most cases, by those who are borrowers themselves" (Cary 1845, 13).[5]

---

3. These figures, which include appearances in the records as both principals and endorsers, are probably underestimations, because sloppy (or perhaps deceptive) bookkeeping practices appear to have hidden additional loans to these individuals (Bill Book A, Wakefield Bank, Rhode Island Historical Society Manuscript Collections). See also Directors' and Stockholders' Minute Book, 1834–65, Wakefield Bank, Fleet National Bank Archives, Fleet National Bank, Slater Trust Branch, Pawtucket, RI; and Robinson (1895).

4. Rhode Island, General Assembly, *Acts and Resolves* (January 1837), 89–92.

5. All of the New England states at some point required banks to report to the legislature the percentage of their discounts that went to directors, but these figures were typically so understated as to be virtually useless as indicators of the extent of insider lending. In the first place, vague reporting requirements and a lack of standardized accounting procedures allowed banks considerable leeway in compiling their reports. Second, the totals did not include loans to relatives or business associates of directors. Nor did they include loans to corporations with which the directors were connected. As a consequence, there was often a large discrepancy between the amount of loans a bank officially reported to the legislature and the extent of insider lending actually indicated by its books. In 1828, for example, the Eagle Bank of Bristol reported to the Rhode

## 5.2   Banks as Vehicles for the Accumulation of Capital

It might be hypothesized that the prevalence of insider lending in the early-nineteenth-century economy was a consequence of the scarcity and poor quality of economic information, that because of the difficulties inherent in obtaining reliable data about the financial standing of strangers, bankers restricted their lending to borrowers whose businesses they knew well—their own and those of close relatives and associates. As we shall see, this argument has some validity, but it is unlikely that it completely explains the practice. Many of the banks with concentrated loan portfolios were located in small country towns, where lenders would have been familiar with the business standing of most would-be borrowers—outsiders as well as insiders. That some of these local, outside borrowers might also be deserving of credit is suggested by the records of the Sutton Bank in southern Massachusetts, one of the few cases I have found for which complete lists of applicants for loans (as opposed to just lists of recipients) are extant. In March 1829, for example, the bank received applications for discounts totaling $10,210.36, but approved only a quarter of that amount. Markings on the records indicate that most of the rest of the notes were denied not for lack of creditworthiness, but instead were "laid over" for lack of funds. At the same time, members of the family that controlled the bank (the Wilkinsons) owed more than $80,000, nearly 90 percent of its outstanding loans. The bank lacked funds to lend to others in the community for the simple reason that the Wilkinsons had already absorbed most of its resources.[6]

A more powerful explanation for the prevalence of insider lending was the general scarcity of credit in this capital-poor economy, a scarcity that induced bank directors to take advantage of their positions of authority to channel funds into their own enterprises. Evidence that has survived from several of the region's pioneering banks indicates that their early years were fraught with conflict, as directors with a broad sense of public purpose struggled for control against those seeking to make personal use of the institutions. For example, at the Massachusetts Bank, chartered in 1784 as the first bank in the

---

Island legislature that it had loaned 18 percent of its funds to directors, yet an examination of its records for this period shows that directors were principals on 30 percent (by value) of the notes it discounted, and endorsers on another 25 percent. The Pawtuxet Bank's report to the general assembly in 1842 indicated that its loans to directors amounted to a mere 6 percent of the total, while the Wakefield Bank's report for 1845 showed directors receiving only 14 percent of the loans. Similarly, at approximately the same time as Rhode Island's bank commissioners were finding extensive evidence of insider lending, the maximum proportion of loans to directors reported in the official bank returns was 35 percent (Draw Account Book, Eagle Bank, Fleet National Bank Archives; Rhode Island, General Assembly, *Acts and Resolves,* May 1828, 37a; May 1837, 42a; June 1842, 16a; and October 1845, 40a). Additional evidence on insider lending is scattered throughout this article. See also Lamoreaux (1986) and Beveridge (1985).

6. Applications for Discount, 1828–30, Sutton Bank, MSS 781, Baker Library, Harvard University Graduate School of Business Administration.

region, a group of the original proprietors used their influence to borrow extensively from the bank and to insist that their loans be renewed at will. By the summer of 1785, this behavior had left the bank short of funds, and a reform coalition headed by William Phillips forced the recalcitrant borrowers to sell their stock and withdraw from the institution. Elected president of the bank the next year, Phillips initiated a series of policy changes that prohibited renewals and limited the amounts that any one individual could borrow. The result of these changes can be seen in a list of the bank's discounts for March 1788. By that time only about 17 percent of total loans (by value) went to directors or others with the same last name. Similarly, by 1792 the bank was able to report to the state that its loans to stockholders amounted to a mere 23 percent of capital stock (and therefore even less of total loans). Most of its borrowers, the bank claimed, were "opulent Merchants of extensive business and credit, but a small part of whose property is in the funds of the Bank."[7]

By contrast, in the case of the Providence Bank (chartered in 1791 as the first bank in Rhode Island), the reformers seem to have lost out. Discount records for 1793 and 1798 show the bank's directors getting 75 to 80 percent of the loans, despite the efforts of Moses Brown, the self-appointed conscience of the directors.[8] As late as 1811 Brown was still criticizing the bank's other directors, decrying their laxity in collecting past-due debts from, and granting overdrafts to, themselves, and also complaining about their reluctance to let him see the bank's books: "I have calld on the Officers a number of Times Since to know if the Accts were ready for My Examination. the period has never yet Arived, the reason Suggested for the Delay by the Officers was their not having time."[9]

In other cases, there is evidence of conflict between contending groups of directors, each seeking to use the bank's resources for its own benefit. For instance, around 1810 Eli Brown, a former director of the Hillsborough (New Hampshire) Bank, submitted a petition to the legislature in which he complained that the bank's bylaws had enabled its directors "to fix themselves in power beyond a possibility of removal, and in secret conclave, to manage the business of the Bank for their own private emolument." Denying the charge, director Samuel Bell claimed that he had lost more than he had gained through his connection with the bank, partly because of the heavy debts that Brown himself had incurred when he was a director and that he was now trying to evade by fraudulently conveying his property to other parties (Bell 1810 or 1811).

7. Gras (1937, 26, 53–54, 78, 263, 268–69, 273–76); Discount Book, 1786–88, Massachusetts Bank, Bank of Boston Archives, Bank of Boston, Boston.

8. Discount Book, 1791–93, and Notes and Bills Discounted, 1798, Providence Bank, Fleet National Bank Archives.

9. Letter from Moses Brown to the board of directors of the Providence Bank, 29 September 1811, Moses Brown Papers, Rhode Island Historical Society Manuscript Collections.

Surviving minutes of stockholders' meetings display periodic hints of these struggles for control. The normally placid and poorly attended events would suddenly attract a large turnout, and instead of following the usual practice of reelecting the existing board, the stockholders would split their votes among a number of contending candidates. Sometimes a new group would win election.[10] One of the functions assumed by the regulatory boards that state legislatures began to create during the 1830s was to mediate these struggles for control. Thus, stockholders of the City Bank of Providence, Rhode Island, sought the intervention of the state's bank commissioners in 1837, complaining that the present directors had planned an underhanded scheme to insure their reelection at the next annual meeting.[11]

Groups that were excluded from control of a bank often sought to form institutions of their own. Indeed, as many contemporary writers commented, one of the primary forces driving the expansion of the banking system in the early nineteenth century was the desire to gain privileged access to credit (Appleton 1831, 19; Williams 1840, 16; Rhode Island, General Assembly 1826, 24). By founding his own bank, a businessman not only assured himself a source of funds but at the same time created an effective vehicle for the accumulation of capital. Once a charter for a bank was secured, the rest was easy. Incorporators could subscribe for a controlling interest in the stock, and when the payment for the stock came due, they could borrow the requisite sum from another institution. These loans were easy to obtain, because they were essentially riskless: as soon as the state regulators satisfied themselves that the new bank's capital stock had actually been deposited, the investors could borrow back the money they had tendered for their stock (even using the stock itself as security), and repay the original loan.[12]

At this point, of course, the new bank had virtually no resources to lend to its proprietors, since a large proportion of its capital stock was fictitious. Some funds could be raised by issuing currency, but the Suffolk system limited the amounts that could be obtained in this way by forcing the bank to maintain a deposit of specie to redeem its notes. Deposits by customers, moreover, were not yet an important source of funds for the banking sector (see the balance sheet in table 5.1). In the early nineteenth century banks raised funds

10. See, for example, minutes of the stockholders' meetings of 3 and 12 December 1849, Directors' and Stockholders' Minute Book, 1833–55, American Bank of Providence, Rhode Island Historical Society Manuscript Collections; Directors' and Stockholders' Minutes for 1834 and 1835, People's Bank of Roxbury, MA, Bank of Boston Archives; and Stockholders' Meeting, 6 October 1829, Stockholders' Minute Book, 1825–64, Bunker Hill Bank, MSS 781, Baker Library, Harvard University Graduate School of Business Administration.

11. Letter from Anthony B. Arnold and Caleb Carter to the Rhode Island Bank Commissioners, 2 July 1837, Shepley Collection, vol. 8, 57, Rhode Island Historical Society Manuscript Collections.

12. Legislative investigations generated detailed information about such financial practices, especially in Massachusetts, where a number of newly chartered banks failed in the aftermath of the panic of 1837. See, for example, Massachusetts, General Court (1838, 9–14), and (1840, 28–29). See also Rhode Island, General Assembly (1826, 30–32); and Stokes (1902a, 36).

**Table 5.1**                **Balance Sheet for Massachusetts Banks in 1835 and 1890**

|  | 1835 (%) | 1890 (%) |
|---|---|---|
| Liabilities | | |
| Capital stock | 54.0 | 26.2 |
| Bills in circulation | 16.7 | 4.4 |
| Deposits | 21.2 | 45.5 |
| Due to other banks | 6.2 | 12.8 |
| Other | 1.9 | 11.1 |
| Assets | | |
| Loans and discounts | 85.9 | 68.5 |
| Specie | 2.0 | 4.0 |
| Due from other banks | 6.7 | 11.9 |
| Other | 5.4 | 15.6 |

*Sources:* Massachusetts, Secretary of the Commonwealth (1835); U.S. Congress, House (1890), 252–53.

primarily through the sale of stock, for which, as we will see, there were many willing purchasers. As a result, once the original investors had stabilized their bank's position, they were usually able to sell off some of their shareholdings. The proceeds from the sale might be used to repay their stock loans at the bank, or else they could pocket the money and substitute some new security (usually an endorser) in place of the stock, in this manner perpetuating their lines of credit. Over time, as the bank established a market for its securities, they could raise additional funds by increasing the bank's capitalization and selling new shares.

Records of the Eagle Bank of Bristol illustrate the ease with which organizers could unload their investments. When the bank was chartered in 1818, large blocks of stock were bought by members of the DWolf family, as well as other prominent citizens of the town, most of whom promptly borrowed back their purchase money on the security of the stock itself. The bank's transfer book shows that, over the next few years, some of these early investors sold off a substantial portion of their holdings. By 1823, for example, Robert Rogers, Jr., had reduced his holdings from 300 shares to 146, Charles DWolf, Jr., from 320 to 143, and George DWolf from 250 to nothing (though he retained liberal borrowing privileges at the bank through the influence of other family members). Minutes of the directors' meetings show that these men were usually not required to repay their stock loans when they sold their holdings, but instead were allowed to offer new security in the form of an endorser. Hence, through this series of transactions, they were able to transform their initial promise to buy stock into wealth (equal to the amount of the stock they later sold) and, at the same time, maintain an equivalent line of credit.[13]

Subsequent losses caused by the failure of George DWolf and his associates

13. Directors' and Stockholders' Minute Book, 1814–46, Stock Transfer Book, 1818–84, and Stock Book, 1818–1900, Eagle Bank, Fleet National Bank Archives.

prevented the Eagle Bank from proceeding to the next stage and raising its capitalization, but the histories of other banks show how successful this strategy of accumulation could be. When the American Bank of Providence was chartered in 1833, for example, it issued only $193,000 of its authorized capital stock of $500,000. Two years later, however, the bank's stockholders voted to increase its capitalization to $300,000. In 1839 they voted to raise it once again, this time to $400,000, and in 1845 to $500,000. In 1851 the stockholders petitioned the general assembly for permission to increase the bank's authorized capital to $1,000,000, and state banking records indicate that a mere four years later American's paid-in capital amounted to $983,750. The bank's stockholders thereupon submitted another petition to the legislature—this time to increase the capitalization to $2,000,000.[14]

Nor was this an isolated example. In Boston alone eleven banks were able to increase their initial capitalization by at least 50 percent between 1820 and 1850. In the rest of the state, forty-two banks had a similar record. All in all, New Englanders displayed an impressive willingness to put their savings into bank stock during this period. The amount invested in the region's banks increased 101 percent during the 1830-to-1837 boom and another 97 percent during the expansionary 1850s. Over the entire period 1820 to 1860, investment in bank stock registered more than a sevenfold increase (see table 5.2). To put these numbers in perspective, the stock of manufacturing capital increased only 63 percent over the decade of the 1850s. By 1860 the paid-in capital of the region's numerous banks amounted to nearly half the accumulated stock of manufacturing capital in the region (Massachusetts, General Court 1850, 4–19; Fenstermaker 1965, 186–247; Sylla 1975, 249–52; U.S. Census Office 1854, 179; U.S. Census Office 1872, 798).

## 5.3   Banks as Investment Clubs

The rapidity with which capital flowed into bank stock in this period is intriguing, particularly given the extent to which banks engaged in insider lending. We know that the practice was common knowledge. Newspaper editorials and pamphlets harangued about it, government commissions investigated it, and state legislatures repeatedly tried to limit it (Lamoreaux 1989a). Why then were investors not scared away? Why did they not worry that bank directors would allow their judgment to be clouded by their own need for funds—would channel excessive amounts of loans into their own enterprises?

One reason why reports of insider lending had so little effect on the flow of capital into banking was that many large purchases of bank stock were made by insurance companies, savings banks, and other institutions whose investment decisions were controlled by the same groups of men who dominated

---

14. Directors' and Stockholders' Minute Book, 1833–55, American Bank of Providence; Rhode Island, Secretary of State (1855, 5).

**Table 5.2**   **Number and Paid-in Capital Stock of Banks in New England, 1820–60**

| Year | Maine | Massachusetts | New Hampshire | Rhode Island | New England[a] |
|------|-------|---------------|---------------|--------------|----------------|
| 1820 | 1.65 | 10.60 | 1.00 | 3.06 | 16.82 |
|      | (15) | (28) | (10) | (31) | (87) |
| 1830 | 2.45 | 19.30 | 2.10 | 6.07 | 34.77 |
|      | (18) | (63) | (21) | (46) | (172) |
| 1837 | 5.46 | 38.28 | 2.84 | 9.85 | 66.44 |
|      | (55) | (129) | (27) | (62) | (323) |
| 1850 | 3.10 | 34.63 | 2.19 | 11.21 | 62.87 |
|      | (32) | (119) | (23) | (61) | (300) |
| 1860 | 7.51 | 64.52 | 5.02 | 20.87 | 123.56 |
|      | (68) | (174) | (52) | (91) | (505) |

*Sources:* Fenstermaker (1965), 186–247; Sylla (1975), 249–52.
Note: Numbers of banks are in parentheses. Capital is in millions of dollars.
[a]Includes Connecticut and Vermont.

the banks. Thus the Providence Insurance Company, controlled by the Browns, was by 1814 the largest stockholder in the Providence Bank, also controlled by the Browns. Similarly, the Rhode Island Insurance Company, chartered in 1803 in association with the Newport Bank, owned half the latter's stock. More generally, legislatures often deliberately chartered insurance companies in conjunction with specific banks. They also frequently granted charters for savings institutions to groups that had already founded commercial banks, with the two organizations sharing a building, clerical staff, and more importantly, many of the same officers and directors. These arrangements were so prevalent by the 1850s that Massachusetts' banking commissioners expressed reservations about them. In Rhode Island, as late as 1870, nine of the eleven savings institutions in the city of Providence each shared at least four directors with a commercial bank; for these nine, the average number of common directors was seven. Finally, other capital-accumulating institutions also established interlocking directorates with banks. In addition to being president of the Pawtuxet Bank, for example, James Rhodes was president of the Rhode Island Society for the Encouragement of Domestic Industry, an organization that invested heavily in his bank's stock.[15]

But interlocking directorates between banks and other institutions cannot completely explain the flow of capital into banking, because many individuals and institutions without such connections were also heavy purchasers of bank stock. In 1840, for example, bank regulators in Maine published complete

15. Directors' and Stockholders' Minute Book, 1815–85, Pawtuxet Bank. Lists of directors were taken from the *Providence Journal,* scattered issues throughout 1870, the *Providence City Directory* (1870), and the *Rhode Island Business Directory* (1872). See also Stokes (1902a, 15–16); Redlich (1947, 32–33); and *Bankers' Magazine and Statistical Register* 3(May 1854):871. For a discussion of the interlocking directorates employed by the Boston Associates to raise capital for their businesses, see Peter Dobkin Hall (1974–75).

lists of the stockholders of each bank in the state. Analysis of these lists shows that on average only 35 percent of a bank's stock was owned by directors, other individuals with the same last name, and local institutions whose boards of directors might overlap with the bank's. Although some individuals whose last names differed from those of the directors might also have been closely associated with the board, these results suggest that a large proportion of each bank's capital stock was held by outsiders (Maine, Legislature 1840a, 1840b).

Banks could, of course, compensate outside investors for any risks that might be associated with insider lending by offering them a higher rate of return. Bank stock did pay reasonably good dividends during this period. For example, based on the par value of their stock, Boston banks paid out 5.64 percent per year on the average over the period 1831 to 1845, despite the long depression that began in 1839. During the next decade and a half their dividends averaged 7.31 percent per year, while the dividends of country banks in Massachusetts averaged 7.24 percent over the same period. Rhode Island banks paid dividends averaging 6.7 percent per year from 1837 to 1860. Maine banks paid 7.27 percent per year between 1850 and 1859. New Hampshire records are incomplete, but they suggest dividends in excess of 7.5 percent over the decade 1846 to 1855 (Martin 1898, 98–99; Stokes 1902b, 320–21; Rockoff 1990, 32; New Hampshire, Bank Commissioners 1846–56).

These dividend rates were by no means spectacular, however, and indeed it is questionable whether they were high enough to have compensated investors for much in the way of added risk. J. Van Fenstermaker, R. Phil Malone, and Stanley R. Stansell calculated the returns that could be earned on the stock of Boston banks evaluated at actual market prices. Although shrewd investors who bought stock at the lowest recorded price in a given year and then sold it at the next year's highest price could do very well, on the average the rate of return that investors could earn on bank stock was less than the yield on comparatively riskless instruments such as Massachusetts municipal securities or U.S. government bonds (Fenstermaker, Malone, and Stansell 1988). Investors who bought their stock at the time of the initial offering, when prices were usually low, undoubtedly earned significantly higher returns. Nonetheless, the existence of a market for the stock at prices that reduced yields to the level of comparatively riskless securities suggests that, insider lending notwithstanding, bank stock seems to have to have been perceived as a safe repository for funds.[16]

Other evidence confirms this supposition. Bank stock was one of the few securities in which Massachusetts allowed its savings institutions to invest their deposits during this period. In addition, so common was it for men to buy stock with an eye to the future needs of their widows and orphans, that by 1851, about a quarter of the stock of Massachusetts banks was held by

16. Preferential access to credit may have been another incentive to buy stock, but bank records show that most small shareholders never borrowed from their banks.

women, guardians, trustees, and administrators of estates (Massachusetts, General Court 1836, 319, and 1851, 94). Bankers, moreover, seem to have deliberately cultivated this image of safety for their stock. During times of low earnings they were reluctant to cut dividend rates, sometimes, as Massachusetts' bank commissioners repeatedly complained, dipping into surplus resources in order to sustain dividends at a level in excess of current earnings (Lake 1932, 168–70).

If insider lending was really perceived as a danger, moreover, stockholders could have done something about it. Virtually all bank charters in this period gave disproportionate power to small investors by limiting the number of votes that those with large numbers of shares could exercise. In addition, as time went on the rights of stockholders who were not directors received more explicit protection. For instance, in 1840 a Massachusetts statute limited to ten the number of proxy votes a director or bank officer could cast; other stockholders were permitted up to fifty. In 1843 the legislature also granted stockholders the right, upon the vote of at least one-eighth of their members, to investigate the soundness of their bank. Finally, in 1851, the legislature put the state's bank commissioners at the service of stockholders. Whereas previously only the commissioners themselves (or the governor) could trigger a bank examination, now a request from five stockholders was sufficient to compel the commissioners to "make a full investigation of the affairs of such corporation."[17]

Occasionally, stockholders did make use of their powers to regulate insider lending by directors. At the Atlantic Bank of Boston, for example, they passed bylaws specifying that "no loan shall be made to, nor any money deposited with, any Director, under any colour or pretence whatever, free of interest, or at less rate of interest than is required of other persons generally." They also prohibited loans to directors "without other security, than the obligation or responsibility of any one Director and his partner or partners in trade," and forbade directors to overdraw their accounts. After the panic of 1837, the bank's stockholders responded to a rash of bank failures in the state by voting to limit loans to any one individual or firm to 15 percent of capital. They also voted to appoint annually a committee of "Stockholders who are not Directors" to examine the books of the bank.[18]

Such activism was relatively rare, however. Minutes of annual meetings show that stockholders almost never challenged their directors' decisions about lending policy or, for that matter, anything else. Moreover, not only did they generally display little concern about insider lending; there is evidence that they positively approved of the practice. After 1851, Massachusetts law

17. Massachusetts, General Court (1836, 308–20); Massachusetts, *Laws,* 14:302–6, 515–17; Massachusetts, *Acts and Resolves* (1840, 208; 1843, 56–58; 1851, 625–28).

18. Stockholders' Bylaws, 18 March 1828, Stockholders' Meetings, 1 October 1838 and 5 October 1840, Stockholders' Minute Book, 1828–64, Atlantic Bank, Boston, MA, Bank of Boston Archives.

required stockholders to ratify by a formal vote loans to directors in excess of the statutory limit of 30 percent of the bank's capital stock. Surviving records suggest that stockholders willingly granted such approval. Even at the Atlantic Bank they voted repeatedly to raise the limit to 50 percent of capital.[19]

The indulgence with which stockholders treated insider lending is easier to understand once one appreciates the importance of reputation in this information-scarce economy. A glance at the credit reports collected by R. G. Dun and Company, for example, shows that character could be as important as net worth in eliciting a favorable rating. Men who were considered good credit risks were typically described in the reports as "honorable," "trustworthy," and "prompt" in their payment of debts. Conversely, those who got into financial difficulties and defaulted on their obligations might never regain the trust of the business community. Credit reports often ended with an individual's failure, the absence of subsequent entries symbolically recording the borrower's financial death. In the relatively rare event that the listing continued, it was typically full of warnings—"unsafe," "careless of credit," "improvident"—and the resulting inability to raise funds led almost inevitably to a subsequent failure.[20]

Not surprisingly, businessmen went to great lengths to safeguard their reputations, sometimes to the extent of taking on debts that they had no real legal obligation to pay off. John James Dixwell, president of the Massachusetts Bank, is a case in point. He had encouraged the bank to loan substantial sums of money to the Boston Brick Manufacturing Company, where he was also president. When the company failed in 1855, Dixwell felt that it was incumbent on him to assume its obligations to the bank, even though he was not a signatory on any of its notes. The other directors accepted the payment, expressing "the highest respect for that delicate sense of honor" which their president had displayed. Dixwell's reputation survived the incident intact, and he was able to retain his position at the bank, serving as president for almost two decades more (Gras 1937, 128, 494–95, 502–4).

As Dixwell's case suggests, bankers' regard for their own reputations could operate to protect the interests of stockholders. In addition, the fact that banks in this period were for all practical purposes group-managed enterprises, whose directors collectively assumed responsibility for allocating loans, enhanced the workings of this mechanism. If one director overextended himself and endangered the institution by borrowing excessive sums of money, all of the others stood to suffer. Not only would a bank failure cost them their pre-

19. Stockholders' Meetings, 4 October 1852, 3 October 1853, and 2 October 1854 (ibid). See also the annual October meetings of the Shoe and Leather Dealers' Bank of Boston from 1852 to 1859, Stockholders' Minute Book, 1836–64, Bank of Boston Archives; Gras (1937, 122); Warner (1892, 13–14); National City Bank of Lynn, MA (1904, 36).

20. For examples, see Rhode Island vol. 2, 63; vol. 9, 121, 176, 393, 403; vol. 15, 51, 53; in R. G. Dun and Company Collection, Baker Library, Harvard University Graduate School of Business Administration.

ferred access to credit, but it threatened their reputations as well. As a result, bank insiders might be expected to monitor closely each other's borrowing habits. Given the poor quality of information in this period, moreover, such monitoring of insiders by insiders may actually have been less risky than extending credit to perfect strangers. Although bank directors might have occasionally given way to temptation and loaned too much of their funds to themselves, they also had much more information about the businesses of those with whom they were personally connected—information that enabled them to make more informed decisions about loan amounts than they could in dealing with strangers. Over the long run, this information advantage could lower losses from bad debts, as Andrew Beveridge found when he studied insider lending at the Cheshire Provident Institution for Savings in Keene, New Hampshire. Over the period 1833 to 1897, Beveridge calculated, 98 percent of all funds loaned to people who were personally connected with the bank were paid back, as opposed to 90 percent of all other loans (Beveridge 1985, 402).

Finally, in order to understand the willingness of stockholders in this period to condone insider lending, one must appreciate the role banks played in providing small investors with a safe way to participate in the gains from industrialization. The great textile mills of the Boston Associates earned handsome returns throughout this period, but their stock was closely held by members of the group and rarely appeared on the market (Martin 1898, 126). Some of the smaller textile enterprises that sprang up throughout the region were also quite profitable, but many were not, and large numbers of them actually failed. In Rhode Island, for example, approximately two-fifths of the textile mills in the state closed in 1819 and another 15 percent failed in the late 1820s. The latter crisis also brought down many of the state's textile machinery producers (Coleman 1969, 88–89, 91–92, 100–103). Direct investment in these smaller enterprises was a risky proposition and was perceived by investors as such, as is evidenced by the difficulties in raising capital that the few that incorporated themselves had. Thus a corporate charter secured in 1835 by Gamaliel Gay for a silk manufacturing enterprise in Rhode Island never became operational because the firm was unable to attract the necessary support. Most of the other manufacturing corporations chartered in the state in the first half of the nineteenth century suffered similar fates (Coleman 1969, 114–17).

Investments in manufacturing were, in fact, so risky—and also provided so little opportunity for economies of scale—that few entrepreneurs specialized in them exclusively. Most of the men who developed textile mills in the region also invested in commerce, real estate, and/or transportation ventures. It is well known that important merchant groups like the Boston Associates in Massachusetts and the Brown family in Rhode Island followed a strategy of diversification. What is not so often recognized, however, is that many less familiar entrepreneurs pursued similar plans. Thus Samuel Weston and Abner Coburn, founders of the Somerset Bank in Maine, in 1825 had extensive investments in local mills, timberlands, lumbering, and railroads. Stephen Harris, one of the organizers of the Centreville Bank in Warwick, Rhode Island, had a medical practice, a pharmaceutical dispensary and grocery business, large textile-mill investments, a farm, and a limestone quarry. Similarly, the men that controlled the Cheshire Provident Institution for Savings in Keene, New Hampshire, were involved in a variety of enterprises ranging from textile mills to railroads to local utilities (First National Bank of Skowhegan, Maine 1925, 57, 65–69; Basham 1973, 2–3, 21–23; Beveridge 1985, 396).

The problem, of course, with such a strategy of diversification was that it required considerable amounts of capital—amounts that were typically beyond the reach of all but the wealthiest merchant families. Banks helped to solve this problem for less affluent groups by providing them with the wherewithal to diversify their interests. At the same time, they enabled the men, women, and institutions that purchased their stock to achieve a similar level of diversification by buying what was in essence a share of the group's total investments. Because bank loans in this period were usually secured by the endorsements of respected businessmen rather than by specific items of collateral, they were backed by all the resources (the full diversified portfolios) of both the maker of the loan and his endorser(s).

Of course, the phenomenon I am describing here is in a sense simply the familiar one of financial intermediation. The practice of insider lending gave this well-known banking function an important twist, however, because purchasers of bank stock knew that they were investing in the diversified enterprises of the particular group that controlled the bank—not in some anonymously diversified portfolio. In other words, the practice of insider lending conveyed information to the public about the nature of a bank's investments, and this information enabled investors to make important choices—to decide, for example, whether to pursue the less risky option of entrusting their funds to members of the established elite, or to take a chance with aspiring entrepreneurs.

That investors did indeed make use of such information is suggested by the widely different prices commanded by the stock of each bank in the year immediately following its organization, that is, before it could establish its own earnings record. For example, the initial selling price of the stock issued by the seven banks chartered in Boston in 1836 (par value $100) ranged from $75 to $100, using each bank's lowest quotation, or $94 to $100, using each bank's highest (Martin 1898, 97–101).[21] Over time, of course, the price commanded by a bank's stock reflected its actual record of earnings, but investors' assessment of the character of the group that controlled the bank remained important. For Boston banks in 1854, for example, the dividend record of the past ten years explained only about 26 percent of the cross-sectional variation

---

21. Martin reported only the highest and lowest quotations for each year. He provided no information about the quantities sold at each price. Nor did he calculate an average price for the year.

in stock prices (compared to a common par value of $100), using the year's lowest quotations, and 52 percent of the variation using the highest. The addition of a variable for the year in which each bank was chartered (a crude proxy for the character of the bank's directors, since the most prestigious merchants received charters first) added about 15 to 20 percentage points to the explanatory power of the equation, with the oldest banks generally displaying the highest stock prices (see table 5.3). Given the crudeness of the proxy, it is likely that much of the remaining variance can also be explained by differences in the public's assessment of the character of the banks' directors and their business interests.

In sum, although the prevalence of insider lending cannot be explained simply as a response to the scarcity of information in the early-nineteenth-century economy, the practice did have important implications for the flow of information in the economy. Bank managers knew a lot about the business of their primary borrowers—themselves and their close relatives and associates. Moreover, the fact that a large proportion of each bank's loans went to insiders gave potential investors useful information about the kinds of assets that backed up its portfolio. Indeed, it would not be too farfetched to argue that early commercial banks were in essence investment clubs, the counterparts of our modern mutual funds. The sale of bank stock enabled small savers to buy shares in a diversified portfolio of investments whose character differed in important and known ways from one institution to the next. It thus gave small investors a way of participating in the gains from industrialization without

**Table 5.3**    **Determinants of the Price of Bank Stock in Boston in 1854**

| Independent Variables | Dependent Variables | |
|---|---|---|
| | Highest Stock Quotation (1854) | Lowest Stock Quotation (1854) |
| Constant | 338.84*** | 397.42*** |
| | (4.47) | (4.27) |
| Average dividend rate | 4.65*** | 3.43*** |
| (1846–54) | (7.37) | (4.42) |
| Year bank was chartered | −0.144** | −0.18** |
| | (−3.45) | (−3.43) |
| Adjusted $R^2$ | 0.623 | 0.420 |
| $F$-test probability | 0.000 | 0.000 |
| Number of observations    36 | | |

*Sources:* Martin (1898, 97–101); Fenstermaker (1965, 139–49).

*Note:* $T$-statistics are in parentheses.

*Significant at the .10 level.

**Significant at the .05 level.

***Significant at the .01 level.

exposing them to serious risks. At the same time, banks provided entrepreneurs with a mechanism they could use to tap the community's savings and channel the proceeds into industrial development.

## 5.4   The Decline of Insider Lending

This early-nineteenth-century banking system contained the seeds of its own destruction, however. Economic development and the tremendous expansion that occurred in the number and size of banks transformed New England from a capital-scarce to a capital-rich economy. Development also reduced the risks involved in specialization, making it easier for firms to raise funds for their ventures directly, without the assistance of financial intermediaries. Both of these changes in turn operated to reduce the incidence of insider lending. Since funds were now more widely available, bank directors had less need to draw on their own institutions for loans. Although insider lending by no means disappeared (many directors still used their positions to obtain funds, and some banks continued to operate exclusively in the interests of their directors), records that are extant from the last two decades of the nineteenth century suggest that it was now much more common for insiders to account for less than 20 percent of a bank's total loans.[22]

A good example is the case of the Providence Bank, which was dominated for more than a century after its 1791 founding by the interrelated Brown, Ives, and Goddard families. As we have already seen, in the years immediately following its organization, the bank's lendable funds were largely absorbed by insiders. Over time, however, as the region's credit markets matured and the family's textile ventures became themselves important generators of capital, the Browns turned less frequently to their bank for funds. Thanks to the diaries of the Goddard Brothers Company, the firm that managed the Browns' various textile enterprises, the family's relationship with the bank can be followed for the last quarter of the nineteenth century in particularly close detail. William Goddard, a senior partner in the firm, was president of the Providence Bank for most of this period.[23]

The diaries show that Brown-family enterprises continued in the late nineteenth century to use the Providence National Bank for a variety of purposes.[24] The family's textile businesses kept funds on deposit there, and one of them,

22. Reports of national bank examiners to the comptroller of the currency indicate that directors of Boston banks accounted on the average for about 9 percent of their banks' loans in the early 1890s. These figures did not include loans to relatives or to corporations with which the directors were connected. For specific examples supporting the 20 percent figure that are based on banks' internal records, see Lamoreaux (1989b). The records of the U.S. Comptroller of the Currency, Examination Division, are stored in the National Archives in Washington, Record Group 101.

23. Goddard Brothers Diaries, Brown and Ives Manufacturing Records, MSS 9, subgroup 10, series D, Rhode Island Historical Society Manuscript Collections. See also Hedges (1968, 255–56).

24. Like many other banks, the Providence Bank reorganized under the new National Banking Acts and took a new name, the Providence National Bank.

the Lonsdale Company, routinely had its payroll made up at the bank. The records also show that Goddard Brothers occasionally drew upon the bank for loans, sometimes of substantial size. For example, in November 1879 the diaries record, "We discount at Prov. Nat¹ Bank + Prov. Ins for Savings all Bills Receivable due Dec + Jan belonging to Lonsdale + Hope Co." A few years later, in November 1886, the notation appears, "Bk lends all its money to L Co + H Co @ 5%. Money still scarce about here."[25]

Goddard Brothers was, however, just as likely to be in the position of the bank's creditor, as its debtor. In July 1881 the firm loaned the Providence National Bank $50,000 on call so that it could meet heavy drafts by the Providence Institution for Savings. A few days later the diaries noted, "The bank does little business as it owes $150000 to L Co + this is remittance day." In 1889 Goddard Brothers once again helped the bank meet heavy demands by the savings institution for funds.[26]

Indeed, the general position of the Brown family's enterprises with respect to the money markets was that of a creditor. For the better part of each year, revenue from sales poured into the Goddard Brothers' counting house, and the firm's main problem was to find suitable investment outlets.[27] Only during the fall cotton-buying season did the family's enterprises ever have substantial need for credit, but even then they were much less likely to borrow from the Providence National Bank than they were from other institutions, especially in Boston. According to notations in the diaries, Goddard Brothers negotiated loans totaling approximately $4,479,000 from banks and other kinds of financial intermediaries between 1878 and 1898. Of this amount only about $333,000 (7 percent) came from the Providence National Bank. Another $563,000 (13 percent) came from the Providence Institution for Savings, which the family also dominated, and $740,000 (17 percent) from the Rhode Island Hospital Trust Company, an institution that the family had helped to create but did not control. All of the remainder came from Boston institutions, which supplied the firm with approximately $2,793,000 in loans, 63 percent of its total borrowing.[28]

Goddard Brothers turned to Boston banks for loans because, as the diaries suggest, it found interest rates in that city generally lower than in Providence.[29] Family members, it seems, would rather borrow out of town at good rates than use their leverage as insiders at the Providence National Bank to

25. Goddard Brothers Diaries, vol. 2, 17 November 1879, and vol. 9, 22 November 1886.

26. Ibid., vol. 4, 26 July 1881 and 1 August 1881, and vol. 12, 23 October 1889.

27. A large portion of the diary entries are taken up with notations of purchases of commercial paper or money loaned on call. But see especially ibid., vol. 8, 24 April 1885, and vol. 12, 13 June 1889.

28. Amounts for three loans (two from Providence National Bank, one from the Providence Institution for Savings, and one from an unnamed Boston institution) were not given. I estimated the missing amounts by calculating the average size of the loans from each source (ibid., vols. 1–21).

29. See, for example, ibid., vol. 1, 23 December 1878, and vol. 21, 24 January 1898.

obtain favorable terms for their enterprises. It seems that they preferred to protect their bank's earnings (and also the dividends on their extensive stock-holdings) by loaning out the bank's funds at the market rate of interest to creditworthy borrowers, even to their business rivals. According to an entry for October 1896, "our enemies have been borrowing heavily of Prov Bk  In all they will have taken 50000 each or 200,000 on notes maturing this year at 6%." The diarist seemed pleased with the result, for he went on in the next sentence to note, "The City [of Providence] deposit is very convenient to us." For the Browns, banking had become by the late nineteenth century a business in its own right, an investment to be carefully managed and prized for its good, steady yields.[30]

The Providence National Bank is perhaps an extreme example of the changes that were occurring in the banking sector, because the Brown family's ventures were so extraordinarily successful that they could command favor-able credit terms in Boston as well as Providence. But as the century pro-gressed, an increasing number of banks found themselves for a variety of rea-sons with resources in excess of the needs of the parties that controlled them and sometimes even beyond the requirements of the local community. Some banks had extra funds because their directors (like the Browns) were able to generate most of their capital internally or could turn to outside sources of funding. Other banks were so successful in attracting lendable resources that they overshot local needs. And sometimes banks had surplus funds because the groups that had originally founded them were no longer actively involved in business, either as a result of business troubles, an inability to pass on the enterprise to the next generation, or some other cause.

Whatever the reason, the appearance of these surplus funds had a snowball-ing effect that operated to reduce the incidence of insider lending in the econ-omy in general. To the extent that banks had surplus funds that could be loaned to outsiders, the funding opportunities for those who were insiders in other banks increased. Moreover, to the extent that these insiders did in fact turn to other institutions for loans, they freed up funds in their care to be loaned to ventures in which they had no personal interest, which in turn freed up funds at still other institutions for similar purposes.

## 5.5    The Problem of Collecting Information about Creditworthiness

As banks increased the proportion of funds they loaned to outsiders, the problem of evaluating the creditworthiness of would-be borrowers took on

---

30. Ibid., vol. 19, 9 October 1896. The Providence National Bank paid dividends of 10 percent from 1870 to 1876, 7 percent from 1877 to 1879, and 8 percent from 1880 to 1900. By 1880, the Brown, Ives, and Goddard family group owned 61 percent of the bank's stock (Directors' and Stockholders' Minute Books, 1865–80, 1880–96, 1896–1915, and Stock Ledger, 1857–85, Providence National Bank, Fleet National Bank Archives).

new seriousness. When bankers loaned their funds primarily to insiders, they dealt with businessmen whose strengths and weaknesses were well known to them. But once bankers began to loan their funds to those with whom they had no personal connections—once they began to accommodate customers in distant communities—they had to develop new ways of distinguishing worthy borrowers from the great mass of applicants.

Bankers attempted to cope with this new information problem in a number of ways. In the first place, they displayed a heightened interest in the business of discounting what was called "real" commercial paper—that is, notes issued in the course of actual commercial transactions (e.g., sales by a manufacturer to a wholesaler). Such loans were considered desirable because (it was believed) they were self-liquidating: once the wholesaler disposed of the goods he had bought from the manufacturer, he would be able to redeem the IOU he had issued to cover the purchase (West 1977, 136–62; Mintz 1945, 206–10). More to the point, such loans were also thought to minimize information problems. Because the manufacturer had to scrutinize the wholesaler's standing before he would risk his own credit by endorsing the note, bankers felt that it was usually not necessary for them to conduct further credit investigations. As the conservative Chicago banker James B. Forgan instructed an audience of bank employees in Providence, "The strength of the promise is not in this case of prime importance, and need not therefore be as closely considered" (Forgan 1920, 8).

Some commentators went so far as to argue that, because commercial paper bore a one-to-one correspondence to the actual wealth-generating activities of the economy, it was for all practical purposes as good as gold. As one writer explained, "Commodities are, after all, the only things that are really wealth. . . . [I]t is only by convertibility into food, fuel, clothing, and shelter that anything becomes of value. Gold is wealth because of its convertibility; and in the same way, credit is wealth" (Woodlock 1907, 23–24). If credit based on real bills was tantamount to wealth, it mattered little to whom a bank granted its discounts. So long as all the notes in its portfolio were bona fide commercial paper, the bank was safe. Information problems were thus minimized.

By the last quarter of the nineteenth century, however, commercial paper of this type was increasingly difficult to come by. In response to the monetary disturbances of the Civil War era, manufacturers began to encourage customers to pay for goods in cash by offering them price discounts. Buyers responded to these incentives by changing the way they borrowed on the credit markets. Rather than paying for their purchases with an IOU, which the seller then endorsed and discounted at a bank (making it two-name or "real" commercial paper), buyers began to issue IOUs in advance of purchases in order to take advantage of the discounts. The result was a decline in the proportion of real bills on the market and a corresponding increase in what was called single-name paper. Backed only by the promise of the maker, single-name paper was effectively unsecured and was not directly linked to the completion of any particular commercial transaction. Whether it was a good investment or not depended on the financial soundness of the maker (James 1978, 55–59; West 1977, 157–62).

The shift to this new kind of instrument coincided with the development of a national market for commercial paper, which compounded bankers' problems in evaluating the worth of these notes. In the early nineteenth century borrowers had typically restricted their dealings to one or two local banks, which as a consequence always had a good sense of their customers' total obligations. But now that firms could issue their IOUs through note brokers, who would market them to banks and other financial intermediaries across the country, banks lost their ability to assess a customer's total indebtedness. As an article in *Bankers' Magazine* reminded readers, by negotiating their loans through bill brokers, borrowers were "able to float much more paper in many cases than they could if they depended on one or two banks for funds. Herein is the risk of this new mode of lending money; a bank is utterly at sea concerning the ability of the borrower" (48[July 1893]:163–64).

Banks therefore had to find other ways of coping with their growing information problems. One solution that was commonly adopted was to require borrowers to put up collateral for loans (ibid. 39[August 1884]:113–22). Because the National Banking Acts prohibited banks from loaning on the security of real estate, collateral necessarily consisted for the most part of securities that commanded a ready market on the exchanges. As a result, this type of loan was most useful to businesses that themselves issued marketable securities (the best examples were the railroads—industrial securities were rarely traded on the exchanges before the turn of the century) and for those engaged in the buying and selling of stocks and bonds. But collateral loans could be of only limited use to most other borrowers, for the obvious reason that businesses that had the surplus funds to invest in marketable securities were not likely to be the ones most in need of funds. Not surprisingly, then, despite their obvious advantages for banks, collateral loans remained only a small part of their total portfolios. As late as 1890, 64 percent of the loans granted by Boston's national banks were still based entirely on personal security (U.S. Congress, House 1900, 141).

Another way that banks coped with their growing information problems was to insist that borrowers maintain deposits of a certain minimum size with the bank. While this requirement may initially have been a mechanism that enabled banks surreptitiously to earn interest in excess of the usury ceiling, by the last few decades of the century falling interest rates had made the usury laws increasingly irrelevant. The practice seems to have continued more than anything else for the information it communicated about borrowers' creditworthiness, and for the discipline it imposed on debtors' balance sheets. As one banker argued in *Rhodes' Journal of Banking*, "The *best* paper to accept is that offered by firms or individuals who are in the habit of carrying balances with their bank from whom the accommodation should be obtained. There appears to me *no* better means to determine the amount of risk a bank incurs than by regulating its loans according to the average balance carried" (20[May 1893]:486–89). Another banker pointed out that the requirement to maintain compensating balances helped to prevent losses by insuring that customers had a "cash reserve for emergencies" (Forgan 1920, 17).

But the protection that was offered by borrowers' deposits was limited at best. Although the relationship between the deposit and the loan amount varied so much from one institution to the next that commentators were loath to generalize, the ratio was likely to have been small, especially after the competition for deposits heated up in the latter part of the century. Commentators repeatedly complained that banks attempted to lure new depositors by promising them excessive lines of credit (Barrett 1907, 285; Forgan 1920, 17).[31]

In any event, none of the methods thus far described did much to reduce the heavy losses that banks were experiencing in the last few decades of the century. Minutes of directors' meetings reveal that, beginning in the mid-1870s, banks faced soaring numbers of unpaid and overdue loans (the overwhelming majority of them involving outsiders), and bank examiners' reports show no improvement over the remainder of the century.[32] Although much of the problem undoubtedly resulted from the rocky state of the economy in this period, bankers were desperate to improve the situation. By the 1890s, they had become convinced that "by far the greater part of losses incurred by banks on commercial paper could have been avoided had their officers been possessed of sufficient information regarding the applicants at the time the loan was asked for."[33]

One thing was clear: bankers could no longer afford to base their credit decisions on the general reputation of a borrower for wealth and character. Even country bankers were now likely to be misled by the personal knowledge they thought they had about their borrowers' businesses, as one such banker

31. Bank records are usually silent about these arrangements. The one example I have come across was an agreement noted in the minutes of the Shawmut National Bank, specifying that an out-of-town firm would be granted a line of credit of $40,000 secured by collateral. It was expected that in return the firm would keep on deposit an amount equivalent to 20 percent of its debt (Directors' Meeting, 27 September 1875, Directors' and Stockholders' Minute Book, 1865–77, Shawmut National Bank, Shawmut Bank Archives, Shawmut Bank, Boston.

32. Only ten of the approximately two hundred problem loans noted in the minutes of six Boston banks between 1880 and 1900 could be traced to the banks' directors. The banks were Atlantic National, Boylston National, Commercial National, Faneuil Hall National, Fourth National, and National City. The records of these banks are all in the Bank of Boston Archives. I traced the firms whose debts were unpaid through the Boston city directories in order to learn the names of all the local partners involved. The trend in losses was calculated from the reports of national bank examiners to the U.S. Comptroller of the Currency, 1876–95 (Boston banks only).

33. *Rhodes' Journal of Banking* 20(June 1893):585–92. See also *Bankers' Magazine* 57(September 1898):384, 413–22.

found when he determined to write into a credit book everything that he "positively knew, or could learn from unquestionable sources" about his borrowers. To his "astonishment" he discovered "how little I really knew." He concluded from his experiment that he and other bankers had been "granting credits on 'general reputation' unworthily."[34]

For years bankers had supplemented their personal knowledge by subscribing to the reports issued by commercial credit agencies such as R. G. Dun and Company. These reports were rarely based on financial statements filed by the firm in question. More frequently they consisted of estimates of the worth of the firm and of the character of its proprietors based on the surmises of local lawyers and businessmen—precisely the kinds of information that bankers were discovering to be inadequate. Not surprisingly, then, by the 1890s bankers were questioning the worth of such reports and arguing that more systematic methods of collecting information were needed. To a large extent, they argued, bankers would have to take charge of this responsibility themselves by organizing credit departments within their organizations and requiring financial statements from all of their customers. These more rigorous procedures would pay off, it was argued, because many applicants for loans were in fact unworthy of credit. In order to demonstrate "the value of a careful investigation of credits," one writer asked a New York bank with a credit department to prepare a summary of its investigation of 1,598 would-be borrowers. "Of these, 798, or practically 50 percent., were unsatisfactory and credit was refused." The implication of the lesson was that without its credit investigation department, the bank would not have been as able to discriminate among the various applicants for loans and would have faced heavy losses as a result.[35]

Writers not only urged banks to require financial statements from their customers, but insisted that these statements be interpreted in a very specific way. A customer's resources should be divided into fixed assets on the one hand, and quick or convertible assets on the other. Only the latter, they argued, were the proper foundation for loans. Moreover, loans should not be granted if a borrower's liabilities exceeded 50 percent of his quick assets, "the so-called 50 per cent. rule." Even on this basis, loans should be granted for only short periods of time, at most six months and preferably less (Cannon 1907, 44, 47; Forgan 1920, 8–10).

How this particular prescription emerged is a matter of some importance, because by definition it ruled out important categories of loans to manufacturers. The emphasis on quick assets meant that much of the capital invested by manufacturers in their businesses, even if unencumbered, would not be con-

34. *Bankers' Magazine* 57(August 1898):286–87. See also *Rhodes' Journal of Banking* 20(February 1893):137–39 and (April 1893):377.
35. *Bankers' Magazine* 47(January 1893):535–36. See also Cannon (1891, 6–8).

sidered a proper basis for loans.[36] At the same time, the insistence on loans of short duration meant that manufacturers could not borrow from banks to finance improvements in plant and equipment that might take a longer period to generate returns.

Many writers justified their emphasis on short-term commercial loans by emphasizing the greater need for liquidity that resulted from the growth of deposit banking. According to a pamphlet issued by the American Institute of Banking, "experience shows that a bank all of whose assets can be converted into cash within a few months without loss is altogether unlikely to be disturbed by lack of confidence, and should it be subjected to unfounded rumors no difficulty is experienced in securing the necessary funds from other banks" (*Loans and Investments* 1916, 12).

But the argument that short-term loans necessarily led to greater liquidity made little sense, as even the writers of this pamphlet seemed to realize. Under conditions of crisis, portfolios consisting entirely of short-term commercial loans could be as difficult to liquidate as those with a significant proportion of long-term loans, because bankers typically had to renew their customers' notes in order to avoid alienating them or precipitating failures that would render the loans themselves uncollectible (ibid., 14–15; Mintz 1945, 216–19). Liquidity needs, bankers recognized, had to be met in other ways, and it was common to recommend that a bank invest 20 percent of its funds in high-grade bonds and securities, "such as are convertible at a moment's notice," and another 20 percent in commercial paper purchased in the open market, which would be free of any pressure for renewal at maturity. With the liquidity of the institution thus safely assured, the bank could loan the remaining 60 percent of its funds locally for the benefit of its customers. But despite the recognition that these assets would generally be unavailable in times of emergency, writers still insisted that "the conclusion should not be drawn, however, that the loans made to such regular customers need not possess the quality of liquidness." Loans to regular customers should also be granted for brief periods only and should be based solely on the firms' short-term assets (*Loans and Investments,* 1916, 14–15; Coman 1907, 66–77).

Careful study of the pamphlets that promoted this advice suggests that at the heart of the matter was concern about information and monitoring problems—not liquidity per se. Short-term loans based on quick assets were desired because they helped to discipline the borrower. Bankers expected "that borrowers will use the proceeds of loans which they are to repay in a few months more wisely than might be the case if the payment were indefinitely deferred." Moreover, because the information contained in a borrower's financial statement reflected current conditions only and was liable to "change rad-

---

36. In the first two decades of the twentieth century, a few writers did express doubts about the formula precisely on these grounds. See, for example, Hogg (1915, 20) and H. G. Moulton (1918).

ically for the worse" with the passage of time, such statements were clearly "a basis of short time credit only" (*Loans and Investments* 1916, 14–15).

## 5.6  The Problem of Communicating Information about Soundness

At the same time as the decline of insider lending made it more difficult for banks to assess the creditworthiness of their borrowers, it also made it more difficult for investors and (now more importantly) depositors to evaluate the soundness of each bank. Now that only a small proportion of loans went to insiders, the identity of a bank's directors conveyed little information to investors about the content of the institution's loan portfolio. Worse still, the identity of the directors also conveyed less and less information about the quality of the bank's management team, since directors tended to lose interest in overseeing a bank once their need for its funds diminished. Indeed, by the last three decades of the nineteenth century, many directors had begun to shirk their responsibilities, failing to attend the regular meetings of the board and delegating increasing amounts of their authority to the bank's executive officers. Attendance reached an all-time low, for example, at the weekly meetings held to scrutinize recent discounts. Only two of the seven directors of the Boylston National Bank of Boston were present at least for 70 percent of the board's meetings in 1880. Only three of the Massachusetts National Bank's nine directors had a similar attendance record, as did only one of the nine directors of the People's National Bank of Roxbury. The pattern, moreover, was the same at many other institutions.[37]

The problem with this negligence was that it opened the way for opportunistic behavior by the bank's management team (the president and/or cashier and the bank's few active directors). These men could use their positions of authority to loan themselves large sums of money without the consent of the rest of the board and, of course, without the knowledge of the general public. Whether these loans were more likely to lead to losses than the insider loans so common in early-nineteenth-century banks is impossible to determine. What is certain is that contemporaries regarded such behavior as increasingly dangerous. By the 1880s it had become a truism that large loans to insiders were the major cause of bank failures. As Comptroller of the Currency William Barret Ridgely insisted in a sentiment that was voiced repeatedly throughout the period, "The practically universal rule is that all failures are due to excess loans to one interest or group of interests, generally owned or controlled by the officers of the bank itself" (quoted in Moxey 1905, 33).

But how were investors and depositors to know which banks were engaged

37. Directors' and Stockholders' Minute Book, 1864–87, Boylston National Bank of Boston; Directors' and Stockholders' Minute Book, 1865–83, Massachusetts National Bank of Boston; Directors' and Stockholders' Minute Book, 1864–83, People's National Bank of Roxbury, MA; all in Bank of Boston Archives. The generalization is based on my reading of directors' minute books for a large number of banks in the region.

in such dangerous practices? And how were banks that eschewed such practices to communicate this fact to the public at large? The question was not merely an academic one, for at stake was the banks' ability to raise funds. Moreover, unless the public was able to distinguish among the various banks, the failure of any one of them threatened to undermine public confidence in the banking system as a whole and with it the public's willingness to hold deposits. As Charles W. Calomiris and Gary Gorton have pointed out, information asymmetries made it difficult for depositors to monitor the performance of individual banks. Whenever depositors believed that some banks were in danger of failing but were unable to identify the particular institutions at risk, they might withdraw their savings indiscriminately, precipitating a system-wide panic.[38]

Contemporary bankers understood this danger all too well. As one writer in *Bankers' Magazine* explained, "We are in a most important sense directly responsible for each other, and cannot avoid being disturbed by the ignorance, selfishness or immoral conduct of our most remote members." Or, as another writer succinctly put it, "Every bank that fails through mismanagement weakens the surrounding ones." The danger was dramatically illustrated in early 1884 when several failures, "all attributable to the madness of speculation by bank officers," caused depositors to panic. In Vermont, for example, the failure of the First National Bank of St. Albans (allegedly caused by an "unfortunate speculation in stocks by its president and cashier") led to a run on the National Union Bank of Swanton, even though professionals regarded the solvency of the latter bank as undoubted: "To meet only $52,000 due depositors, it held $117,000 of good, short time paper." That same year the *Bankers' Magazine* despaired that "many business men are suspicious of other banks, and, by withdrawing their deposits, are doing their utmost to bring on the very condition of things they deplore."[39]

38. Calomiris and Gorton (1991). One writer claimed that it was "much more difficult to secure trustworthy information in regard to the standing of a bank than it [was] in regard to the standing of a commercial firm." Although each national bank published a financial statement biannually, these documents contained no information at all about the contents of the banks' loan portfolios. Moreover, the balance sheets of many banks looked roughly similar. For example, in 1885 the average ratio of capital plus surplus to total liabilities for Boston banks was about 35 percent, with nearly half of them falling within the range of 30 to 40 percent. At the same time, the fact that five of the nine banks with ratios below 25 percent were among the most successful in the city in attracting deposits suggests that savers may not have paid much attention to such information anyway (*Rhodes Journal of Banking* 15[March 1888]:232; U.S. Congress, House, 1885, 62–83).

39. *Bankers' Magazine* 38(May 1884):886, 38(June 1884):901–2, 39(July 1884):45, and 42(August 1887):83. William Goddard himself painfully learned this lesson in the late 1870s, when a savings-bank panic spread to the rock-solid Providence Institution for Savings. Over the course of the run the savings bank lost nearly $500,000, in deposits. On the worst day of the panic about $195,000 was withdrawn. That night the Providence National Bank stayed open until 10:30 in order to pay checks drawn on it by the savings institution. Cash ran low, and Goddard had to arrange for $425,000 to be shipped express from New York. See Goddard Brothers Diaries, vol. 1, 8, 12, 26, 27, and 29 April 1878; Directors' Meeting, 27 April 1878, Directors' and Stockholders' Minute Book, 1865–80, Providence National Bank, Fleet National Bank Archives; *Providence Journal* (29 April 1878):2.

Just as their predecessors in the early nineteenth century had developed the Suffolk system to guard against the monetary excesses of the country banks, bankers responded in similar fashion to this new danger by attempting to regulate the behavior of their colleagues. The Boston Clearing House, the region's first such institution, was originally founded in 1855 to facilitate the settling of accounts among the city's many banks. But its potential usefulness as an instrument of regulation soon became apparent. In addition to clearing checks, the organization could be used to instill public confidence as well as to prevent runs on its membership by serving as a lender of last resort for temporarily insolvent banks, thereby safeguarding the public's deposits. Since this service was only available to members, moreover, admission to the clearing house became a prize that could be offered as a reward for good management practices or denied as a punishment for financial transgressions (Gorton 1985; Gorton and Mullineaux 1987). The Pacific National Bank of Boston, for example, was excluded from the clearing house because the city's leading bankers disapproved of its management and "decidedly and successfully opposed its admission."[40]

Unlike the Suffolk system, however, the clearing house was of only limited effectiveness as a disciplinary tool. In the first place, banks like Pacific National typically arranged to clear their checks through allied member institutions, a practice that potentially jeopardized the latter's safety. When the Pacific National Bank failed in 1881, for example, its correspondent, Central National, faced heavy losses and had to be rescued by the associated banks (Patten 1896, 357). Second, the organization could not afford to be overly selective, because denying membership to a large number of banks would have undermined clearing-house effectiveness both in clearing checks and maintaining public confidence in the banking system (Bolles 1890). Third, the kinds of general balance-sheet information that the clearing houses routinely collected did not provide any information about loan portfolios. Although clearing-house officials had the authority to conduct a full examination of each bank's affairs, such powers were usually reserved for emergencies.

Moreover, even when information about unsound practices surfaced, clearing-house officials might deliberately ignore the danger signals. The case of the Maverick National Bank in Boston (which collapsed as a result of large loans to support the speculative investments of its president, Asa P. Potter, and several of its directors) shows that they could be so worried about financial crises that they would rather overlook the transgressions of member banks than rock the boat and risk precipitating any failures. Certainly, when Potter's partner, Irving A. Evans, went bankrupt and committed suicide a month before the Maverick's collapse, rumors quickly spread that the bank itself was in

40. Patten (1896, 357). At the time of the Pacific National failure, Patten was cashier at Boston's State National Bank, a member of the clearing house. On the admission policies of clearing houses, see also Carroll (1895, 132–33). According to a *Manual* put out by the Maverick National Bank (1887, 93), seven other New England cities had clearing houses by the late 1880s.

trouble. The clearing house, however, took no action until the Winthrop Bank, of which Evans's brother was president, refused to honor one of the Maverick's certified checks. (Potter later claimed that the brother blamed him for the suicide and used this means to exact revenge.) Other clearing-house members were appalled by the Winthrop's action, but the cat was now out of the bag, and the association had no choice but to initiate an investigation, which culminated with the pronouncement that the Maverick National Bank was indeed insolvent.[41]

Government regulators also proved to be of little use to clearing houses in controlling the behavior of individual bankers. Although the National Banking Acts prohibited loans to any one individual, firm, or corporation in excess of 10 percent of a bank's capital, this provision was relatively easy to evade and difficult to enforce. The only sanction the comptroller of the currency had at his disposal was to institute proceedings to revoke the offending bank's charter, a remedy far too drastic to be invoked with any frequency. As a result, the statutory limit notwithstanding, over 40 percent of the national banks reporting to the comptroller in June 1900 had made at least one loan that exceeded 10 percent of their capital.[42] The most the comptroller could do was to make regular examinations and communicate the results to the banks' officers and directors. But what the banks did with this information depended mainly on the character of their boards of directors and the extent to which board members exercised any oversight over managers' decisions.

## 5.7   Specialization in Short-Term Commercial Lending

Thus one solution to the problem of dangerous banking practices was to encourage directors to become more vigilant. Trade journals from the 1880s were filled with articles urging directors to pay closer attention to their duties—to attend board meetings more frequently, to examine the books of their banks with greater regularity, and to "watch the conduct of their president and manager."[43] These exhortations, plus a growing tendency for creditors to sue the directors of failed banks for negligence, seem to have produced a rise in attendance at directors' meetings. To return to the original examples, by 1895 all six directors of the Boylston National Bank of Boston were present at 80 percent or more of the meetings, and four were there at least 90 percent of the time. Attendance was still low at the Massachusetts National Bank, but at People's in Roxbury four of the directors attended at least 70 percent of the meetings, as opposed to only one in 1880. To encourage this trend, many

41. *Boston Evening Transcript* (2 November 1891):1–2, and (3 November 1891):8.
42. *Bankers' Magazine* 37(December 1882):445; Barrett (1907, 289).
43. *Bankers' Magazine* 36(December 1881):414–16, 36(April 1882):733–35, 36(June 1882):892–94, 39(October 1884:241–44, 42(August 1887):81–84; 42(December 1887):409–13; *Rhodes' Journal of Banking* 12(April 1885):259–60.

banks began to pay their directors a nominal sum, usually $2 (sometimes more), for each meeting attended.[44]

In order for this increased attentiveness to have any consequence, however, directors had to be educated about sound banking practices. In addition, there had to be a set of agreed-upon standards—particularly a set of objective criteria for loans—that directors could use to monitor managers' performance. In the case of collateral loans, objective criteria were relatively easy to establish, because the securities markets provided an evaluative mechanism. Hence, the securities of closely held corporations had at all cost to be avoided. Because they were not traded on the exchanges, their worth was difficult to establish, and this uncertainty made it possible for bank officers to overvalue the assets of enterprises with which they themselves were associated. A rash of bank failures in the early 1880s dramatically illustrated the dangers involved:

> The banks which lately failed loaned on very poor security, and other banks have lost by doing the same thing—by accepting the bonds and stocks of incomplete enterprises, and which perhaps were earning no dividends. But the saddest feature of the recent disclosures is that bank officers were led to do these things because of their pecuniary interest in the enterprises that received the money. They well knew in most of these cases, probably, that the securities were of a hazardous nature. And they never would have accepted such securities, except for their own interest in these outside undertakings.[45]

Such willful misjudgment was more difficult to guard against in the case of unsecured loans, but bankers' faith in the objective worth of real commercial paper helped them to devise another set of lending criteria that they felt would obviate the problem. Although they recognized that real commercial paper was increasingly scarce, they believed that banks could create an equally effective substitute by restricting their business to short-term loans based on quick assets only. We have already seen how this type of loan was embraced as a solution to the problem of evaluating the creditworthiness of outside borrowers. That it might also be embraced as a solution to the objectivity problem can be seen from a pamphlet by E. T. Coman, entitled "Requisites of a Good Loan." Like other writers at the time, Coman recommended that banks should invest 20 percent of their funds in high-grade bonds and securities and another 20 percent in commercial paper purchased in the open market. Such investments would seem to insure that the banks had enough liquid assets to meet most exigencies, yet Coman nonetheless insisted that their remaining loans

44. Directors' and Stockholders' Minute Book, 1887–1909, Boylston National Bank; Directors' and Stockholders' Minute Book, 1883–1900, Massachusetts National Bank; Directors' and Stockholders' Minute Book, 1883–98, People's National Bank. The generalization about remuneration is based on my reading of minute books for a large number of banks in the region.

45. *Bankers' Magazine* 38(June 1884):908. See also Bradley (1907, 62–66).

should be based only on borrowers' "current business," by which he meant advances on "the market value of commodities in the process of conversion into money." If not specified for sixty or ninety days, such loans "should mature upon the definite happening of an event which is of reasonable certainty of occurrence . . . , the maturity of a crop, the completion of a contract." Loans of indeterminate length, he suggested, were a recipe for disaster. Especially to be avoided were "loans which have the character of a permanent investment in the business of the borrower" (Coman 1907, 69–71).

It is clear from the remainder of the pamphlet that the author, who goes on to fret about the problem of insider lending, made these recommendations not primarily for the purpose of insuring liquidity, but because he believed that they were the best means of insuring that loans would be granted according to objective criteria, such that a banker could exercise "no arbitrary discretion when he extends or refuses accommodation to the borrower" (ibid., 66). By adopting a standard for loans that resembled as closely as possible the ideal of real commercial paper, banks could avoid the entanglements between borrower and lender that distorted the latter's judgment and potentially undermined the security of the banking system.

As Coman's pamphlet suggested, long-term loans were considered prima facie evidence of the existence of such potentially disastrous entanglements between borrowers and lenders. Hence as bankers redefined the boundaries of their business during the latter years of the century, they proscribed this type of lending entirely. James B. Forgan underscored this point in 1898: "One of the most fundamental principles of good banking is that the bank should not furnish the capital for its customers to do business upon. The customer should possess his own capital, and require assistance from the bank only at certain seasons and for specific purposes" (*Bankers' Magazine* 57[September 1898]:384). Comptroller of the Currency Hugh McCulloch put the matter even more succinctly in a statement that was repeatedly quoted in the practical banking literature: "Banks are not loan offices. It is no part of their business to furnish their customers with capital" (quoted in Barrett 1907, 305).

## 5.8 Theory and Practice

There is no question that, by the end of the century, these principles had come to dominate all discussions in the practical banking literature. But whether bank managers in fact adhered to them in their daily business activities is much more difficult to determine. There simply are no internal bank records from this period that report the actual criteria employed in evaluating individual applications for loans.

That directors did make use of the new rules to monitor the performance of their managers is, however, suggested by the records of the National Shawmut Bank, the largest bank in Boston, the result of a merger of ten of the city's banks. The Shawmut's lending business was normally handled on a day-today basis by an executive committee, whose decisions the board of directors assembled weekly to ratify. Each year, however, the board appointed its own agents to scrutinize the state of the bank's loan and investment portfolios. In the reports of these examiners, one finds clear evidence that the principles set down in the practical banking literature were actually being applied. In 1903, for example, the examiners chastised the bank's managers for accepting as collateral securities that were not actively traded on the market: "We disapprove in loaning on the stock of a Corporation where we are loaning direct to the Corporation, especially to Officers, except on listed and active and saleable stocks." The examiners also devoted a significant portion of their report to criticizing "the large and apparently permanent Loans to Corporations and Individuals which appear like furnishing a steady Capital for business enterprises." To reduce the number of such loans the examiners recommended "converting a certain class of Time Loans that usually have to be renewed at the option of the borrower, and a part of what we call Steady Demand Loans, into Loans that when they come due cannot possibly have any claims on the Bank." To this end they advised the executive committee to make purchases "in the open market of Commercial paper and Collateral Loans."[46]

Yet even if we grant, as the Shawmut evidence seems to suggest, that these new principles were indeed finding their way into everyday banking practice, we still need to assess the extent to which they actually shaped loan portfolios. Writing in the second decade of the twentieth century, the economist H. G. Moulton attacked the (by then) conventional wisdom of the practical banking literature by arguing that banks should play an active role in supporting manufacturing investment. In order to demonstrate that such a role would not undermine the safety of the banking system, he undertook to show that a considerable portion of existing loans already financed such investment—that "commercial banks are prone to ignore, in practice, the distinction between commercial and investment business" (Moulton 1918, 639). Moulton conceded that banks decided whether to make unsecured loans by calculating the ratio of a firm's debt obligations to its quick assets. He also admitted that such loans were rarely granted for periods longer than six months. But he argued that many short-term loans were regularly renewed, and that once a loan was granted, banks had no control over the use to which the borrower put the funds. As a practical matter, the proceeds of a loan could be used just as easily to pay for investments in plant and equipment as to finance goods in the stream of production. Based on his own (undescribed) "investigations extending over a period of several years," Moulton claimed that as much as 20 percent of the banking sector's unsecured commercial loans were used for investment purposes (ibid., 648).

Moulton's assertions are difficult to verify, because most of the bank records

---

46. Report of the Committee to Examine the Loans and Securities of the Bank, 23 April 1903, Directors' Minute Book, 1898–1903, National Shawmut Bank.

that are extant contain only scattered data on loans, with no information at all about their terms or about the kinds of security that backed them up. There is, however, a brief run of complete loan records for the Suffolk National Bank in Boston.[47] Analysis of these records shows that 54 percent of the bank's portfolio consisted of short-term loans based on personal security, and that it is unlikely that many of these loans could have supported investments in plant and equipment. Fully two-thirds (by value) were notes purchased on the commercial-paper market, that is, bought from individuals or firms that served neither as principals nor endorsers for the notes. Although many of the signatories on these loans were manufacturers, they were not themselves customers of the bank and hence could not expect their notes to be renewed at maturity. In fact, only 19 percent of the bank's loan portfolio consisted of notes backed by personal security that were discounted for the benefit of customers who were signatories, and less than half of this amount involved manufacturing enterprises.

It is, of course, possible that the Suffolk National Bank was unusually specialized in the commercial lending business, and that the loan portfolios of other institutions would look quite different. But the (much less complete) evidence on loans that is available for other banks in Massachusetts and Rhode Island suggests otherwise. The problem with these records is that it is impossible to distinguish loans to regular customers from short-term commercial paper bought in the open market. But a proxy for this distinction can be constructed by assuming that all loans to local firms (that is, loans whose principals or endorsers were listed in local city directories) were loans to customers, and that all other loans consisted of purchased commercial paper. Such a calculation reveals that loans to local customers who were manufacturers ranged form 0 to at most 20 percent of portfolios, with most banks clustering between 14 and 20 percent. There is no reason to assume, moreover, that all of the loans in this category supported investments in fixed capital. A large proportion undoubtedly financed bills receivable.[48]

47. Discount Register, 1899–1902, vol. 75, Discounted Notes Balance, 1900–1902, vol. 101, Discount Ledger, 1901–2, vol. 102, Suffolk Bank, Boston, MA, MSS 781, Baker Library, Harvard University Graduate School of Business Administration. I analyzed all loans granted in the months of January, April, July, and October 1901.

48. At least some information on loans is available for the following banks: Shoe and Leather National Bank of Boston, 1887; Monument National Bank of Charlestown, Boston, 1905; National Bank of Rhode Island, Newport, 1888; First National Bank of Warren, RI, 1886; National Hope Bank, Warren, RI, 1889; National Warren Bank, RI, 1888 and 1898; National Niantic Bank, Westerly, RI, 1893; and First National Bank of Bristol, RI, 1898. See Directors' and Stockholders' Minute Book, 1885–93, Shoe and Leather National Bank, Bank of Boston Archives; loose sheets in Directors' Minute Book, 1892–1905, Monument National Bank, MSS 781, Baker Library, Harvard University Graduate School of Business Administration. The remainder of the records are located at the Fleet National Bank Archives. See Directors' Minute Book, 1862–1902, National Bank of Rhode Island; Directors' and Stockholders' Minute Book, 1864–89, First National Bank of Warren; Directors' and Stockholders' Minute Book, 1873–92, National Hope Bank; Directors' and Stockholders' Minute Book, 1887–99, National Warren Bank; Directors' and Stockholders' Minute Book, 1892–1905, National Niantic Bank; Directors' and Stockholders' Minute Book, 1865–1901, First National Bank of Bristol, RI.

It is, of course, true, as Moulton also pointed out, that collateral loans to brokers and other intermediaries who dealt in the securities markets could be construed as supporting capital formation, because they indirectly underwrote the investment activities of the firms that issued the securities in the first place (Moulton 1918, 651–54). Eighty-four percent (by value) of the Suffolk's collateral loans (38 percent of its total portfolio) were of this type. But what is interesting about these loans was precisely how indirect the relationship between banks and capital formation was. Whereas early-nineteenth-century banks had granted large loans to support the investment activities of their officers and directors, late-nineteenth-century bankers responded to the information problems created by their arm's length dealings by eschewing anything that smacked of a direct investment in their customers' enterprises. Instead they insisted that loans backed by personal security be based on quick assets only and that loans backed by collateral security be based on readily marketable securities. In the case of both types of loans, moreover, bankers seem by the turn of the century to have preferred increasingly to escape the mutual obligations of the customer relationship and do much of their business through brokers. Although banks thus relinquished their ability to monitor or influence borrowers' behavior, such specialization enabled them to reduce risk by shifting it to other kinds of intermediaries. As one banker fantasized, "Some day [I] will have a bank (about the time of the millennium) which will . . . make no loans direct, but will only buy notes through the brokers; where collateral is used, that will be held by guarantee companies who shall endorse. It will thus be able to stop lending on any name without reflecting on the party's credit" (*Rhodes' Journal of Banking* 20[February 1893]:138–39).

# References

Appleton, Nathan. 1831. *An examination of the banking system of Massachusetts, in reference to the renewal of the bank charters*. Boston: Stimpson and Clapp.
Barrett, Albert R. 1907. *Modern banking methods and practical bank bookkeeping*. Fifth edition. New York: Bankers Publishing Co.
Basham, Susan M. 1973. The Greene Manufacturing Company: A case study of cotton manufacturing in Warwick, Rhode Island, during the early nineteenth century. Photocopy. Rhode Island Historical Society Library, Providence.
Bell, Samuel. 1810 or 1811. *An answer to the petition of Eli Brown, complaining of misconduct, &c. &c. of the directors and agents of the Hillsborough Bank*. Amherst, NH: R. Boylston.
Beveridge, Andrew A. 1985. Local lending practice: Borrowers in a small northeastern industrial city, 1832–1915. *Journal of Economic History* 45:393–403.
Bolles, A. S. 1890. The functions of clearing houses: The New York Clearing House controversy. In *Proceedings of the Convention of the American Bankers' Association*, 127–31. New York: William B. Greene.
Bradley, J. T. 1907. Securities that are not securities. In *Practical problems in banking and currency*, ed. Walter Henry Hull, 62–66. New York: Macmillan.

Calomiris, Charles W., and Gary Gorton. 1991. The origins of banking panics: Models, facts, and bank regulation. In *Financial markets and financial crises*, ed. R. Glenn Hubbard, 109–73. Chicago: University of Chicago Press.

Cannon, James G. 1891. *An ideal bank*. New York: privately printed.

———. 1907. Bank credits. In *Practical problems in banking and currency*, ed. Walter Henry Hull, 43–55. New York: Macmillan.

Carroll, Edward, Jr. 1895. *Principles and practice of finance: A practical guide for bankers, merchants, and lawyers*. New York: G. P. Putnam's Sons.

Cary, Thomas G. 1845. *A practical view of the business of banking*. Boston: privately printed.

Coleman, Peter J. 1969. *The transformation of Rhode Island, 1790–1860*. Providence: Brown University Press.

Coman, E. T. 1907. Requisites of a good loan. In *Practical problems in banking and currency*, ed. Walter Henry Hull, 66–77. New York: Macmillan.

Fenstermaker, J. Van. 1965. *The development of American commercial banking, 1782–1837*. Kent, OH: Bureau of Economic and Business Research, Kent State University.

Fenstermaker, J. Van, R. Phil Malone, and Stanley R. Stansell. 1988. An analysis of commercial bank common stock returns: 1802–1897. *Applied Economics* 20:813–41.

First National Bank of Skowhegan, Maine. 1925. *A century of service, 1825–1925: The First National Bank of Skowhegan, Maine*. Skowhegan, ME: privately printed.

Forgan, James B. 1920. *A good note*. 1903 edition. Chicago: privately printed.

Gorton, Gary. 1985. Clearinghouses and the origin of central banking in the United States. *Journal of Economic History* 45:277–83.

Gorton, Gary, and Donald J. Mullineaux. 1987. The joint production of confidence: Endogenous regulation and nineteenth-century commercial-bank clearinghouses. *Journal of Money, Credit, and Banking* 19:457–68.

Gras, N. S. B. 1937. *The Massachusetts First National Bank of Boston, 1784–1934*. Cambridge: Harvard University Press.

Hall, Peter Dobkin. 1974–75. The model of Boston charity: A theory of charitable benevolence and class development. *Science and Society* 38:464–77.

Hedges, James B. 1968. *The Browns of Providence Plantations*. Vol. 2, *The nineteenth century*. Providence: Brown University Press.

Hogg, Albert N. 1915. *The sixth sense*. Philadelphia: Corn Exchange National Bank.

James, John A. 1978. *Money and capital markets in postbellum America*. Princeton: Princeton University Press.

Lake, Wilfred Stanley. 1932. The history of banking regulation in Massachusetts, 1784–1860. Ph.D. diss., Harvard University.

Lamoreaux, Naomi R. 1986. Banks, kinship, and economic development: The New England case. *Journal of Economic History* 46:647–67.

———. 1989a. Banks and insider lending in Jacksonian New England: A window on social structure and values. Manuscript. Brown University.

———. 1989b. From entrepreneurs to bankers: The professionalization of banking in late–nineteenth-century New England. Manuscript. Brown University.

*Loans and investments*. 1916. New York: American Institute of Banking.

Maine. Legislature. 1840a. *List of stockholders in the banks of Maine*. State Documents.

———. 1840b. *Report of the bank commissioners*. House Doc. 7.

Martin, Joseph G. 1898. *A century of finance: Martin's history of the Boston stock and money markets*. Boston: privately printed.

Massachusetts. General Court. 1836. *The revised statutes of the Commonwealth of Massachusetts*. Boston: Dutton and Wentworth.

————. 1838. *Report relating to Kilby Bank*. Senate Doc. 34.

————. 1839. *Report of the bank commissioners*. Senate Doc. 5.

————. 1840. *Report of the bank commissioners*. Senate Doc. 7.

————. 1850. *List of banks chartered in Massachusetts*. House Doc. 93.

————. 1851. *Final report of the bank commissioners*. Senate Doc. 11.

Massachusetts. Secretary of the Commonwealth. 1835. *Abstract from the returns of banks in Massachusetts*. Boston: Dutton and Wentworth.

Maverick National Bank. 1887. *Manual*. Boston: Wright and Potter.

Mintz, Lloyd W. 1945. *A history of banking theory in Great Britain and the United States*. Chicago: University of Chicago Press.

Moulton, H. G. 1918. Commercial banking and capital formation. *Journal of Political Economy* 26:484–508, 638–63, 705–31, 849–81.

Moxey, Edward Preston. 1905. Bank defalcations: Their causes and cures. *Annals of the American Academy of Political and Social Science* 25:32–42.

National City Bank of Lynn, Massachusetts. 1904. *Semi-centennial of the National City Bank of Lynn*. Lynn: privately printed.

New Hampshire. Bank Commissioners. 1846–56. *Annual Reports*.

Patten, Claudius. 1896. *The methods and machinery of practical banking*. Seventh edition. New York: Bradford Rhodes and Co.

Redlich, Fritz. 1947. *The molding of American banking: Men and ideas*. Part 1. New York: Hafner Publishing Co.

Rhode Island. General Assembly. 1826. *Report of the Committee to Inquire into the Expediency of Increasing the Banking Capital*. Providence: Smith and Parmenter.

Rhode Island. Secretary of State. 1855. *Abstract exhibiting the condition of the banks*. Providence.

Robinson, Caroline E. 1895. *The Hazard family of Rhode Island, 1635–1894*. Boston: privately printed.

Rockoff, Hugh. 1990. The capital market in the 1850s. NBER Working Paper Series on Historical Factors in Long-Run Growth, no. 11.

Smith, Norman Walker. 1967. A history of commercial banking in New Hampshire, 1792–1843. Ph.D. diss., University of Wisconsin.

Stokes, Howard Kemble. 1902a. *Chartered banking in Rhode Island, 1791–1900*. Providence: Preston and Rounds.

————. 1902b. Public and private finance. In *State of Rhode Island and Providence Plantations at the end of the century: A history,* ed. Edward Field, 3:173–322. Boston: Mason Publishing Co.

Sylla, Richard E. 1975. *The American capital market, 1846–1914: A study of the effects of public policy on economic development*. New York: Arno Press.

U.S. Census Office. 1854. *Statistical view of the United States . . . ; Being a compendium of the seventh census*. Washington, DC: Beverley Tucker.

————. 1872. *Compendium of the ninth census*. Washington, DC: Government Printing Office.

U.S. Congress. House. 1885. *Annual report of the Comptroller of the Currency*. 49th Cong., 1st sess., Ex. Doc. 3.

————. 1890. *Annual report of the Comptroller of the Currency*. 51st Cong., 2d sess., Ex. Doc. 3, vol. 1.

————. 1900. *Annual report of the Comptroller of the Currency*. 56th Cong., 2d sess., Ex. Doc. 10, vol. 1.

Warner, Caleb H. 1892. *The National Bank of Commerce of Boston*. Cambridge, MA: privately printed.

West, Robert Craig. 1977. *Banking reform and the Federal Reserve, 1863–1923*. Ithaca: Cornell University Press.

Williams, Henry [A Citizen of Boston, pseud.]. 1840. *Remarks on banks and banking; and the skeleton of a project for a national bank.* Boston: Torrey and Blair.
Woodlock, Thomas F. 1907. Banking conditions in Wall Street. In *Practical problems in banking and currency,* ed. Walter Henry Hull, 23–37. New York: Macmillan.

## Comment     Charles W. Calomiris

Naomi Lamoreaux's portrayal of New England banking emphasizes several intriguing features of the changing structure and role of New England's banks. I would call attention to three major themes in the paper. (1) In the early history of the system "insiders" played a fundamental role in ownership and management, obtained preferential treatment in access to funds, and accounted for a large share of bank loans. (2) "Outsiders" (including unsophisticated investors) during the early history of New England banking were not just debt holders (as many historical and theoretical studies of other times and places lead one to expect), but in many cases accounted for the majority of stock ownership in banks. (3) By the late nineteenth century the reliance on insider ownership and control had waned, insiders were far less important as an outlet for bank loans, and financing came to rely less on capital and more on debt.

A central point of Lamoreaux's paper is that the early financing and loan-allocation structures of New England banks should not be studied in isolation; they are best understood as a combined response to the need to finance productive local investments in an environment of "capital scarcity," given that other means for external finance were lacking. Furthermore, she argues that the change in bank financing structure and loan allocation over time support that view. The decline in the reliance on insider ownership, management, and borrowing coincides with an increased reliance on debt, and a change in the way banks gathered information about their new primarily "arm's length" borrowers.

What I especially like about this paper is that the evidence it contains helps to tie together three important literatures: the theoretical literature on the optimal form of bank finance in environments of asymmetric information, the empirical literature on the evolution of banking in the United States, and the historical literature on changing regional concentration of industrialization over the nineteenth century.

I will discuss how I think these three literatures are linked, using evidence presented in the paper and some additional evidence. In doing so, I will (1) provide generally supportive descriptive evidence, (2) recast and add to the argument linking the peculiarity of the two sides of early New England banks'

Charles W. Calomiris is visiting associate professor of finance at the Wharton School, University of Pennsylvania.

balance sheets, and (3) show that—consistent with the theoretical model I will discuss—New England's *cities* during the first half of the nineteenth century were the main outlier with respect to the loan allocations and financing structure of U.S. banking.

## Industry and Banks in New England Relative to the United States

Let me begin with a discussion of the literature on changes in industrial location during the nineteenth century. New England banks (especially those in Boston and Providence) initially were an important vehicle for financing the golden age of New England industrial growth. As investment opportunities shifted to other regions, New England's banks changed their role from financing investment to financing commercial activities and investing in securities. As is well known, small groups of New England's entrepreneurs set up a complex interlinked network of banks and industrial enterprises during the period of early industrialization. This network was mainly designed to help finance growing industry during an early stage when entrepreneurs lacked sufficient investment funds.

The reasons behind the early concentration of industry in New England has been the focus of much research—by Field, Hekman, Goldin and Sokoloff, and many others.[1] These authors point to a combination of factors—low-cost labor displaced from agriculture as the West opened, and agglomeration economies (or Marshallian factor-market externalities) that made Boston an especially good location to develop new techniques. Boston and vicinity was where cheap unskilled labor, skilled artisans who could manufacture and service innovative (and changing) machinery, and concentrations of capital could all meet and collaborate easily.

Hekman's map of industrial location emphasized the importance of proximity to Boston's factor markets during the early phase of technological development and capital accumulation in cotton textiles.[2] He, and later Wright,[3] argued that the shift of industry away from Boston and toward the South in the 1880s and 1890s reflected lower costs of unskilled labor in the South, and a mature (and therefore) "transportable" manufacturing technology that no longer required proximity to skilled machinists. Factories, entrepreneurs, and capital moved South and West in the late nineteenth century as economic opportunities, transportation cost declines, and factor-market price differentials propelled them out of the Northeast. It is therefore natural that New England's big-city bankers would change their allocation of funds more toward com-

1. Alexander Field, "Sectoral Shift in Antebellum Massachusetts: A Reconsideration," *Explorations in Economic History* 15(1978):146–71; John S. Hekman, "The Product Cycle and New England Textiles," *Quarterly Journal of Economics* 94(1980):697–717; Claudia Goldin and Kenneth Sokoloff, "Women, Children, and Industrialization in the Early Republic: Evidence from the Manufacturing Census," *Journal of Economic History* 42(1982):741–74.

2. Hekman, "Product Cycle," fig. 1.

3. Gavin Wright, "Cheap Labor and Southern Textiles before 1880," *Journal of Economic History* 39(1979):655–80.

merce and more distant investments. Additionally, as New England firms grew, their internally generated cash flow increased relative to their investment opportunities, reducing their demands for borrowing. An interesting example of this turning outward was a propensity of state-chartered banks in New England to invest in western mortgage pools in the latter quarter of the century. Gary Gorton and I discovered this while sifting through state bank superintendent reports from the 1890s. When the western land bust came, it seems New England state-chartered banks were among the hardest hit of eastern state-chartered banks.

Thus far I have argued that the transition from financing local capital accumulation to other activities, which Lamoreaux argues occurred, makes sense within the overall context of the history of changes in industrial expansion in various regions of the United States. But this does not explain why industrial entrepreneurs in New England during the early nineteenth century should have *owned and controlled* banks, nor why banks in New England cities had such higher ratios of capital to assets relative to other banks.

Before discussing explanations for these unusual aspects of early New England banking, it is worth noting that New England's *cities* were the exception to the rule in their propensities to make so many loans to insiders and to rely on capital as their primary means of finance.

First, on the question of loans to insiders, scattered data that are available suggest that states outside New England had much lower proportions of loans to insiders. For example, according to the reports of the superintendent of banking in New York State for 1845, only 6 percent of assets took the form of loans to insiders. By 1854 in New York City loans to directors amounted to roughly 4.8 percent of total assets, while for the state as a whole insider loans were 4.6 percent of total assets. Many states (Ohio, for example) specifically limited loans to insiders, and in many cases 10 percent was considered a large number.

On the question of reliance on capital finance, again New England—and its cities in particular—seems to be a national outlier. In a recent paper, Kahn and I pointed out that New England's banks had much lower specie ratios and much higher capital ratios than other northeastern states' banks in 1850.[4] We also found that these patterns varied greatly by bank location within each state. Holding urbanization constant, New England and other states have similar reliance on capital, except in the large cities (Boston and Providence) where the reliance on capital far exceeds that of Baltimore, New York City, or Philadelphia.

Table 5C.1 draws on data from state superintendents' reports to compare and contrast the financing structure of banks in New York, Massachusetts, and Pennsylvania for three dates in the nineteenth century. The essential messages

---

4. Charles W. Calomiris and Charles M. Kahn, "The Efficiency of Cooperative Interbank Relations: The Suffolk System," manuscript, Northwestern University, 1990.

**Table 5C.1    Bank Growth and Financing**

|  | 1836–37 | | | | 1854–55 | | | 1900[a] | | |
|---|---|---|---|---|---|---|---|---|---|---|
|  | NY 1/37 | PA[b] 1/37 | MA 10/36 | BUS 1/37 | NY 9/54 | PA[b] 11/54 | MA 8/55 | NY | PA | MA |
| D/A | 0.14 | 0.20 | 0.22 | 0.02 | 0.34 | 0.24 | 0.17 | 0.56 | 0.62 | 0.54 |
| N/A | 0.20 | 0.22 | 0.16 | 0.10 | 0.13 | 0.34 | 0.22 | 0.02 | 0.04 | 0.04 |
| C/A | 0.30 | 0.38 | 0.51 | 0.29 | 0.35 | 0.26 | 0.49 | 0.08 | 0.12 | 0.15 |
| C&S/A | 0.35 | 0.42 | 0.56 | 0.34 | 0.38 | — | 0.54 | 0.17 | 0.23 | 0.24 |
| IB/A | 0.16 | 0.12 | 0.08 | 0.28 | 0.09 | 0.04 | 0.06 | 0.23 | 0.11 | 0.15 |
| a |  |  |  |  | 2.2 | 1.8 | 1.7 | 11.0 | 9.4 | 5.2 |
| n |  |  |  |  | 1.4 | 2.8 | 2.3 | 1.3 | 1.0 | 1.0 |
| d |  |  |  |  | 5.4 | 0.6 | 1.3 | 17.9 | 24.5 | 16.5 |
| c |  |  |  |  | 2.6 | 1.2 | 1.6 | 2.6 | 4.3 | 1.7 |
| c&s |  |  |  |  | 2.4 | — | 1.7 | 4.9 | 7.2 [c] | 2.3 |
| A | 108 | 62 | 68 | 119 | 237 | 112 | 112 | 2,609 | 1,053 | 585 |
| n/a |  |  |  |  | 0.6 | 1.6 | 1.4 | 0.1 | 0.1 | 0.2 |
| d/a |  |  |  |  | 2.5 | 0.3 | 0.8 | 1.6 | 2.6 | 3.2 |
| c/a |  |  |  |  | 1.2 | 0.7 | 0.9 | 0.2 | 0.5 | 0.3 |
| c&s/a |  |  |  |  | 1.1 | — | 1.0 | 0.5 | 0.8 | 0.4 |

*Sources:* U.S. Congress, House, *Condition of Banks throughout the Union*, 25th Cong., 1st Sess., Ex. Doc. 111 (1837); U.S. Congress, House, *Condition of Banks throughout the Union*, 34th Cong., 1st Sess., Ex. Doc. 102 (1855); Board of Governors of the Federal Reserve System, *All Bank Statistics* (Washington, DC, 1959).

*Note:* Lowercase letters denote ratio of current level to previous period's levels. D = individuals' deposits; N = bank notes outstanding; C = capital; S = surplus; IB = deposits of other banks; A = total assets.

[a]Data include national and state banks.

[b]Data exclude Bank of the United States (BUS).

[c]Assuming 4 percent surplus-to-assets in 1854 (the ratio in 1837).

of this table are (1) in 1836 and 1854 Massachusetts banks had a much higher reliance on capital to finance assets; (2) from 1836 to 1854 the reliance on capital was little changed in New York or Massachusetts, with balanced growth in all financing components in Massachusetts (in contrast to New York's increased reliance on deposits, and Pennsylvania's increased reliance on notes); (3) by 1900, all three states had converged to a fairly homogeneous financial structure, with Massachusetts and Pennsylvania showing an especially strong "catching up" in deposit banking.

But the heavy reliance on capital in the early phase of banking growth in Massachusetts shown in table 5C.1 is entirely attributable to Boston. If Boston banks are removed from the sample, the capital ratio of Massachusetts banks falls from 51 percent to 33 percent. This is comparable to a 35 percent capital ratio of banks in New York state located outside New York City.

These facts suggest that a theoretical explanation of the reliance of banks on capital should explain the peculiarity of New England's cities in the early period. Another fact that the model should explain is that the greater reliance on bank capital did not require higher returns to stock ownership. Indeed, dividends for New England banks (in and outside Boston) are lower than those of Philadelphia or New York City banks.[5] In other words, banks in New England were able to float more stock at lower cost than banks elsewhere, while at the same time lending more of their money to insiders.

## Modeling Bank Ownership Structure and Financing Structure

I return now to the two central puzzles of New England banking to be explained—namely, the high reliance on capital by banks in Providence and Boston, and the relative importance of loans to insiders (those who own a substantial share of the bank and control its operations).

In explaining the preferential treatment afforded insiders, Lamoreaux dismisses the argument that outsiders were too costly to screen and monitor, noting first that they were typically part of the same local community, and second, that many outsiders' loan applications were rejected not on the grounds of poor credit risk, but because the insiders preferred to lend to themselves and "lay over" the requests of outsiders. Indeed, Lamoreaux argues that "one of the primary forces driving the expansion of the banking system in the early nineteenth century was the desire to gain privileged access to credit." In other words, part of the value of starting a bank was owning a loan supply option for your own business.

This is certainly a reasonable idea, given the potential information problems involved in financing growing enterprises through other means than the bank (foreign or out-of-state borrowing, direct corporate stock flotations in foreign or out-of-state markets, etc.).

Assuming there was a credit-supply benefit to insiders from organizing

5. Ibid.

banks to make loans to them, how does one explain (1) that insiders will hold a substantial fraction of the bank (an even larger fraction relative to their own wealth) and (2) that outsiders provide a readier market for bank stock than in other states, rather than debt, and at lower yields than in other states? This second fact seems all the more puzzling given the potential for cheating outsiders through fraudulent or excessively risky insider lending. After all, many arguments for the prevalence of bank reliance on debt financing under asymmetric information view debt as limiting the banker's behavior to protect the interests of the outsider.[6]

I think many of the pieces necessary to make a reasonable argument are provided in Lamoreaux's paper. The argument for why capital was feasible in New England seems to have three parts: (1) small stockholders were given disproportionate power in voting as a check on insider abuse (note that the fact that this power was not used very often could simply be an indication that it was a very effective check); (2) much of bank stock was owned by people in the know who were not loan recipients, thus providing a mechanism (through stock demand) to keep insiders behaving properly; and (3) insiders or their associated enterprises (including savings banks) held substantial amounts of bank stock, which would have been reduced by fraudulent or excessively risky lending to insiders.

Thus part of the explanation for why widows and orphans were willing to hold bank stock is that enough insiders and sophisticated investors were also doing so. Kahn and I make a similar argument for the prevalence of bank stock in New England at low yields.[7] We argue that institutional peculiarities in New England (notably the Suffolk system) facilitated incentive-compatible monitoring by informed parties. A central point here is the old saw that "where there's no conflict, there's no interest." Environments where asymmetric information is important imply benefits from some subset of the debt or equity holders monitoring the managers. The trick is to provide an incentive for the right people to do the right amount of costly monitoring.[8]

As nineteenth-century contemporaries and banking historians since Redlich have stressed, New England bankers seem to have solved the problem of creating incentive-compatible monitoring extraordinarily well. Lamoreaux's detailed evidence allows us to speculate more specifically on how incentives for monitoring were created. Incentive-compatible monitoring seems to have occurred at two levels: within the banking firm and among financial institutions. In both cases, there were clear gains to be had by relatively informed parties in limiting excessive risk-taking by insiders at the expense of outsiders.

6. Charles W. Calomiris and Charles M. Kahn, "The Role of Demandable Debt in Structuring Optimal Banking Arrangements," *American Economic Review* 81(1991):497–513; Charles W. Calomiris, Charles M. Kahn, and Stefan Krasa, "Optimal Contingent Bank Liquidation under Moral Hazard," Federal Reserve Bank of Chicago Working Paper WP–13 (April 1991).

7. Calomiris and Kahn, "Efficiency of Cooperative Interbank Relations."

8. Described in Calomiris and Kahn, "Role of Demandable Debt"; Calomiris, Kahn, and Krasa, "Optimal Contingent Bank Liquidation."

First, at the level of the banking firm, insiders had incentives to monitor each other. Importantly, not all insiders desired funds at any one point in time. Insiders who wished access to funds tomorrow would want to preserve the solvency and reputation of the bank today. So long as the value to insiders of continued access to funds is sufficiently great, insiders will have incentives to monitor one another and protect the long-run interests of the bank. They would not be amenable to side payments from today's insider borrowers at the expense of the bank's overall health. According to this argument, so long as there are *several* insiders running the bank, they will restrain any one insider's attempt to use the bank as a vehicle to finance an unworthy project. Moreover, as Lamoreaux correctly argues, short-term loans can provide an effective means to limit risk taking by borrowers too, allowing early intervention to correct borrowers' abuses.

This argument helps to explain the feasibility of New England's early reliance on capital. Because the future loan-supply option was so valuable to the insiders, they expended the information costs necessary to ensure proper allocation of funds. In other states, and in New England by the late nineteenth century, the value of the credit-supply option may not have been as high, and thus capital finance and insider lending would not have been accompanied by the appropriate degree of monitoring among insiders.

It is interesting to note that this is precisely the same principle employed by the Grameen Bank of Bangladesh for ensuring that farmers repay government loans.[9] Groups of landless farmers form loan cooperatives, with each farmer taking turns at borrowing. The group members' incentives to screen and monitor each other depend on the value of the government-subsidized loan-supply option, which is conditional on the continuing performance of the previous borrowers in the group. If any member of the group defaults, the entire group is redlined in the future. Actual default rates on loans are extremely small (1 percent).

As both Lamoreaux and Calomiris and Kahn[10] emphasize, there was also a significant *interbank* monitoring network at work in New England. The interlacing of the balance sheets of the savings banks and commercial banks, and the interlacing of commercial bank liabilities through the Suffolk system, created strong incentives for banks to regulate each other (as in the Suffolk system) and monitor each other. The gains from doing so for the Suffolk system were the joint product of a higher demand for New England bank notes (wider circulation at lower rates of discount), while the benefits to the savings banks and insurance companies from monitoring followed from their direct investments in commercial banks.

Gorton, myself, Schweikart, and Kahn have argued that there are many

9. See Mahabub Hossain, *Credit for the Rural Poor: The Experience of the Grameen Bank in Bangladesh* (Dacca: Bangladesh Institute for Development Studies, 1984).
10. Calomiris and Kahn, "Role of Demandable Debt."

other examples of successful interbank monitoring to provide a joint benefit, including city clearing houses, mutual guarantee systems (in antebellum Ohio and Indiana), and branch-banking systems (particularly in the antebellum South).[11] What sometimes limited the potential for interbank coordination, however, was the number of banks and the geographical dispersion of banks, under unit banking. Once the number of potential monitors becomes too great, the incentives to invest in information that benefits the group becomes too low, because the individual benefit to the monitor is too watered down. Moreover, distant banks have a hard time observing each other's actions, in contrast to a small number of branching banks whose locations overlap throughout an area.

Lamoreaux is somewhat skeptical of the potential for interbank monitoring to discipline member banks, based on a few examples of clearing-house failures to detect and act upon unsound practices. I think the weight of evidence from the studies cited above, and the logic of self-regulation within clearing houses, run contrary to her conclusion that "the clearing house was of only limited effectiveness as a disciplinary tool." I conclude from Lamoreaux's examples only that the clearing house, like any good regulatory apparatus, is liable to make a few mistakes. A self-regulatory banking system that never experiences a bank failure is probably overly restrictive.

I believe that the peculiarity of New England's city banks can be attributed to incentive-compatible monitoring among borrower-insiders and among banks. The feasibility of such monitoring may have been greater in cities for two reasons. First, because cities were better areas for entrepreneurs to locate,[12] insiders' loan-supply options may have had higher value. Second, cities had a higher concentration of banks and, therefore, facilitated interbank monitoring and discipline.[13]

Reduced interbank coordination may be an important element in explaining the demise of New England banking's reliance on capital (along with the reduction at the individual bank level in the value of the loan-supply option). As the number of banks grew, mechanisms for coordinating their behavior became harder to enforce, except in cities, where limited numbers and geographical overlap encouraged the development of city clearing houses.

11. Gary Gorton, "Clearinghouses and the Origin of Central Banking in the U.S.," *Journal of Economic History* 45(1985):277–83; Gary Gorton, "Self-Regulating Bank Coalitions," manuscript, The Wharton School, University of Pennsylvania, 1989; Charles W. Calomiris, "Is Deposit Insurance Necessary? A Historical Perspective," *Journal of Economic History* 50(1990):283–95; Charles W. Calomiris and Larry Schweikart, "The Panic of 1857: Origins, Transmission, and Containment," *Journal of Economic History* (1991); Charles W. Calomiris and Charles M. Kahn, "Cooperative Arrangements for the Regulation of Banking by Banks," *Illinois Business Review* (Summer 1990):8–13.

12. As argued in Hekman, "Product Cycle."

13. Note the continuing importance of clearing-house self-regulation in cities throughout the nineteenth century, discussed in James G. Cannon, *Clearing Houses* (Washington, DC: Government Printing Office, 1910), and Gorton, "Clearinghouses" and "Self-Regulating Bank Coalitions."

## Conclusion

To sum up, the reliance on capital, insider lending, and the ready market for bank stock among outsiders were jointly sustainable in New England during the first half of the nineteenth century primarily because opportunities for entrepreneurs were great, and institutional relations among financial institutions provided interbank discipline. As opportunities waned, and perhaps as institutional discipline became more costly, banks increasingly turned to other more typical means of solving agency problems, which included a greater reliance on demandable debt.

As Lamoreaux shows, this transformation coincided with a reduction in insider lending, less direct involvement of directors in bank affairs (hence, less conflict and less interest), and the development of credit evaluation techniques once outsiders became more important as a source of loan demand.[14] It also coincided with a move toward greater diversification and a preference for mark-to-market portfolios, which would have been less desirable when banks were financing insiders.

This paper has added greatly to my understanding of the information problems and special early opportunities that underlay the unusual balance-sheet and financial-returns data for New England relative to other regions. I hope in the future we can convince Lamoreaux to provide a similarly detailed look at other regions. It would be particularly interesting to date the increasing involvement of New York City and Philadelphia banks in the securities markets (which I would guess becomes pronounced in the 1850s), and to see how this affected (if at all) the structure of bank balance sheets.

14. Lance E. Davis was among the first to emphasize these changes in lending practices within New England. See "Sources of Industrial Finance: The American Textile Industry, A Case Study," *Explorations in Entrepreneurial History* 9 (1957): 190–203; and "The New England Textile Mills and the Capital Markets: A Study of Industrial Borrowing, 1840–1960," *Journal of Economic History* 20 (1960): 1–30.

# 6     Did J. P. Morgan's Men Add Value?

## An Economist's Perspective on Financial Capitalism

J. Bradford De Long

## 6.1   Introduction

The pre–World War I period saw the heyday of "financial capitalism" in the United States: securities issues in particular and the investment banking business in general were concentrated in the hands of a very few investment bankers—of which the partnership of J. P. Morgan and Company was by far the largest and most prominent—who played substantial roles on corporate boards of directors. This form of association between finance and industry had costs: it created conflicts of interest that investment bankers could exploit for their own profit. It also had benefits, at least from the owners' perspective:[1] investment banker representation on boards allowed bankers to assess the performance of firm managers, quickly replace managers whose performance was unsatisfactory, and signal to investors that a company was fundamentally sound.

The Morgan-dominated "money trust" thus filled an important monitoring role in the years before World War I. In 1910–12 the presence on one's board of directors of a partner in J. P. Morgan and Company added about 30 percent to common stock equity value. The overwhelming proportion of this increase in value came from the fact that Morgan companies performed better than others similarly situated.

J. Bradford De Long is an assistant professor of economics at Harvard University and a faculty research fellow of the National Bureau of Economic Research.

The author would like to thank George Alter, Michael Bordo, David Corbett, Greg Clark, Naomi Lamoreaux, Bill Lazonick, Thomas McCraw, Elyse Rotella, Charles Sabel, Mike Spagat, Robert Waldmann, Eugene White, especially Dan Raff and Peter Temin, and many others for helpful discussions and comments, and Hoang Quan Vu for excellent research assistance.

1. As opposed to the workers' or consumers' perspective. Some of the increased value came from improved productive efficiency. Some came from an increased ability to exercise monopoly power.

Some share of the increase in value almost surely arose because investment banker representation on the boards of competing companies aided the formation of oligopoly. But the development of similar institutions in other countries that, like the Gilded Age United States, experienced exceptionally rapid economic growth—Germany and Japan are the most prominent examples—suggests that a large share of the value added may have arisen because "financial capitalism" improved the functioning of financial markets as social capital-allocation mechanisms.

This paper is organized as follows. Section 6.2 lays out the major issues that arise when taking an economist's perspective on the turn-of-the-century "money trust." Section 6.3 presents Progressive and finance historian perspectives and argues that they leave the most interesting questions unaddressed. Section 6.4 lays out the money trust's contemporary view of itself, and interprets it in a way that promises to resolve the anomalies pointed out in section 6.2. Section 6.5 argues that the money trust's view of itself is by and large supported by the available quantitative evidence. Section 6.6 considers two very brief case studies, International Harvester and AT&T. Section 6.7 considers extensions and related issues, and section 6.8 offers conclusions.

## 6.2   An Economist's Perspective on the Money Trust

In the years before World War I, a corporate security flotation worth more than $10 million invariably passed through one of a very few investment banks—J. P. Morgan and Company; Kuhn, Loeb, and Company; the First National Bank; the National City Bank; Kidder, Peabody, and Company; and Lee, Higginson, and Company.[2] The partners and directors of these institutions were directors, voting trustees, or major stockholders of corporations with a total capitalization—debt plus equity—including subsidiaries, of nearly $30 billion (Brandeis 1914). In perspective, this sum bore the same relation to the size of the U.S. economy then that $7.5 trillion bears today: it amounted to one and a half years' national product and 40 percent of the country's produced capital (Goldsmith 1954).

The investment banking oligarchs profited immensely from their middleman role. Typical fees on mergers and restructurings ranged between 4 and 10

---

2. When questioned by Samuel Untermyer, chief counsel and guiding spirit of the investigating Pujo Committee (chaired by Louisiana representative Arsène Pujo), First National Bank chairman George F. Baker was "unable to name a single issue of as much as $10,000,000 . . . that had been made within ten years without the participation or cooperation of one of the members" of the small group of dominant investment banks (Pujo Committee 1913b). Securities issues then amounted to about $500 million a year.

percent of the capital value of the businesses involved.[3] The commissions on U.S. Steel were as large a share of the economy then as $15 billion would be today. Today Wall Street's investment banking firms are strained to the limit by deals that are, in proportion to the size of the economy, only one-tenth as large.

Wall Street finance before World War I was thus several orders of magnitude more concentrated than it has been at any time since. This concentration of finance was a major political flashpoint. Progressives feared this money trust in finance as an evil much more dangerous than any monopoly in an individual industry. The financial dominance of the money trust allowed it to charge high fees and so levy a destructive tax on the productive classes, and the high profits earned by the money trust were distributed to buy influence to keep its dominance.[4] Historians of financial markets have exhibited a strong revisionist tendency to reject the Progressive critique: many have argued that, since there were few barriers to entry in finance, monopoly power was impossible to exercise and that the dominance of Morgan and the other oligarchs should be viewed as reflecting their excellence at innovation and as financial entrepreneurs.

Progressives write the history of American finance around the turn of the century as a series of frauds and conflicts of interest (Brandeis 1914; Untermyer 1915; Pecora 1939). Finance historians and biographers tend to write it as a series of individual acts of entrepreneurial vision: J. P. Morgan at the Morgan partnership (see Hovey 1912; Satterlee 1935; Allen 1949; Chernow 1990) and Jacob Schiff at Kuhn, Loeb (Adler 1921, 1928) saw the opportunity for a certain merger or restructuring or reorganization before anyone else, carried it through, and reaped the rewards of ingenuity and enterprise (see also Redlich 1951).

But from an economist's standpoint neither of these ways of telling the story fully captures how it really happened. Ingenuity and enterprise produce high profits in the short run, but such high short-run profits then attract imitators and competitors. The imitators and competitors copy the organizations and operating procedures of the first-moving innovators, and compete away the initial high profits. *Sustained* high profit rates and sustained market dominance require not only ingenuity and enterprise but also substantial "barriers to entry." Sustained high profits are possible only if there are factors that make

3. The lower figure comes from the investment banker share of the very straightforward International Harvester merger. The upper figure comes from the investment banker share of U.S. Steel. It does not include the investment banker share of previous combinations bringing together various subparts of the future U.S. Steel.

4. Many historians have often been more approving of the large financial organizations and deals of the Gilded Age. See Chandler (1990). In addition, Gerschenkron (1962) argued that the heavy capital requirements of modern technologies required large firms and larger banks. Davis (1963, 1966) wondered whether Great Britain's economic decline might be linked to its failure to develop "finance capitalist" institutions.

it costly for competitors to enter the business, and difficult for competitors to match existing firms' capabilities.

Yet neither Progressives nor finance historians have addressed what such "barriers to entry" were. No one has maintained that Morgan and Company and Kuhn, Loeb earned mere "normal" rates of return on their capital in the years before World War I. Such high profits should have induced much of the potential competition to become actual—or, at a bare minimum, the threat of new entry and subsequent competition should have induced Morgan and Company and its peers to moderate their fees—unless the existing investment banking firms had organizational capabilities and competitive advantages that new entrants could not effectively match.

From an economist's standpoint, therefore, the combination of no visible barriers to entry, sustained dominance by a tight oligarchy of firms, and extraordinarily high profit rates is anomalous. On the progressive reading of the situation, the Morgan partnership and its peers should have earned high profits in the present while experiencing a rapid erosion of market share—as did U.S. Steel, Morgan's dominant firm in the steel-making industry, which earned high profits but experienced a very rapid erosion of its market share to Bethlehem Steel and others in the years before the Great Depression. On finance historians' reading, competition between the Morgan partnership, its investment banking peers, and additional potential investment banking competitors should have kept Morgan and Company from earning sustained supernormal profits in the first place.

Thus the key to understanding American finance around the turn of the century is to find an answer to the following question: What were the barriers to entry that prevented new firms from matching the capabilities of Morgan and Company and its peers? There must have been some way that they created value for customers that potential competitors could not match. The story of American finance at the turn of the century cannot be coherently and completely told without detailing the origins and functioning of the Morgan partnership's competitive advantage.

This paper tries to specify the source and nature of Morgan and Company's competitive advantage. In the process, it puts some empirical meat on the theoretical bones of the relationship between finance and industry. And it tries to untangle the question of what the money trust actually was.

Such a study is of obvious historical interest. Morgan and Company must have had some striking competitive edge in order to maintain its dominance over American finance at the turn of the century: if not, such a profitable business should have seen the rapid arrival of new competitors to reduce the magnitude of the wealth to be earned. The Morgan-headed "money trust" remained a fixed point for more than a generation, while all was in flux around it.

Such a study could be of direct interest to those concerned with the regulation of today's securities markets. Perhaps the forces that allowed Morgan and

Company to become the focus of the turn-of-the-century capital market are still at work today. In such a case, how the turn-of-the-century market functioned carries information about how today's markets ought to function.[5]

The conclusions reached on the source of the money trust's competitive advantage are most hospitable to a view of the relation between finance and industry often identified with Lester Thurow (1986). The Morgan partnership and its peers saw themselves—and other participants in the pre-World War I securities industry saw them—as filling a crucial "monitoring" and "signaling" intermediary role between firms and investors in a world where information about firms' underlying values and the quality of their managers was scarce. In such a world it was valuable for a firm to have the stamp of approval from Morgan and Company (with its established reputation) and to have its managers watched over by Morgan's men from their posts on the board of directors. The presence of Morgan's men meant that when a firm got into trouble—whether because of "excessive competition" or management mistakes—action would be taken to restore profitability. The presence of one of Morgan's men may also have reassured investors that a firm appearing well-managed and with bright prospects actually was well-managed and did have bright prospects.

On this interpretation, the structure of information is the key to understanding turn-of-the-century Wall Street. Individual investors are, essentially, without reliable information about firms' prospects and their managers and without power to adequately monitor and control the executives who manage the firms in which they invest. By serving as an honest (albeit expensive) broker, a dominant investment bank can channel investors' funds into and choose executives to run firms, collect high fees, and yet on net provide value to investors. In such a situation, a firm's reputation as an honest broker becomes a very important asset—an asset that must be safeguarded by actually being an honest broker, and an asset that a potential competitor will find it very hard to match.

High concentration in investment banking may have played a role in supporting "financial capitalism." A firm with a large market share may reap large benefits from a good reputation. If reputations as honest brokers are sufficiently fragile, a firm with a large market share will find it most profitable in the long run to strive to be above suspicion in every short run: it will not imperil its reputation for the sake of higher short-run profits in any one deal as long as the finance industry's future and its own market share appear secure.

---

5. On the other hand, perhaps styles of management, means of gathering information, and shareholders' ability to discipline rogue management have all changed sufficiently that capital market institutions that were effective in 1900 would be ineffective today. A look, however, at Germany and Japan—which appear to have kept many "finance capitalist" institutions throughout the past century—leads one to suspect that institutions that were effective in 1900 would still be effective in 1990. These issues are briefly touched on in section 6.7.

By contrast, a firm with a small market share may well decide to "cash in" its reputation by luring investors into a profitable deal that is unsound—as Standard Oil magnates H. H. Rogers and William Rockefeller may have done with the Amalgamated Copper Corporation (Lawson 1906). With a small market share, the future returns expected from a reputation as an honest broker might also be small, and less than the present benefits from exploiting to the fullest one unsound deal. If investors follow this chain of reasoning and conclude that a firm with a small market share has little incentive to be an "honest broker," such small firms will find themselves unable to compete with Morgan and Company or with Kuhn, Loeb, for no one will trust them not to sacrifice their long-run reputation for immediate profits. The large market share of the Morgan partnership and its expected future profits served, in a sense, as a performance bond that the Morgan partnership could post, but that other, smaller potential competitors could not.

The disadvantages of financial concentration stressed by Progressives were certainly present. Conflicts of interest were frequent and potentially severe. Often "Morganization" meant the creation of value for shareholders by the extraction of monopoly rents from consumers: if Westinghouse and General Electric share controlling directors, their competition is unlikely to be too intense.[6] And First National Bank chairman George F. Baker sat on the boards of six railroads that together carried 80 percent and owned 90 percent of Pennsylvania anthracite. But there were positives on the other side—positives apparently strong enough to support Morgan dominance over potential competitors for more than a generation. The breaking of financier control over managers in the interwar period raised a new worry: is it better for managers to be unmonitored and effectively their own bosses than for them to be responsible to financiers (Berle and Means 1932)?[7]

### 6.3  Progressive and Finance Historian Perspectives on the Money Trust

Concern over this "money trust"—the concentration of the business of issuing the securities of large corporations in the hands of a few investment

---

6. An explicit watchword in Morgan reorganizations was "community of interest": as long as the Pennsylvania Railroad held a large block of Erie Railroad stock, the Pennsylvania would suffer if its actions undercut the profits of the Erie. On the other hand, as Kolko (1963) points out, industries in which financiers could preserve monopoly by strangling competitors at birth were almost nonexistent. And Brandeis allowed that "lately . . . the Westinghouse people were complaining that the General Electric's competition was unfair" even though Lamont was a director of one and Steele a director of the other (see Lamont 1913).

7. An issue present but unnoted in the Pujo report. On the one hand, the report stresses how shareholder apathy allows investment bankers to exercise dominant roles in choosing directors with only a minority of the stock. On the other hand, it calls for direct election of directors and managers by the small shareholders. The possibility that shareholder apathy combined with the elimination of financial capitalism would produce destructive managerial autonomy is not considered.

banks led by the Morgan partnership, and the associated presence of investment bankers on boards of directors—dominated public policy debate over the securities industry for the first third of this century. The debate was resolved only by the Great Depression. The presumed link between the stock market crash and the Depression left the securities industry without political defenders. The Glass-Steagall Act broke the links between board membership, investment banking, and commercial banking–based management of asset portfolios that had marked American finance between 1890 and 1930 (Seligman 1982).

In retrospect, it is surprising that "financial capitalism" in America lasted so long, given the heat of the political hostility to it. The money trust was subject to two major congressional investigations, the first in 1912–13 by a special House committee chaired by Arsène Pujo and counseled by Samuel Untermyer (triggered by the approach of a presidential election and Minnesota congressman Charles Lindbergh's denunciation of the money trust; see Huertas and Cleveland 1987);[8] the second in 1932–33 by the Senate Banking Committee counseled by Ferdinand Pecora.

### 6.3.1   The Progressive Perspective

Progressives like Louis Brandeis were sure that the Morgan and Company–headed money trust exercised enormous control over industry, and that such control was a bad thing. Brandeis, ever sensitive to conflicts of interest, saw the money trust as a "concentration of distinct functions . . . beneficent when separately administered [but] . . . dangerous . . . when combined" (Brandeis 1914, 6). The money trust's possession of monopoly power in the business of issuing securities imposed an unreasonable tax on all companies raising money in the capital market. And the links between corporate boards, investment bankers, and portfolio managers—First National Bank head George F. Baker was on the board of AT&T and the prime mover behind AT&T's appointment of Theodore N. Vail as its president; Morgan partner George W. Perkins was also a director of New York Life, which invested heavily in securities underwritten by the Morgan partnership—created a serious conflict of interest. Corporations sought to get as much for their securities as possible, and saving institutions sought to obtain high returns.

Investment bankers like Baker and Perkins were thus in a position to sacrifice the interests of one set of principals to the other—or to increase the spread they received as middlemen.[9] Perkins, testifying before Pujo and Untermyer, believed that he could determine whether a deal had come to him in his capac-

---

8. Lindbergh's son Charles, the aviator, was to marry the daughter of then Morgan partner Dwight Morrow, later U.S. ambassador to Mexico.

9. For Brandeis, the freezing of individual initiative because few dared to run the risk of crossing Morgan appears to have been an equally serious problem. As Brandeis said to Lamont, "You may not realize it, but you are feared, and I believe the effect of your position is toward paralysis rather than expansion" (Lamont 1913).

ity as vice-president of New York Life or as partner of Morgan and Company and bargain accordingly. Others disagreed, including National City Bank president Frank Vanderlip, who wrote, "There were times . . . when I opposed underwriting fees because I felt they were too high. As a director [of the Union Pacific] I believed my obligation of trusteeship ran to the stockholders, and not to [railroad president E. H.] Harriman. I have in mind recollections of occasions when it was pointed out to me, in a hurt tone, that the City Bank was sharing in those underwriting profits that I thought were too fat" (Vanderlip and Sparkes 1935, 204–5). The Progressive position on how to cure the evils of the money trust called for the systematic prohibition of all such conflicts of interest. Such a prohibition, Brandeis argued, would "not be an innovation. It will merely give full legal sanction to the fundamental law . . . that 'No man can serve two masters'. . . . [N]o rule of law has . . . been more rigorously applied than that which prohibits a trustee from occupying inconsistent positions. . . . And a director of a corporation is . . . a trustee" (Brandeis 1914, 56).

Progressives thus believed that the money trust's dominance over finance and its exploitation of conflicts of interest reinforced one another. Exploitation of conflicts of interest generated funds necessary to reward those who cooperated with present deals. And fear of the power of the money trust to freeze one out of future deals restrained potential competitors.[10] But firms sought Morgan at least as much as the reverse. For example, it is difficult for the Progressive interpretation to account for the eagerness of the McCormick and Deering interests to involve the Morgan partnership in their merger into International Harvester if the partnership's raison d'être was the exploitation of conflicts of interest.[11]

### 6.3.2 Finance Historian Perspectives

By contrast, many finance historians today argue that there never was a "money trust" in Brandeis's sense.[12] Vincent Carosso, for example, whose knowledge of the history and day-to-day workings of the Morgan partnership is unequalled, argues that investment bankers did not have a lock on their traditional clients. He argues instead that there was "very frequently interfer-

---

10. Brandeis said that his belief in the power of the money trust came "from my own experience. . . . I found that the policy of the New Haven . . . was loading it down so that . . . it could not possibly bear the burden. . . . I went to some of the leading Boston bankers. . . . I said—'If this thing continues, the New Haven is going to be bankrupt. Won't you please act in this manner and call Mr. Morgan's attention to it.' Their reply . . . was that they would not dare to . . . that the New Haven was Mr. Morgan's particular pet, that he resented any interference . . . and that it would be as much as their financial life was worth to try to poke their fingers in" (Lamont 1913).

11. The McCormicks, at least, did worry about involving the Morgan partnership. They feared that their interests would be sacrificed to those of U.S. Steel, but decided to go ahead anyway with the merger on Morgan's terms. In fact, Morgan partner George W. Perkins did make some attempts to sacrifice International Harvester interests to those of U.S. Steel and the Morgan partnership (see Carstensen 1989, and section 6.6).

12. In this they take a different tack than earlier historians like Fritz Redlich (1951).

ence or attempted interference" in banker-client relationships, as Kuhn, Loeb head Jacob Schiff told Samuel Untermyer (Carosso 1970; Pujo Committee 1913b).[13] Carosso further points out that Untermyer knew that there was no "unlawful industrial combination" in finance, and could only proceed by re-defining "money trust" as a "loose, elastic term" meaning a "close . . . under-standing among the men who dominate the financial destinies of our country and who wield fabulous power . . . through their control of corporate funds belonging to other people" (Carosso 1970, 139). He concludes that Unter-myers was unable to demonstrate "the existence of a money trust . . . even in the sense in which . . . [he] defined it" (ibid., 151), for investment bankers did not "purposely act together; and even if they had, they would have been unable to impose their will upon the other directors . . . always more numer-ous than the representatives of Wall Street" (ibid., 151–52).

In a similar vein, Huertas and Cleveland (1987) argue that the industry in which Morgan and his peers were engaged was contestable: anyone could accept a block of securities, and then knock on doors until he found willing buyers who would take the placement. They see Pujo Committee counsel Un-termyer, at least, as guilty of bad faith in his investigation.[14] For "aspiring politician" Untermyer, Huertas and Cleveland say, the "appointment was a godsend."[15] But unfortunately, "not knowing . . . such an opportunity would come his way, Untermyer had stated in November 1910 . . . [that] 'monopo-lies and substantial domination of industries . . . could be counted on the fingers of your hand,' and he [had] attacked 'political partisans who seek to make personal and Party capital out of a demagogic appeal to the unthink-ing' " (Huertas and Cleveland 1987; citing Kolko 1963, 359 n. 53).[16]

13. The majority of the Pujo Committee interpreted Schiff's evidence differently than Carosso, focusing instead on Schiff's assertion that he did "not think that another banking house of the standing of J. P. Morgan and Company would accept an offer of the Union Pacific Company to negotiate its securities while it [Union Pacific] was in the hands of Kuhn, Loeb, and Co." The committee concluded that there was little competition in the business of underwriting securities for large companies in the sense of attempts by competitor investment banks to disrupt existing banker-client relationships (Pujo Committee 1913c; Untermyer 1915). The minority report took the Morgan partnership's view (Pujo Committee 1913a).

14. On the other hand, no one (with the exception of New York, New Haven, and Hartford president Mellen, who suggested Brandeis was working for Boston interests who wanted to loot the railroad) has challenged Brandeis's good faith.

15. Reading the transcripts of the hearings makes one more favorably disposed toward the finance historian view. It is easy to dislike Untermyer and Pecora, the counsels of the two congres-sional investigations. Neither had a "theory of the case." In Untermyer's 1907 hearings Morgan is first pilloried for having issued clearing-house loan certificates during the panic of 1907 (thus illegally assuming the role of a central bank) and then pilloried for not having issued enough clearing-house certificates (Pujo Committee 1913b). Both Untermyer and Pecora (1939) appear more interested in generating headlines than in laying the factual groundwork for legislation in the public interest. It is much easier to like and respect Brandeis, and to respect Morgan.

16. It is also possible that Untermyer's conversion to progressivism was partly driven by a desire for revenge against the Rockefeller interests, which had outmaneuvered him in dealings surrounding the formation of Amalgamated Copper. Huertas and Cleveland do not address such issues, perhaps because this sword would cut both ways. James Stillman's successor as City Bank

But the finance historian perspective is as incomplete as the Progressive perspective. Progressives could not account for why owner-managers outside of Morgan influence would ever wish to enter it. The historians of finance do not account for the Morgan partnership's high profits. On their reading, market discipline left the Morgan partnership little freedom of action. But such market pressures should have led Morgan and Company to moderate its fees as well.

## 6.4 The Money Trust's Perspective on Itself

Morgan's supporters and ideologues at the time—for example, the writer and journalist John Moody, founder of Moody's Investment Service—would have rejected the finance historian position that there was no money trust and did reject the Progressive position that the money trust survived by exploiting conflicts of interest. Instead, Moody argued that there was a functioning money trust and that its existence was a good thing: supervision of firm managers by financiers was necessary given the need of enterprises for capital and the need of investors for trustworthy intermediaries to handle the selection of firms in which to invest (Moody 1904, 1912).

Without domination of boards of directors by the investment banking oligarchs, there would be no effective way for scattered individual shareholders to monitor the performance of corporate managers. Only investment bankers could effectively monitor firm managers, and so the presence of investment bankers on boards signaled to ultimate investors that the firm management was competent and industrious. Some executives preferred to avoid Morgan control if possible. Richmond Terminal executive W. P. Clyde, for example, was alleged to have told Morgan in a private meeting that "I've bought Richmond Terminal at 7 or 8 and sold it at 15 twice in the last few years. I see no reason why I shouldn't do it again." And he tried to block the inclusion of the Richmond Terminal within the sphere of Morgan's influence.

Moody's positive view of the money trust was not his own invention. His view was more or less the consensus view held by the securities industry and was a commonplace in the early literature on investment banking. Willis and Bogen's early investment banking textbook, for example, argued that the

> investment banker, intimately concerned as he is with the affairs of the corporation for which he has sold bonds, since the continued meeting of the obligation on these bonds is essential to the maintenance of the investment banker's prestige, often takes . . . a voice in control as a matter of

president, Frank Vanderlip, judged City Bank deals in which William Rockefeller appeared on both sides as "the means of some of the worst abuses that occurred in Wall Street" (Vanderlip and Sparkes 1935). Huertas and Cleveland do not pursue the tangled relationships between Untermyer, the Rockefeller interests, and the National City Bank (Lawson 1906).

course. . . . This kind of power over the affairs of the borrowing enterprise represents the correlative of the moral responsibility which he has assumed toward the holder of the bonds or stock he has sold. . . . [T]his management function . . . gives the buyer . . . an assurance that the banker has knowledge of what is being done by the borrowing concern, and also of better management . . . [and] explains why investors . . . place so much stress, in purchasing securities, on the character and reputation of the house of issue. . . . The history of American business has hitherto been marked by a steady increase in the influence of the investment banker for these reasons. (Willis and Bogen 1929, 31).

The same assessment was made more pithily by New York, New Haven, and Hartford president Charles Mellen, in a private conversation with journalist C. W. Barron: "I wear the Morgan collar, but I am proud of it" (Pound and Moore 1931, 273).[17]

This assessment of the situation was also the official view of the industry. Morgan himself is quoted as giving the answer "Your railroad? Your railroad belongs to my clients" to railroad executives who did not know their place. The partnership of Morgan and Company responded to Pujo by writing an open letter giving their view of the functioning of the securities market. This pamphlet (primarily written by Morgan partner Henry Davison) argued that the reason the partnership had control over investors' funds was "thousands of investors . . . seeking . . . securities . . . have neither the knowledge nor the opportunity for investigating a great . . . enterprise" (Davison 1913, 18). They "look to a banking house to perform those functions and to give its stamp of approval." Morgan and Company's approval had become "a large factor which inspires confidence in the investor and leads him to purchase." The practice of banker representation on boards

has arisen not from a desire on the part of the banker to manage the daily affairs of the corporation or to purchase its securities more cheaply than he otherwise would; but rather because of his moral responsibility as sponsor for the corporation's securities, to keep an eye upon its policies and to protect the interests of investors in the securities of that corporation. . . . Inquiry will readily develop the fact that the members of the leading banking houses . . . are besought continually to act as directors . . . and that in general they enter only those boards which the opinion of the investing

17. A statement made in private and off the record—Barron's notes of his conversations were later found, edited, and published. A similar impression of Mellen's relationship to Morgan is given by Brandeis (in Lamont 1913), who recalls that he "hit upon a matter . . . of manifest advantage to the [New Haven rail]road, and through a friend I submitted it to Mr. Mellen. Mr. Mellen sent back word that he would submit it promptly to Mr. Morgan. . . . Mellen's reply was that Mr. Morgan did not think well of the matter. . . . At my behest, my friend went back to Mr. Mellen . . . asking if he would not submit it to Mr. Morgan once more. Mr. Mellen said—'What, go to Mr. Morgan a second time on a matter, after he has already expressed his opinion on it? No one would even dream of it!'"

public requires them to enter, as evidence of good faith that they are willing to have their names publicly associated with the management. (Ibid., 17)[18]

Morgan and Company, moreover, argued that their influence over investors' choice of securities was not dangerous because it was disciplined by the market. If the firm lost its reputation for "character"—placed investors in securities that were profitable to it but offered poor returns—or another firm acquired a reputation as a superior judge of risk, Morgan control would disappear:

> The public, that is the depositors, are the ones who entrust bankers with such influence and power as they today have in every civilized land, and the public is unlikely to entrust that power to weak or evil hands. Your counsel asked more than one witness whether the present power held by bankers . . . would not be a menace if it lay in evil hands. . . . The only genuine power which an individual . . . can gain is that arising from the confidence reposed in him . . . by the community. . . . [M]en are entrusted with such heavy responsibilities because of the confidence which their records have established, and only so long as their records are unblemished do they retain such trusts. These . . . axioms . . . apply . . . more emphatically . . . to banking than to any other form of commerce. To banking the confidence of the community is the breath from which it draws its life. The past is full of examples where the slightest suspicion as to the conservatism, or the methods of a bank's management, has destroyed confidence and drawn away its deposits overnight. (Ibid., 25–26)

The investment bankers thus claimed that their oligarchy and their presence on boards had three benefits: First, investment banker representation on a board warranted that the firm was managed by capable and energetic executives. Promising and well-managed businesses would thus be able to issue securities on more favorable terms with investment banker representation.

Second, investment banker representation provided an easy way to learn about the performance of managers and to dismiss them if they failed to measure up. The investment banking oligarchs provided an effective mechanism for monitoring executives and replacing those who performed badly; in Morgan and Company's view such monitoring and supervision were more easily performed on the board than off it.

Third, the concentration of the business improved the functioning of the market. The wealth and dominant position of the Morgan partnership de-

---

18. Lamont provided Brandeis with a similar justification of Morgan representation on boards, saying that "as you realize, we have generally drifted onto these various railroad and industrial boards because we had first undertaken to place a large block of the corporation's securities with our clients, and we felt a sense of responsibility to those clients which we fulfilled by keeping an eye upon the corporation in which they had invested. We have felt that that was a strong factor in enabling us to market these securities, and while the responsibility was a very onerous one, nevertheless, we shouldered it. Don't you think there is quite a little in that point?" Brandeis agreed that it was an important point but saw no reason why bankers needed to exercise control rather than merely gather information (see Lamont 1913).

pended on its reputation for "character." A firm with a large market share could never be tempted to sacrifice its reputation for the sake of the profits of any one deal because such an unsound deal could destroy its reputation as an honest broker—the Morgan partnership said that its reputation could disappear "overnight." A firm with a small market share might sacrifice future reputation for present profits.

It is somewhat ironic that firm defenders of private privilege, property, and capitalism like Moody and Davison wound up advocating a system for the assessment and allocation of investment that appears in many respects, from an early-twentieth-century perspective at least, "socialist." The forty-five employees of Morgan and Company approved and vetoed proposed top managers, decided what securities they would underwrite, and thus implicitly decided what securities would be issued and what lines of business should receive additional capital. Savers followed their advice. And the net effect appears similar to what would be done by a centralized investment planning directorate. The major difference is that the judgment of Morgan and his partners was substituted for that of some bureaucracy in deciding which investment projects were to be undertaken.[19] Instead of being decided by a market, the allocation of investment and the choice of firm managers was decided by a hierarchy, albeit a loose one (and one that felt itself subject to market discipline in the long run, in which the partnership can gain or lose its reputation for "character").[20]

The Morgan partnership's stress on the importance of its reputation provides an answer to the question of what was the money trust's competitive edge. High profit rates could coexist with ease of entry into investment banking because there was no rapid way for new firms to acquire that "reputation" that was the Morgan partnership's chief institutional asset. Progressives never supplied an answer to the question of why firms and investors continued to use the Morgan partnership, given the high fees it charged and the fact that you could never be sure when you hired Morgan and Company that it would

19. This is not quite right. On the one hand, Morgan and Company were shareholders' agents, not the public's. On the other hand, Morgan and Company had a strong incentive to run an efficient operation and make the "correct" investment decisions from shareholders' point of view: they faced competition from Kuhn, Loeb, from National City, and from others. Bureaucracies, by contrast, have many other objectives than the accomplishment of their legally mandated mission.

20. This identification of an investment banking partnership's reputation as an honest broker as (from the resource allocation side) a valuable social asset and (from the market structure side) a sizable barrier to entry raises the question of how the Morgan partnership acquired its reputation in the first place. It appears to have grown up slowly. The London banking house of George Peabody and Company specialized in selling American state bonds to European investors. Peabody and Company was very anxious that the bonds it sold turn out to be good investments—even contributing "campaign contributions" to Daniel Webster to induce him to make speeches for debt repayment (Chernow 1990). After J. S. Morgan joined Peabody and Company, the house branched out from state government bonds to selling American railroad securities to European investors. The reputation gained was then also applied by J. S. and J. P. Morgan to selling American railroad securities to American investors, and then by J. P. Morgan to selling American industrial securities to American investors (Navin and Sears 1955).

act in your interest when your interest came into conflict with the interests of its other clients. Finance historians never explained the sources of the money trust's high fees. Morgan and Company did give an answer to both questions: firms and investors come to us because they know that we have been honest brokers in the past—and they know that they can trust us because we have too much invested in the business to risk by failing to be honest brokers in the present.

The negative effects of financial capitalism stressed by Progressives are not blotted out by these investment banker arguments that the structure of pre-Depression American finance served useful economic purposes.[21] The conflicts of interest identified remain conflicts of interest; the high fees and relative absence of competition for different firms' business remain a tax on the provision of capital to the industrial sector. But the financial capitalists saw themselves as creating value, at least for shareholders. And given that a reputation as a competent analyst and an honest broker is difficult to develop and can be a valuable social asset, domination of turn-of-the-century financial markets by the Morgan partnership and its peers may have been better than the alternative.

## 6.5  The Value of Morgan's Men

Examination of the cross-sectional pattern of the market values of Morgan-influenced corporations supports the claim that Morgan influence was associated with enhanced value. According to the lists compiled by the Pujo investigation, in 1912 Morgan or his partners sat on the boards of twenty manufacturing, mining, distribution, transport, or utility companies that had actively quoted common stocks—three utilities, nine railroads, and eight other companies. Data on these twenty companies, and on sixty-two other control companies of similar size, were collected for 1911 and 1912 from *Poor's Manuals* of railroad, industrial, and utility securities.[22]

Table 6.1 reports regressions of the average relative price of the firm's common stock (relative to its book value) on whether the firm's board of directors

---

21. For Brandeis, at least, the key objection was in large part not economic but political and psychological. Brandeis tends to speak not of efficiency and productivity but of experimentation and individualism. He told Lamont that he saw J. P. Morgan's power as "dangerous, highly dangerous. The reason, I think, is that it hampers the freedom of the individual. The only way that we are going to work out our problems in this country is to have the individual free, not free to do unlicensed things, but free to work and to trade without the fear of some gigantic power threatening to engulf him every moment, whether that power be a monopoly in oil or in credit" (see Lamont 1913).

22. Partners in Boston investment banks like Lee, Higginson, and Company or Kidder, Peabody served on too few boards of directors apart from Morgan partners to allow for the quantitative estimation of a "Lee" or a "Kidder" premium. Kuhn, Loeb did not insist on holding board memberships in corporations under its influence, so it is more difficult to track the extent of its active involvement in monitoring corporations. For these reasons this section deals with J. P. Morgan and Company alone.

**Table 6.1**              **The Value of Having a Morgan Partner as a Board Member**

| Morgan Partner[a] | Utility Company? | Other Variables | | Adjusted $R^2$ | SEE |
|---|---|---|---|---|---|
| 0.259 | | | | 0.021 | 0.834 |
| (0.161) | | | | | |
| 0.270* | 0.281 | | | 0.038 | 0.830 |
| (0.161) | (0.197) | | | | |
| 0.253* | 0.107 | −1.834* | Earnings/price | 0.270 | 0.730 |
| (0.144) | (0.175) | (0.304) | | | |
| 0.375* | 0.441* | 1.680* | Log book/par value | 0.180 | 0.777 |
| (0.151) | (0.186) | (0.374) | | | |
| 0.055 | 0.155 | 0.569* | Log earnings/book | 0.236 | 0.726 |
| (0.102) | (0.124) | (0.073) | | | |

*Source:* As described in text.

*Note:* Dependent variable is log of average 1911–12 stock price relative to book value (eighty-two observations, including twenty Morgan companies). Standard errors in parentheses.

[a]Corporate board contains a partner of J. P. Morgan and Company.

*$P(t) < .05$ (one-tailed).

---

included a Morgan partner and on control variables. The first thing to note is that standard errors are large: the set of Morgan companies contains only twenty, and the spread of returns within this set is very large. Since these twenty companies are the only source of variation for identifying the Morgan influence coefficients, gathering more data would not lead to a more precise estimate of the Morgan influence coefficient.

One implication of the high standard errors on the Morgan influence coefficient is that its estimates are very sensitive to the treatment of outliers. The International Mercantile Marine Company's common stock had a return of − 25 percent per year over the decade before World War I. Had this promotion been a success, the estimates of the Morgan influence coefficient would have been higher by an additional 15 to 20 percent. Similarly, if the New York, New Haven, and Hartford's price had collapsed in 1911 rather than two years later (Staples 1954), the estimated Morgan influence coefficient would have been from 5 to 8 percent less.

The first row of table 6.1 shows that corporations with a Morgan partner on their boards of directors have a logarithm of common stock $q$—the ratio of the common stock's market value to the book value of common stockholders' equity—higher than other companies by 0.259, corresponding to a 30 percent increase in the common stock's market value. This coefficient is imprecisely estimated: an analyst who began with completely diffuse prior beliefs about this coefficient and examined row one would conclude that there were nine chances out of ten that the true effect on the stock price of having a Morgan partner sitting on the board of directors was positive, but would be confident only that there were two chances out of three that the true effect was between 10 and 40 percent.

The second row adds a dummy variable for whether the company is a utility. Utilities have higher ratios of price to book value than railroads or industrials in this period.[23] Inclusion of the utility dummy does not materially affect the size of the Morgan influence variable, but does push it across the line of statistical significance at the .05 level (although there are still only two chances in three that the effect is between 10 and 40 percent of common stock value).

The estimated impact of adding a Morgan partner does not seem out of line if one considers how much Morgan's financial services cost. For International Harvester—a simple and straightforward deal—the investment bankers' share was about 4 percent of the capital value floated (equal in value to 8 percent of the post-1906 common stock). For U.S. Steel the investment bankers' share was 10 percent (in value 30 percent of the common stock). Such large fees can be justified—if they can be justified—only if the unique value added by this particular group of financiers is substantial. If the Morgan influence coefficient does reflect a true increase in value, not just the result of chance, then investment banking fees appear to take up a sizable chunk, but not all, of the increased value.

Row three shows that the Morgan influence coefficient is not affected by the inclusion in the regression of the corporation's earnings/price ratio. If Morgan companies were selling for higher prices on the stock market because Morgan influence allowed the exploitation of monopoly power, we would expect Morgan companies to have a high earnings/price ratio: earning in the present would be high, but prices would not rise in proportion because investors would look forward to the long-run erosion of monopoly power in the face of new entry. In this case, we would find in row three that companies with high earnings/price ratios had high ratios of price to book value, and that inclusion of the earnings/price ratio reduced the Morgan influence coefficient. This is not so, but this test is weak: all that can be said is that the cross-sectional data do not speak strongly for the hypothesis that Morgan influence raises shareholder value because it allowed the exercise of monopoly power.

Row four shows that the Morgan influence coefficient is not materially affected by the inclusion in the regression of the ratio of common stock book to par value. This ratio is a measure of the corporation's accumulated surplus. It is thus a proxy for the long-run growth of the company—of how much earnings have been in excess of dividends since the creation of the firm's current capital structure. If Morgan influence was associated with high value because Morgan limited his long-run associations to profitable and rapidly growing companies, then inclusion of the ratio of book to par value should reduce the size of the Morgan influence coefficient. Instead, the Morgan influence coef-

23. Experimentation with a railroad dummy variable found no significant effect.

ficient rises. In row four, there appear to be two chances in three that the true effect is between 25 and 70 percent.

Row five shows the effect of adding the return on capital—the ratio of earnings to book value—to the regression. The estimated Morgan partner coefficient declines to almost nothing (it is always imprecisely estimated). Figure 6.1 plots the data underlying the regression in row five. The gray lines mark the average values of the log price/book and earnings/book values for non-Morgan companies. They divide the graph into quadrants.

Figure 6.1 shows why the estimated Morgan influence coefficient becomes indistinguishable from zero in the row five specification. Of the twenty Morgan companies, fifteen have higher market prices relative to book values than the average non-Morgan company. All fifteen of these also have higher ratios of earnings to book value than the average non-Morgan company. Three Morgan companies have both lower than average prices and lower than average earnings—the Chicago-Great Western, the Erie, and the Southern railroads. Two Morgan companies have higher than average earnings but lower than average prices—the Baldwin Locomotive Company and the International Mercantile Marine.

This suggests that, to the extent that Morgan partners added value, they did so by making the companies they monitored more profitable, not by significantly raising the share price paid for a company of given profitability. It also accounts for why inclusion of the earnings/book value reduces the estimated Morgan influence coefficient so severely. In this sample, having a high price/book value, having high earnings/book, and having a Morgan partner on the board of directors are all strongly associated. Given that a firm has a high ratio

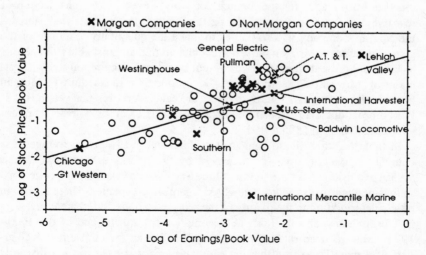

**Fig. 6.1   Relative prices and earnings of Morgan and non-Morgan companies, 1910–12**

of current earnings to book value, there is not much additional information about its relative stock price that can be deduced from the fact that it also has a Morgan partner on its board of directors.

It is particularly striking that Morgan companies have high ratios of earnings to book values, given that Morgan companies are reputed to have had abnormally high book values. One of Brandeis's most frequent criticisms of money trust practices was the overstatement of book values through "watering" the stock. Book values in "Morganized" companies thus represented not the cost of the business's physical assets but instead investment bankers' assessments of its earning power (Dewing 1914). Stock watering inflates book values and moves Morgan companies down and to the left in figure 6.1. It is thus very noteworthy that the Morgan-influenced companies are nevertheless clustered in the upper right-hand corner of the figure.

The regression in row five of table 6.1 is subject to differing interpretations, however, and is "fragile" in the sense of resting to a large degree on the performance of the outlying extremes of Morgan's financial empire. A key role in generating the estimates is played by the one extreme negative outlier: the International Mercantile Marine Company. The conclusion that the Morgan influence does not increase the price paid for companies of given profitability is reversed if one uses nonparametric tests that downweight extreme observations—in this case the International Mercantile Marine.

Figure 6.1 also shows that, of the twenty Morgan-influenced companies, fifteen have higher stock prices than would be predicted by the estimated regression line for the non-Morgan companies. Such a division would happen by chance only one time in a hundred if the Morgan influence were truly zero. Thus this nonparametric view can reject the null hypothesis that the Morgan touch did not matter for the median company—even in the specification of row five—at the .01 level. But the performance of the International Mercantile Marine Company was so bad as to make the quantitative estimate of the geometric average Morgan influence coefficient indistinguishable from zero.

Table 6.2 presents nominal rates of return realized on common stock investments in "Morganized" corporations. For corporations that acquired a Morgan board member after 1895, rates of return are calculated from that year to 1913. For corporations that had Morgan board members as of 1895, rates of return are calculated from 1895 to 1913.

In table 6.2 there is no sign that stockholders received, on average, less than fair market returns—as measured by the returns earned by Cowles's (1938) extension backward in time of the Standard and Poor's composite portfolio—on their investments in newly Morganized companies. There is no sign of any deterioration in the quality of the reorganizations undertaken: investors in Westinghouse and in Baldwin Locomotive toward the end of the 1900–1913 period realized rates of return that were higher than those realized earlier. And there is no sign that the Morgan name was used to trick investors

**Table 6.2  Stock Market Rates of Return on "Morganized" Companies**

| Company | Date Morganized | Cumulative Return to 1913 | Rate of Return (%) | Stock Market Return [b] | Commercial Paper Return [b] (%) | Excess Returns [a] (%) | |
|---|---|---|---|---|---|---|---|
| | | | | | | Commercial Paper | Stock Market |
| *Nonrailroad* | | | | | | | |
| Adams Express | 1895 | 3.66 | 7.21 | 7.96 | 4.61 | 2.60 | −0.75 |
| AT&T | 1908 | 1.52 | 8.37 | 7.96 | 4.61 | 3.76 | 0.41 |
| Baldwin Locomotive | 1911 | 1.56 | 22.23 | 7.96 | 4.61 | 17.62 | 14.27 |
| General Electric | 1895 | 15.63 | 15.27 | 7.96 | 4.61 | 10.66 | 7.31 |
| International Mercantile Marine | 1902 | 0.07 | −24.85 | 7.96 | 4.61 | −29.46 | −32.81 |
| International Harvester | 1902 | 2.23 | 7.30 | 7.96 | 4.61 | 2.69 | −0.66 |
| Public Service Corp of New Jersey | 1911 | 1.14 | 6.64 | 7.96 | 4.61 | 2.03 | −1.32 |
| Pullman | 1895 | 8.82 | 12.09 | 7.96 | 4.61 | 7.48 | 4.13 |
| U.S. Steel | 1901 | 2.59 | 7.94 | 7.96 | 4.61 | 3.33 | −0.02 |
| Westinghouse | 1908 | 2.57 | 18.85 | 7.96 | 4.61 | 14.24 | 10.89 |
| Average | | | 8.46 | 7.96 | 4.61 | 3.85 | 0.50 |
| (standard error) | | | (4.04) | | | | |
| *Railroad* | | | | | | | |
| Atchison, Topeka, and Santa Fe | 1895 | 13.54 | 14.48 | 7.96 | 4.61 | 9.87 | 6.52 |
| Erie | 1896 | 1.88 | 3.73 | 7.96 | 4.61 | −0.88 | −4.23 |
| New York, New Haven, and Hartford | 1895 | 2.53 | 5.16 | 7.96 | 4.61 | 0.55 | −2.80 |
| Reading | 1897 | 10.09 | 14.45 | 7.96 | 4.61 | 9.84 | 6.49 |
| Southern | 1895 | 2.18 | 4.33 | 7.96 | 4.61 | −0.28 | −3.63 |
| Average | | | 10.90 | 7.96 | 4.61 | 6.29 | 2.94 |
| (standard error) | | | (2.47) | | | | |

*Source:* As described in text.

[a]Relative to diversified investments in commercial paper and in the stock market.

[b]Average nominal returns earned over 1890–1914 by stock market investments, as estimated by the Cowles Commission backward extension of the Standard and Poor's Composite portfolio, and by investments in high-grade commercial paper.

into buying unsound and overpriced unduly "watered" stock:[24] the prices at which the Morgan syndicates offered common stock in Morgan-influenced companies appear to have been on average fair prices.

Together, tables 6.1 and 6.2 support the Morgan partnership's claim that it played a productive and valuable role in the corporations it influenced. Stockholders in Morgan corporations do not appear to have overpaid for their investments. Morgan companies sold at higher multiples of book value than other companies, and they did so not because of the advertising value of the Morgan name but because they earned higher returns on capital.

Regressions, of course, cannot sort out the causal chain. It could be that the addition of a Morgan partner to the board leads to the replacement of bad and the shaping-up of good managers. It could be that Morgan partners joined the board only if they had confidence in the management, and that Morgan and Company were skillful investors but had no effect on the performance of the economy as a whole.

Event studies of the short-run effect on asset values of the announcement of Morgan interest in a company could sort out the chain of causation and reveal investors' expectations of the value of the Morgan touch. But too many "Morganized" companies were closely or privately held before the Morgan interests took a hand. Their pre-Morgan values cannot be ascertained. We know what such event studies would show: owners must have expected to reap profits from reorganizations and restructurings even net of the Morgan partnership's commissions or they would not have invited the Morgan partnership in. But our inability to perform event studies on our sample means that we do not know how much investors thought the Morgan touch was worth.

The next section tries to shed some light on these questions of causation by examining what Morgan influence really was, and trying to determine how the Morgan partnership exercised its monitoring and control functions in the cases of individual operating companies (table 6.3).

## 6.6   International Harvester and AT&T

In both of the cases considered here, investment bankers played an active and powerful but limited role. They took pains to ensure that the firms had the right managers but otherwise left the management alone. It is not fair to criticize these two case studies on the grounds that they examine successes—that in other firms investment banker intervention failed to create value. As section 6.5 has shown, the typical Morganized firm was, in fact, a success. It produced higher stock market values without inducing investors to overpay. It is, however, fair to criticize these two case studies as examples in which value may have been created primarily as a result of the creation of monopoly power: the relative roles of monopoly and efficiency in the "Morganization

24. A hypothesis advocated by Dewing (1914).

**Table 6.3        Companies under Morgan Influence on the Eve of World War I**

| | |
|---|---|
| Adams Express Co. | New York, New Haven, and Hartford Railroad |
| AT&T | Northern Pacific Railroad |
| Atchison, Topeka, and Santa Fe Railroad | New York Central Railroad |
| Baldwin Locomotive Co. | Pere Marquette Railroad[a] |
| Chicago–Great Western Railroad | Philadelphia Rapid Transit Co. |
| Erie Railroad | Public Service Corp. of New Jersey |
| General Electric Co. | Pullman Co. |
| International Agricultural Co.[a] | Reading Railroad |
| International Mercantile Marine Co. | Southern Railroad |
| International Harvester Co. | U.S. Steel Co. |
| Lehigh Valley Railroad | Westinghouse Co. |

[a]Not included in regressions; satisfactory data unavailable.

premium" cannot be determined in a fashion convincing enough to overcome prior beliefs.

### 6.6.1   International Harvester

An opening to consolidate the farm machinery industry appeared at the beginning of the 1900s. The McCormick firm—established by the inventor of the reaper, Cyrus H. McCormick—had been under heavy competitive pressure from the rapidly expanding Deering firm. William Deering's children were much less interested in running their firm and establishing competitive predominance over McCormick. The three sons of the founding Mc-Cormick—Cyrus, Stanley, and Harold—were also eager to see a reorganization of the industry. But each family was also strongly averse to handing control of their firm over to the other (McCormick 1931; Carstensen 1989).

There did appear to be substantial economies of scale to be gained by integrating the firms' production operations. U.S. Steel head Elbert Gary (a close adviser of the Deering family) told the McCormicks that he estimated that the stock of the amalgamated firm would be worth 35 percent more than the stock of the two separate firms. Moreover, he attributed this gain to efficiency, writing that "this increase would not be fictitious but real value, owing to the fact that by a combination they would secure stability of prices and diminishing expenses even though they did not secure increased average prices" (Garraty 1960, 128).

If monopoly power did allow the new, integrated firm to increase its average prices, the extra profits from amalgamation would of course be higher. J. P. Morgan and Company felt that such monopoly power would easily be gained, and that as a result the McCormicks should not worry that using Wall Street money to combine the firms would harm their reputation with their farmer customers: after all, the Morgan partners remarked, the farmers had no choice but to buy farm machinery.

Morgan partner George W. Perkins explained to the brothers the terms under which Morgan and Company would take charge of the deal. Perkins emphasized that "Morgan would . . . insist on choosing all officers and directors of the new company" and that "this point . . . Morgan and Company have found indispensable in making their combinations" (Garraty 1960, 133). The McCormicks, the Deerings, and the owners of two other, smaller firms included in the new International Harvester Corporations took all the stock of the new company; since no issue of securities was required, Morgan and Company charged less than their normal fee—they took only 3 percent of the company up front in fees. After organization, Morgan and Company retained ultimate control over the firm. All stock was committed to a voting trust, the trustees of which were one McCormick, one Deering, and Perkins.

The McCormicks had some doubts about committing themselves to the hands of the Morgan partnership. They feared that Harvester interests would be subordinated to those of U.S. Steel or to the Morgan partnership in general (Carstensen 1989). Their fears were well founded: Perkins did place International Harvester money on deposit with the Morgan bank interest-free, and he did unsuccessfully attempt to have International Harvester sell steel properties developed by the Deerings to U.S. Steel for a fire-sale price.[25]

For the first few years of its operation, the performance of International Harvester was disappointing. Rationalization of the firm's product lines was blocked; integration of production proceeded only very slowly (U.S. Department of Commerce 1913). In 1906 Perkins removed remaining McCormick and Deering family members from management and replaced them with salaried professionals. The younger Cyrus H. McCormick alone remained as head of the company. According to Garraty (1960), "the younger element in the company" was advanced to positions of greater influence, and thereafter International Harvester's performance was more satisfactory.

### 6.6.2    AT&T

Banker influence on AT&T can be clearly seen in one action: the return to the Bell System and accession to power of Theodore N. Vail. Vail had been hired for the telephone company by Alexander Graham Bell's father-in-law, Gardiner Hubbard, at the end of the 1870s. He performed very well as general manager of American Bell and as president of its long-distance subsidiary during the initial expansion of the telephone network to the urban East and Midwest (Paine 1921; Danielan 1939).

In 1887, however, Vail resigned. A growing dissatisfaction "with his posi-

---

25. The McCormicks took offense. Their lawyers wrote that Perkins was (unconsciously) biased in favor of the U.S. Steel interests, and that this unconscious bias was even worse than dishonesty, for "a dishonest man is at least prudent." The McCormicks wanted the Deering steel properties to be purchased by International Harvester at fire-sale prices and then sold to U.S. Steel for what the traffic would bear (see Carstensen 1989).

tion at this period was due . . . to the company's reluctance to spend money in keeping the service at maximum" and rapidly expanding the network. Vail had wished to pay low dividends and to plow retained earnings back into the rapid creation of a single comprehensive national telephone network. The major stockholders and their nominees, for example John E. Hudson, president of American Bell from 1889 to 1900, had a different view. They saw that they owned a money machine; they thought this money machine should pay high dividends. After a clash of views Vail left the company, unwilling to be the chief implementer of competitive strategies with which he disagreed. The 1887 annual report made no mention of his resignation or indeed of his services to the company at all, suggesting a high degree of strain and bad feelings (Brooks 1976).

After the expiration of Bell's key patents, Hudson's presidency, and to a lesser extent that of his immediate successors, saw a steady loss of market share to a large group of alternative, local telephone networks. American Bell did pay high dividends. American Bell did not, however, move to consolidate its nationwide natural monopoly.

A general consensus within the reorganized Bell System, now headed by AT&T, toward a shift to renewed rapid expansion developed in the first years of this century. Frederick Fish (president of AT&T from 1902 to 1907) went to the markets to raise money for renewed expansion.

The subsequent securities issues gave the investment bankers their opening. The company's massive financing requirements, and the fact that it had become difficult to raise money as the panic of 1907 drew near, brought the Bell System close to default. The investment bankers' price for continuing to finance the company was that its next president should be someone they trusted: Theodore N. Vail. First National Bank president and Morgan ally George F. Baker had been very impressed with Vail's performance in other dealings. Vail's past record at the telephone company was well known. And who better to head up a company now devoted to rapid nationwide expansion than a man who had been advocating such a competitive strategy twenty years earlier?

Vail did for AT&T what he was installed to do. He oversaw its expansion to a true nationwide telephone system. And he turned out to be very skillful at keeping the government and public convinced that AT&T was a productive natural—and not an exploitative artificial—monopoly. In the choice of Vail, as in the creation of International Harvester, investment bankers appear to have exerted their influence in a positive direction both from the perspective of shareholders' long-run interest and from the perspective of the long-run economic growth of the United States.

Other case studies could be chosen to paint a different picture. The International Mercantile Marine Company was a failure from the beginning, and the Charles Mellen-run New York, New Haven, and Hartford Railroad was denounced as unsound and monopolistic by Louis Brandeis for nearly a decade, at the end of which it did indeed collapse.[26] But the performance of Morganized firms was in general good—not bad—and in these two not unrepresentative cases of good performance the Morgan partnership did play a significant role in selecting managers.

## 6.7    Extensions

### 6.7.1    Financial Capitalism in Comparative Perspective

Around the turn of the century Germany and Japan also saw the growth of their securities markets take on a "finance capitalist" pattern. Consider first imperial Germany. In 1914 its largest banks—such as the Deutsche, the Dresdner, and the Darmstädter—dominated the German capital market. Founded in imitation of the French Crédit Mobilier, these banks made it a business principle from the very outset to maintain permanent representation on the boards of directors and to hold a significant number of shares of the companies they promoted.[27]

The role played by the great banks in monitoring and supervising corporate managements was an accepted part of German financial theory in the years before World War I (Riesser 1911). There was a clear sense that this "monitoring" role was a very valuable one. Riesser, for example, saw the German banks as valuable because of "both the continuity of their existence and regard for their 'issue credit,' i.e., the permanent ability of maintaining among the German public a market for new securities issued under their auspices," which "insured a permanent interest on the part of these banks in the [health of the] newly created [corporations] as well as in the securities which they were instrumental in placing on the market (Riesser 1911, 367; see also 343).

In Japan, the prewar *zaibatsu* and their more diffuse postwar *keiretsu* replacements appear to have played a similar role, in which once again the pat-

---

26. In his conversation with Brandeis, Lamont tried very hard to distance Morgan and Company from the New York, New Haven, and Hartford, protesting "but Mr. Brandeis, we don't attempt to manage railroads. . . . Nobody realizes better than we that that is not our function. We give the best counsel that we can in the selection of good men, making mistakes sometimes, as in the case of Mellen, but on the whole doing fairly well, and we give our very best advice on financial policy. . . . [The] expansion of the New Haven was due, and solely due, to Mr. Mellen's own policy and initiative, and . . . the mistakes which Mr. Morgan and his fellow directors made . . . [were] not of initiation, but of almost blindly following and endorsing Mellen's policies. Mr. Morgan had that large nature which led him almost blindly to have faith in a man when once it was established" (Lamont 1913).

27. Many have argued that the influence exerted by the great banks on industry was substantial: the Deutsche Bank had its representatives on the boards of 159 companies in 1912. Great banks were at once promoting syndicates and originating syndicates, acceptance houses, and sources of short- and long-term commercial credit. In the words of Feis (1964, 63), "the holders of shares in a German Great Bank were participants in an investment trust (among many other things). . . . The risks arising from immobilization of resources" through their commitment to the development of industry "the banks met . . . through their large capital . . . their retention of control [and] . . . subsidiary companies especially founded for this purpose."

tern of influence of finance over industry is reminiscent of Morgan and Company (Hoshi, Kashyap, and Scharfstein 1989). The bank and the trading company of a given enterprise group exercise influence over the policies and senior personnel appointments of the affiliated companies. However, this influence is usually held in abeyance "unless the member company is in difficulties" (Dore 1987; also Thurow 1986).

It is clear that in the United States and in Germany the existence of "finance capitalist" institutions played a significant role in the expansion of managerial capitalism. Investment banker willingness to choose and monitor managers appears to have aided founding families that were attempting to withdraw from active management of their businesses and to diversify their holdings (Atack 1985; Chandler 1990).

Chandler (1990) draws a sharp contrast between wide share ownership distributed by investment banks and salaried managers in Germany and the United States, and the more "personal capitalism" in which founding families preserve substantial equity stakes and managerial positions that prevailed in Great Britain.[28] Yet he also downplays the role of investment banks, especially in the United States where the partnerships were very small business organizations and large deposit banks played a minor role (see White 1983 and 1989; Burr 1927). It may be that investment banks played a key role in allowing founding families to transform their corporations into the professionally managed organizations with diversified stock ownership that were to dominate the twentieth century. Founding families may have been unwilling to sell out and retire from the business unless they could get a fair price. Without a J. P. Morgan to implicitly warrant their property, obtaining a "fair" price from the founding family's perspective may have been difficult. It is possible to speculate that turn-of-the-century finance capitalists played an important role in catalyzing the development of the managerial hierarchies whose importance is stressed by Chandler (1990).

The relative industrial success of Germany, Japan, and Gilded Age United States has its counterpoint in the relative industrial decline of turn-of-the-century Great Britain. As Lewis (1978, 130) puts it, at the end of the nineteenth century "organic chemicals became a German industry; the motor car was pioneered in France and mass-produced in the United States; Britain lagged in the use of electricity, depended on foreign firms established there, and took only a small share of the export market. The telephone, the typewriter, the cash register, and the diesel engine were all exploited by others." Industry after technologically sophisticated industry in which one would have expected British industry, by virtue of Britain's larger industrial base and head start, to have a strong position was dominated by producers from other, follower countries.

---

28. For an insider's view of the pattern of investment banking relationships under such a system of "personal capitalism," see O'Hagan (1929).

Alongside Britain's relative industrial decline went a tremendous surge of capital exports. In 1913 Great Britain's net interests, profits, and dividends from overseas investment amounted to 9.3 percent of gross domestic product. Accumulated balance-of-payments surplus over 1885–1913 amounted to perhaps £2,620 million—110 percent of 1913 gross domestic product. Nominal net overseas assets are equal to the sum of accumulated surplus, the initial position, unrealized (real) capital gains, and inflation, and so may well have been much larger than accumulated surplus. Britain in 1913 had considerably more than an entire year's gross output invested abroad, and its net overseas assets may well have exceeded its total net domestic stock of reproducible capital.

Riesser criticized the pre–World War I organization of British banking and finance because it lacked an equivalent to the monitoring system performed by the industrial cliques in Japan, the great banks in Germany, and the Morgan partners in the United States. He argued that the "complete divorce between stock exchange and deposits . . . causes another great evil, namely, that the banks have never shown any interest in the newly founded companies or in the securities issued by these companies, while it is a distinct advantage of the German system, that the German banks, even if only in the interests of their own issue credit, have been keeping a continuous watch over the development of the companies, which they founded (Riesser 1911, 555).

It is possible to speculate that Britain's surge of overseas investment, its relative industrial decline, and its absence of financial capitalist institutions all go together. If "financial capitalist" institutions did in fact play the role in guiding and warranteeing investments that I have argued they played, the absence of such institutions in Britain may have been a factor contributing to its anomalous combination of healthy domestic savings with anemic domestic investment, large overseas investments, and relative industrial decline. Relative industrial decline in Britain may have played a part in leading financial capitalists to focus their energies elsewhere. J. P. Morgan's father spent at least as much time working in London as in New York. The causal chain seems likely to run in both directions—finance capitalism may help economies grow fast, and fast-growing economies may develop "finance capitalist" institutions—and which direction is the stronger is an open question.[29]

### 6.7.2  The Decline of Financial Capitalism in the United States

Perhaps the Morgan-dominated "finance capitalist" pattern of the 1900s was peculiar to that age, and subsequent changes—chiefly the wider diffusion

29. This line of criticism has been taken up and amplified by many who have seen the financial centers in the City of London as having failed industry. For example, see Ronald Dore (1987). The argument was originally made by Lance Davis (1963). Today (as in the past) the Deutsche Bank votes the shares of many German stockholders, stockholders presumably believing that the bank will do a better job of voting their shares than they would.

of available information to individual stockholders—have eroded the informational advantage of financiers that sustained "finance capitalism" in the
early years of this century. Perhaps the history of U.S. financial markets in the
twentieth century should be written as a history of how informational and
technological changes drive organizational shifts. Perhaps as the twentieth
century passed, the importance of private information declined, the ability of
investors to do their own security analysis grew, and managers' compensation
schemes placed greater weight on stock options and were more closely
aligned with shareholders' interests. In this case it would not be surprising if
the service of monitoring managers provided by Morgan and Company became worth less and less as the century passed.

Yet there is reason to doubt such an interpretation. Historical accounts of
the erosion of financial capitalism in the first half of the twentieth century have
not focused on informational and technological changes that made J. P. Morgan obsolete.[30] Instead, historical accounts emphasize relatively autonomous
political events and psychological shifts in the attitudes of small investors toward the stock market. As historians like Sobel (1965) see it, the first stage in
Morgan's impending decline came in the aftermath of the World War I door-
to-door bond selling campaigns, as Charles Mitchell of the National City
Bank came to recognize that a financial empire does not have to be built by
slowly creating a reputation as a shrewd judge of investments but can be built
through direct salesmanship by uninformed representatives (Peach 1941;
Cowing 1965; Huertas and Cleveland 1987).

The second stage is the popularization of the benefits of common stock
ownership during the 1920s (as urged, for example, by Smith 1924). The
belief that everyone should invest in common stocks, coupled with Mitchell's
high-pressure sales campaigns and the growing possibility that the New Era
might really be a new era of permanent prosperity, helped fuel the stock boom
of the 1920s and made Morgan's or Kuhn, Loeb's willingness to stand behind
a security issue no longer of prime importance. Many investors were willing
to bet along with Samuel Insull that he was a financial genius even without
Morgan's or Kuhn, Loeb's implicit warranty.

The third stage in the decline of "financial capitalism" saw the creation of
the Securities and Exchange Commission and the forcible divorce of bankers
who had the capital to take substantial long-term positions in firms from their

---

30. Another reason to doubt such an interpretation is that much current thinking in finance
argues that the conflict of interest between owners and managers is still a central feature of finance
today. Jensen's (1989) admittedly extreme estimate of these gains in the last decade pegs them as
worth more than half of the total cash dividends paid by the corporate sector. It is possible to argue
that informational and technological changes gradually made "financial capitalism" and an active
market for control obsolete in the first half of this century. It is more difficult to argue that such
changes made "financial capitalism" obsolete in the first half of this century, and that subsequent
changes in information and technology have made "financial capitalism" viable once again in the
1980s.

places on boards of directors from which they could easily monitor managerial performance (Seligman 1982).

This story, traditionally told by historians, is not a story of a shift in the balance of information flows, or in the form of the efficient organization of the relationship between finance and industry. The SEC took the form that it did largely because the populists in Congress had always believed in Untermyer's and Brandeis's critiques of how the bankers used other people's money, not because Untermyer's and Brandeis's critiques had suddenly become more correct than they had been in 1910 (ibid. 1982). The Glass-Steagall Act was passed because of the Great Depression, not because of an increase in ultimate investors' ability to assess and monitor firms. And organizations like the National City Bank and, later, Merrill Lynch appear to have prospered not because they were the best judges of the worth of securities, but because their door-to-door methods were able to directly tap savings that would otherwise have flowed into the life insurance and banking systems, and would presumably have reached the capital market in the hands of more sophisticated money managers.

## 6.8  Conclusions

Many issues have not been addressed. Surely the most important unaddressed issue is the balance between J. P. Morgan's adding shareholder value by improving efficiency as opposed to by creating monopoly. This question is close to unresolvable. No one disputes that the robber barons sought monopoly; no one disputes that the robber barons took advantage of economies of scale. The relative weight to be given these two factors is very hard to assess. And in no case is the evidence strong enough to convincingly overcome prior beliefs of as much strength as historians typically hold on this issue.

This paper, however, has addressed one major element of the Progressive critique of the turn-of-the-century organization of American finance: that financiers' presence on corporate boards of directors allowed them to impose an unwarranted tax on industry by exploiting for their own benefit conflicts of interest. The Progressives' fear was well founded: there were conflicts of interest, and investment bankers did exploit them. But there is also evidence that from shareholders' and owners' standpoints these negatives of financial capitalism were outweighed by positives.

This paper has also pointed out a substantial lacuna in finance historians' interpretations of turn-of-the-century Wall Street. Historians of finance have argued that the Morgan partnership was subject to the discipline of the market, yet they have not explained how active competition is consistent with the very high profits achieved by Morgan and Company. The answer is that the market did not discipline the Morgan partnership in the short run: Morgan and Company was not under pressure to cut its fees in order to keep a possible deal from going to another investment banker. But the market did discipline the Morgan partnership in the long run: the only reason that Morgan and Company were able to keep doing deals and charging high fees was their reputation for good judgment and for giving the ultimate investors in their deals good value. Preservation of this reputation was the primary goal of the partnership and left it with little room to abuse its short-run market power by leading its clients into unsound deals.

In general, a strong argument in economics rests on three supports: First comes a coherent theoretical base laying out the strategies available to and the interests of market participants. Second is concrete evidence that actual individual investors, managers, and bankers understood and acted according to the theoretical logic of the situation. And third comes statistical evidence that such a pattern of action is found not just in isolated anecdotes but is standard operating procedure in the situation.

In this paper the theoretical logic for interpreting Morgan's edge in terms of its hard-to-match reputation as an honest broker and a skillful analyst of risk is clear. Many observers at the time thought that the stamp of approval of Morgan and Company was worth its handsome price and gave confidence. And the large-scale correlation between "finance capitalist" relationships and rapid growth remains intriguing and suggestive. The third support is slightly weaker: there were relatively few Morgan-influenced companies on the eve of World War I, including both successes and disasters. It is not possible to obtain precise estimates of the quantitative value of the Morgan touch, but it is highly likely that it was valuable and that Morgan's influence led to corporations that made higher profits.

Since the decline of the House of Morgan, concern over the relationship between finance and industry in America has centered on two themes. The first is the concern expressed by Berle and Means (1932) that corporate managers had become accountable to no one and would divert corporate wealth and assets to their own selfish purposes. The second is the fear that today investment projects are assessed not by far-seeing investment bankers with a keen sense of fundamentals but by an erratic and flighty stock market committed to the short term. In Keynes's (1936, 160) words: "The spectacle of modern investment markets has sometimes moved me towards the conclusion that to make the purchase of an investment permanent and indissoluble, like a marriage, except for reason of death or other grave cause, might be a useful remedy for our contemporary evils. For this would force the investor to direct his mind to the long-term prospects and to those only." Both of these ills seem to call for large-scale financial institutions to take an interest in firm management by establishing and holding large long-term positions in individual companies. It is an irony that today many of the intellectual children and grandchildren of the Progressives appear to call for a return to "financial capitalism."

# References

Adler, Cyrus. 1921. *Jacob Henry Schiff: A biographical sketch.* New York: privately published.
————. 1928. *Jacob Henry Schiff: His life and letters.* New York: Doubleday, Doran, and Co.
Allen, Frederick Lewis, 1949. *The great Pierpont Morgan.* New York: Harper and Row.
Atack, Jeremy. 1985. Industrial structure and the emergence of the modern industrial corporation. *Explorations in Economic History* 22 (January):29–52.
Berle, Adolf, and Gardiner Means. 1932. *The modern corporation and private property.* New York: Macmillan.
Brandeis, Louis D. 1914. *Other people's money, and how the bankers use it.* New York: Frederick A. Stokes.
Brooks, John. 1976. *Telephone: The first hundred years.* New York: Harper and Row.
Burr, Ann Robeson. 1927. *Portrait of a banker: James Stillman, 1850–1918.* New York: Duffield and Co.
Carosso, Vincent P. 1970. *Investment banking in America: A history.* Cambridge: Harvard University Press.
Carstensen, Fred. 1989. A dishonest man is at least prudent: George W. Perkins and the International Harvester steel properties. Manuscript. University of Connecticut, Storrs.
Chandler, Alfred D., Jr. 1990. *Scale and scope: The dynamics of industrial capitalism.* Cambridge: Harvard University Press.
Chernow, Ron. 1990. *The house of Morgan.* Boston: Atlantic Monthly Press.
Cowing, Cedric B. 1965. *Populists, plungers, and Progressives: A social history of stock and commodity speculation, 1890–1936.* Princeton: Princeton University Press.
Cowles, Alfred, et al. 1938. *Common stock indices.* Chicago: Cowles Commission.
Danielan, N. R. 1939. *AT&T: The story of industrial conquest.* New York: Harper and Brothers.
Davis, Lance. 1963. Capital immobilities and finance capitalism: A study of economic evolution in the United States. *Explorations in Entrepreneurial History* 1(Fall):88–105.
————. 1966. The capital markets and industrial concerns: The U.S. and U.K., a comparative study. *Economic History Review* 19:255–72.
Davison, Henry. 1913. *Letter from Messrs. J. P. Morgan and Co., in response to the invitation of the Sub-Committee (Hon. A. P. Pujo, chairman) of the Committee on Banking and Currency of the House of Representatives.* New York: privately published. Baker Library, Harvard University Graduate School of Business, Thomas W. Lamont Papers, box 210–26.]
Dewing, Arthur. 1914. *The financial policy of corporations.* New York: Ronald Press.
Dore, Ronald. 1987. *Taking Japan seriously: A Confucian perspective on leading economic issues.* Stanford, CA: Stanford University Press.
Feis, Herbert. 1964. *Europe: The world's banker.* New Haven: Yale University Press.
Garraty, John. 1960. *Right-hand man: The life of George W. Perkins.* New York: Harper and Brothers.
Gerschenkron, Alexander. 1962. *Economic backwardness in historical perspective.* Cambridge: Harvard University Press.
Goldsmith, Raymond. 1954. *The balance sheet of the United States.* Princeton: Princeton University Press.
Hoshi, Takeo, Anil Kashyap, and David Scharfstein. 1989. Bank monitoring and in-

vestment: Evidence from the changing structure of Japanese corporate banking relationships. NBER Working Paper, no. 3079.

Hovey, Carl. 1912. *The life story of J. Pierpont Morgan.* London: Heinemann.

Huertas, Thomas, and Harold van B. Cleveland. 1987. *Citibank.* Cambridge: Harvard University Press.

Jensen, Michael. 1989. The eclipse of the public corporation. *Harvard Business Review* (September-October):61–74.

Keynes, John Maynard. 1936. *The general theory of employment, interest, and money.* London: Macmillan and Co.

Kolko, Gabriel. 1963. *The triumph of conservatism.* London: Free Press.

Lamont, Thomas W. 1913. The Brandeis talk. (A conversation between Thomas W. Lamont and Louis D. Brandeis on 2 December 1913.) Baker Library, Harvard University Graduate School of Business, Thomas W. Lamont Papers, box 84. An identical copy is in the Brandeis Papers at Brandeis University.

Lawson, Thomas W. 1906. *Frenzied finance.* New York: Ridgway-Thayer Co.

Lewis, W. Arthur. 1978. *Growth and fluctuations 1870–1914.* London: Allen and Unwin.

McCormick, Cyrus. 1931. *The century of the reaper.* New York: Houghton Mifflin.

Moody, John. 1904. *The truth about the trusts: A description and analysis of the American trust movement.* New York: Moody Publishing Co.

———. 1912. *How to invest money wisely.* New York: Office of John Moody.

Navin, Thomas R., and Marian V. Sears. 1955. The rise of the market for industrial securities, 1887–1902. *Business History Review* 29(June):105–38.

O'Hagan, H. Osborne. 1929. *Leaves from my life.* London: John Lane.

Paine, Albert B. 1921. *Theodore N. Vail: A biography.* New York.

Peach, Nelson. 1941. *The security affiliates of national banks.* Baltimore: Johns Hopkins University Press.

Pecora, Ferdinand. 1939. *Wall Street under oath: The story of our modern money changers.* New York: Simon and Schuster.

Poor's Railroad Manual Company. 1913 and earlier years. *Poor's manual of industrials.* New York: Poor's Railroad Manual Co.

———. 1913 and earlier years. *Poor's manual of public utilities.* New York: Poor's Railroad Manual Co.

———. 1913 and earlier years. *Poor's manual of railroads.* New York: Poor's Railroad Manual Co.

Pound, Arthur, and Samuel Moore, eds. 1931. *More they told Barron.* New York: Harper and Brothers.

Pujo Committee. U.S. Congress. House. Committee on Banking and Currency. 1913a. *Minority report of the committee appointed pursuant to House Resolutions 429 and 504 to investigate the concentration of control of money and credit.* Washington, DC: Government Printing Office.

———. 1913b. *Money trust investigation: Hearings before the committee appointed pursuant to House Resolutions 429 and 504 to investigate the concentration of control of money and credit.* Washington, DC: Government Printing Office.

———. 1913c. *Report of the committee appointed pursuant to House Resolutions 429 and 504 to investigate the concentration of control of money and credit.* Washington, DC: Government Printing Office.

Redlich, Fritz. 1951. *The molding of American banking: Men and ideas.* New York: Hafner Publishing Co.

Riesser, J. 1911. *The German great banks and their concentration in connection with the economic development of Germany.* Washington, DC: Government Printing Office. Also under National Monetary Commission, 61st Cong., 2d sess., S. Doc. 593.

Satterlee, Herbert L. 1935. *J. Pierpont Morgan: An intimate portrait.* New York: Macmillan.

Seligman, Joel. 1982. *The transformation of Wall Street: A history of the Securities and Exchange Commission and modern corporate finance.* Boston: Houghton Mifflin.

Smith, Edgar L. 1924. *Common stocks as long term investments.* New York: Macmillan.

Sobel, Robert. 1965. *The big board: A history of the U.S. stock market.* New York: Free Press.

Staples, Henry Lee. 1954. *The fall of a railroad empire.* Syracuse: Syracuse University Press.

Thurow, Lester. 1986. *The zero-sum solution.* New York: Basic Books.

Untermyer, Samuel. 1915. Speculation on the stock exchanges, and public regulation of the exchanges. *American Economic Review* 5:24–68.

U.S. Department of Commerce. Bureau of Corporations. 1913. *The International Harvester Company.* Washington, DC: Government Printing Office.

Vanderlip, Frank A., and Boyden Sparkes. 1935. *From farm boy to financier.* New York: Appleton-Century.

White, Eugene. 1983. *The regulation and reform of the American banking system, 1900–1929.* Princeton: Princeton University Press.

———. 1989. Regulation, taxes, and the financing of American business 1860–1960. Rutgers University, New Brunswick, NJ.

Willis, H. Parker, and J. I. Bogen. 1929. *Investment banking.* New York: Harper and Brothers.

## Comment    Charles F. Sabel

In the spirit of this conference, De Long's ingenious effort to show that J. P. Morgan and Company served the interests of the investing public and its corporate clients while blocking competitors from sharing its rich fees marks the shift of intellectual perspective from Alfred D. Chandler, Jr.'s, Harvard Business School history of the corporation to what might precipitously be called the New Cambridge Business History. What both schools have in common is the intention to show that even those powerful economic institutions of Gilded Age America, which Populists and Progressives believed had dangerously escaped the control of competition, were subject to a higher discipline. For both, this discipline put pursuit of self-interest in the service of the economy as a whole.

Where they differ, profoundly, is in their understanding of how this discipline worked. Chandler focuses on the way the efficient use of mass-production and continuous-process technologies, manifest particularly in economies of scale, governed the construction and extension of the industrial corporation. Bankers are so far removed from the formative influence of production technology that they can play only a subordinate part in his history,

Charles F. Sabel is Ford International Professor of Political Science at Massachusetts Institute of Technology.

except when (as in the notorious case of U.S. Steel) they or their representatives foolishly interfere with managers' pursuit of the economies of high throughput production.

De Long reflects, in contrast, the temper of the new intellectual times. For his generation of historians, technology is at least as malleable as constraining. Managers may be professionals, but they have selfish interests that can endanger even their own organizations. He is concerned, therefore, with the way the resolution of problems of corporate governance, and especially principals' problems in controlling their agents, form economic institutions that would not exist in a perfectly competitive world. He is drawn, naturally enough, to the study of investment banking as an archetypal case, because the same informational advantages that make an investment bank attractive to its customers invite the bankers to self-dealing and deception. De Long's central argument is that a reputation for honesty, which could only be acquired slowly but lost in a careless or deceitful flash, protected J. P. Morgan against competitive challenges. It also protected the firm's customers against abuses of its dominant market position. A closer look at this argument offers an occasion for noting some of the opportunities, but also the risks, presented by the application of ideas drawn from the new information economics to a fundamental problem of business history.

The following comment is in four parts. The first considers De Long's contention that Morgan did good by its clients and the investing public. It stipulates that, although De Long's arguments are even more dubious than he concedes, there is still sufficient evidence of respect of others' interests to justify curiosity about the question, Why didn't Morgan cheat (more)? The second argues that an explanation based on any straightforward interpretation of the restraining powers of a reputation for reliability is contradicted by the presence of two conspicuously rotten business deals in De Long's small universe of Morgan firms, and that his efforts to explain away the discrepancy as a statistical artifact only make the incongruities more evident. Closer examination of the two bad deals suggests that J. P. Morgan and Company did value its reputation for sound performance, but that the meaning of that concern cannot be grasped by reputation models of corporate behavior that presume that the problems of economic coordination are principally problems of judging the trustworthiness of potential partners.

The third section, therefore, sketches an alternative view of Morgan and Company as a maker of the market for companies—an institution, that is, that shaped the conditions under which industrial assets could be recombined. This view arguably explains everything explained by the reputation model, including the importance of the firm's reputation to its success. But it explains as well the failure of Morgan's business fiascoes to produce the catastrophic results that the reputation model anticipates. Sketchy as it is, this alternative view calls attention to the large class of barriers to entry and restraints on market leaders that result neither from economies of scale nor the costs of establishing a reliable way of signaling trustworthiness. Furthermore, it suggests how to address a question obscured by the reputation view: How do the different ways equally trustworthy makers of markets in corporate control go about their business affect the industrial organization that result?

In a world of manifestly imperfect markets but growing (if unequally distributed) wealth, it is tempting to explain material advances by identifying a mechanism that yokes those with economic power to block progress to the cart of productive efficiency. In the age of mass production, technologically determined economies of scale turned this trick for the Harvard Business School historians (and Karl Marx). In an age that seems to require more and more collaboration within and among firms, regardless of size, it is easy to suspect that the need to acquire and protect a reputation for trustworthiness as a precondition for competitive survival could play a similar disciplinary role. The concluding part offers, by way of summary, some reasons for historians of business to resist this and analogous temptations.

## Who Benefited from Morgan and Company's Services?

If the Progressives were right and Morgan and Company prospered by abusing its economic power, De Long has nothing to explain. Hence his first step is to put the lie to the Progressive view. But even leaving aside the undoubtedly important effects of the firm's international financial activities, and taking the partners' rewards for granted, it is hard to know how wide a net to cast in assessing the firm's performance. An expansive interpretation would assume that Morgan and Company played a decisive role in shaping the American railroad and steel industries. An assessment of the firm's effects would then require an evaluation of its part in the rise and subsequent decline of these industries. A restrictive interpretation would treat Morgan and Company as the provider of specialized financial and consultant services to large corporations. An assessment of the firm's role could then be limited to contrasting the performance of the firm's most important clients with the performance of a comparable but unaffiliated group of corporations. Insofar as the limited finding that Morgan clients outperformed other, similar companies would be sufficient to discomfit the Progressives, De Long reasonably enough concentrates the second and more tractable evaluation. Later, however, we will see that there is a price to pay for his cursory consideration of the first.

Thus De Long compares the stock market performances in 1911–12 of twenty companies—three utilities, nine railroads, and eight others—whose boards of directors included J. P. Morgan or one of his partners, with sixty-two firms of similar size that had not been "Morganized." He finds that the ratio of the market value of a firm's common stock to its book value is about 30 percent higher in Morganized companies than in the unaffiliated ones. This price premium is explained in his estimation by the Morgan firms' superior rates of earnings measured as a percentage of book value. "To the extent that Morgan partners added value," De Long writes, "they did so by making the companies they monitored more profitable." If the performance of the worst-performing company is—implausibly, as we shall see—discounted, then it appears further that at any given level of profitability investors were willing to pay an additional premium for Morgan stocks, presumably because they expected the earnings of such companies to be more secure or to grow faster than those of other equally profitable ones. Finally, the average nominal rates of return on the stock of Morganized companies between 1895 (or the year, if later, in which a Morgan director went on the client's boards) and 1913 correspond to the average rates of return of the market as a whole during that period as gauged by standard indices.

Here I want to enter two of many possible qualifications to these claims. First, as De Long notes at least three times, it is impossible to determine from his calculations the extent to which Morganized companies achieved superior profitability by exploiting monopoly power that their very formation created, rather than by achieving efficiency gains. In many cases typical of the period, furthermore, it will be extremely difficult to distinguish those sources of profitability without undertaking a detailed study of the particular industries and firms at issue. Given economies of scale, the creation of optimally sized production units may require just the kind of concentration of ownership that clears the way to extraction of monopoly rents; and once a firm has the possibility of pursuing either strategy, its actual course of action, as the history of U.S. Steel shows,[1] depends on the managers' ideas of "fair" competition, their expectations regarding the behavior of regulatory authorities, and their concepts of efficiency.

Second, it turns out to be no easier to say precisely what Morganization was than to say what effects it produced. Was inclusion of a Morgan partner on a company's board a necessary and sufficient condition for Morganization? What about firms that hired Morgan and Company to underwrite their securities, but neither chose nor were obliged to offer a directorship to one of the firm's partners? Is their performance distinguishable from that of corporations where Morgan direction was more direct? Or take those instances, which De Long hints at in a footnote (note 20), where Morgan partners served on boards together with partners from other leading investment banks. Were these Morganized in the same way as the others? Did their stocks command a premium because two absolutely trustworthy monitors were on the scene? Or did the presence of rival groups signal the potential for expensive struggles for control? Or, finally, is it possible to distinguish the performance of Morganized firms in which Morgan directors played an active role (as at International Harvester and A.T. & T.) from those—and there surely must have been somewhere the Morgan presence was merely nominal? Perhaps American investors only took notice of an investment bank's possible influence on company per-

---

1. Alfred D. Chandler, Jr., *Scale and Scope: The Dynamics of Industrial Capitalism* (Cambridge: Harvard University Press, 1990).

formance when a Morgan partner went on the company's board, and whenever one of Morgan's men did so, he monitored with alacrity. But it would be nice to know this, or know it cannot be ascertained.

These two lines of criticism strike me as damaging to De Long's project only if he is supposed to be undertaking an estimation of the beneficial effect of investment banking on the U.S. economy in the decade before World War I. If, as I think is plainly nearer the truth, his aim is to show that J. P. Morgan and his clients made surprisingly little use of their undoubted power to bilk the (stock-owning) public, then neither the problem of distinguishing monopoly from efficiency gains nor the broad-bush treatment of Morganization constitute unsurmountable objections, and we are obliged to examine De Long's explanation of their restraint.

### Reputations and Fiascoes

The essence of De Long's explanation of Morgan's prosperous restraint is the idea that some kinds of success can be a safeguard against excess and a defense against imitation. The relevant example is a reputation for reliability or trustworthiness, hard to acquire because no one will entrust a party without such a reputation with a task that supposes trust; but the only way to build the reputation is to execute such tasks in a trustworthy way. The long, slow way out of this trap, as De Long suggests in his résumé of Morgan and Company's origins (note 18), is to demonstrate such able fidelity in the execution of modest assignments that the next client will be reassured enough by the performance to offer riskier work, and so on. Once acquired, finally, the reputation is so valuable that it will not be jeopardized for the gains of any single deception.

Seen this way, it is easy to understand how Morgan and Company, which traded on trust, became a prisoner of what could theoretically have been a calculating display of honesty. Because the reputation was costly to acquire, it constituted a barrier to entry for potential competitors, and it was this barrier that protected Morgan's extraordinary fees and his control of a dominant market position. Modern historians of finance such as Carosso are therefore wrong to think that competition among investment banks rendered talk of a "money trust" a polemical, Progressive exaggeration. But because this same reputation was worthless if abused, Morgan actually had to deliver value for money, and here the Progressive view that the money trust answered only to itself is also incorrect.

This view has three things going for it. It breaks an intellectual stalemate by establishing new stylized facts—there was a money trust in the sense of dominant forms with indubitable power over their clients, but not in the sense of uncontrolled conspiracy—and reconciles them with elegant analytic categories. In doing this, it recasts debate in a way that reveals deep affinities between the new theory and the views of informed contemporaries. An early textbook on investment banking in the United States, De Long notes, already contains the core of the reputation model.[2] Better yet, the same categories that break an intellectual logjam and reestablish more intimate contact with views of key actors also respond to the hopeful promptings of our own times to find a mechanism that disciplines self-interest in the absence of (nearly) perfect competition or technological constraints.

Take it as a sign of pessimism of the intellect and without for the moment further theoretical justification that I believe any theory that good is too good to be true. In this case, at any rate, I am convinced that it is. The reason is simply that, as De Long himself notes, two of the twenty Morganized firms were extremely unsuccessful. Indeed they were in principle unsuccessful enough to ruin the value of the firm's reputation—if, as De Long asserts, that reputation was the equivalent of a performance bond, and hence forfeit if the company did not perform.

Both of the failures were notorious in their time. The first was the International Mercantile Marine Company (IMM), more commonly called the Morgan shipping trust. It was formed in 1902 under Morgan's direction, through the combination of various British and American shipping lines in association with several German carriers also active on the North Atlantic route. The combine never came close to meeting its bankers' expectation that it would consolidate and extend its grip on the growing passenger and freight traffic between Europe and the United States. Among many other problems, Morgan had not foreseen that, when transport was by sea rather than by rail, unscheduled or tramp carriers could enter the trade whenever demand picked up, forcing the scheduled shippers to leave port with empty cargo space even in good times. Morgan, moreover, allowed the IMM to pay exorbitant prices for its constituent properties; the firm's disappointing revenues therefore went mostly to service its fixed debt, with next to nothing left for the owners of its common stock.[3] That stock lost on average one-quarter of the previous year's value each year during the decade before World War I.

The second failure was the bête noire of the Progressives: the New York, New Haven, and Hartford Railroad. J. P. Morgan was native to Hartford, and his family had been associated with the road's predecessor lines for generations before he was elected to the company's board in 1891. His original intention may have been to simply establish an orderly partition of market shares between the New Haven and its northern competitor, the Boston and Maine. But by 1903, when he helped secure Charles Mellen's appointment as the New Haven president, he had become enamored of the idea of creating an integrated regional transport system, including not only the Boston and Maine but also coastal steamship lines and interurban electric trollies. It was Mel-

2. H. Parker Willis and J. I. Bogen, *Investment Banking* (New York: Harper and Brothers, 1929), cited in De Long's paper.

3. Vincent P. Carosso, *The Morgans: Private International Bankers, 1854–1913* (Cambridge: Harvard University Press, 1987), 81–86, 91–93.

len's ruthless acquisition of a 36 percent interest in the Boston and Maine in 1907 that began the long feud between Louis Brandeis—the most sophisticated of the Progressives—and the Morgan interests. But it was the exorbitant price that Mellen paid for his new properties (and the bribes required to facilitate their sale) that brought the grand plan to fall. From 1903 to 1913, the road's bonded debt alone increased from $14 million to an insupportable $242 million. By 1913, in fact, the board of directors forced Mellen to resign. But by then the railroad was so strapped for cash that maintenance of track and rolling stock was reduced below acceptable standards. After a long series of widely publicized accidents, which further enraged its critics, deeply embarrassed the Morgan banks, and alarmed its ridership, the firm omitted its dividend in December of that year.[4]

If investors bought the stocks of Morganized companies on the basis of the reputation model of investment banking, then the failure of these two companies should have caused them to sell all of their stocks. Either Morgan and Company was ignorant of management's missteps and excesses as the partners claimed with respect to Mellen's more lurid activities. But then Morgan and Company was negligent in its responsibility to monitor the behavior of its clients. Or the firm connived with management in operations that put the bank's interests ahead of not only stockholders but many of its business partners as well. But if Morgan and Company felt secure enough behind the screen of its reputation to cheat even once, why should it not cheat again and again? Reputations will not serve as barriers to entry or restraint on self-dealing if they can be spotted without being ruined.

De Long is plainly at loose ends with respect to the cases. His inclination, in effect, is to explain away the IMM case by reestimating the Morgan effect on stock prices with nonparametric tests that discount outliers. But the whole point of reputations in business as he defines them is that they are supposed to insure against the occurrence of (negative) outliers. Evading the problem only calls attention to it.

Facing the fiascoes squarely, on the contrary, shows in my view that the difficulties in De Long's explanation of the Morgans' success are in the particular model of reputation he applies, not in the deeper intuition that trust and reputation plays an important part in explaining the firm's behavior. In fact, what is most surprising about the fiascoes, other than that they occurred at all, is that most of Morgan and Company's mistakes were honest mistakes—misjudgments about business conditions rather than efforts to deceive—and that the firm went to considerable lengths to limit the losses that resulted. As an example of an honest misjudgment, take the matter of overpayment for the constituent properties, a consideration in both the IMM and New Haven cases. The purchase prices reflected expectations about the growth rates of future earnings, as was commonly (and reasonably) the case. When earnings

4. Ibid., 354–56, 607–12.

grew at the expected rate, as in the case of U.S. Steel, things went well, when not, then not. But Morgan's two disastrous predictions arguably resulted from a mindless extrapolation of past experience in the railroad and other industries: witness the failure to anticipate the effects of new entrants such as tramp steamers and later automobiles[5] into markets that the firm wanted to dominate through control of existing properties. If there was deception here, it was as much self-deception as anything else. With regard to the limitation of losses, consider the example of the complex financing of $45 million of New Haven debt, which Morgan undertook at an indeterminate risk to itself and which alone prevented the road from failing or being placed in receivership. Or note that prominent Morgan directors remained on the board of the IMM and continued their efforts to make success of the venture until 1932, when, as world trade collapsed, the bank severed its ties with the company.[6]

Morgan and Company was thus very concerned to protect its reputation for reliability and integrity, even when its reputation defined as a performance bond was forfeit. Why? One way to respond to that question without abandoning the reputation model on which De Long's essay is based would be to define more precisely to whom the bank considered itself as owing its reputation, and how that obligation had to be honored. This means elaborating the view of the bank as an honest broker or—stretching the point in a way that De Long frequently does—honest monitor, balancing the needs of its customers and the investing public. It could be defined instead as, say, a reliable member of the club of financial intermediaries, answerable above all to fellow members. In that case, stock prices might fall without doing irreparable damage to the firm's reputation, but outright failure of one of its companies, including significant write-offs of bonded debt, would. I believe that the more such a notion is elaborated, the closer it comes to a plausible view of all the stylized facts—including now the fact of failure—in which reputation turns out to be a necessary but insufficient condition for explaining Morgan and Company's success. But that is the long way around. The next part starts with a sketch of this more comprehensive view and then distinguishes it from the core idea of the reputation model, however elaborated.

## Morgan and Company as Market Makers

Economic historians usually know, even if economists often do not, that markets do not arise spontaneously. The background rules of exchange, such as contract law or the rules governing liability, as well as the distribution and meaning of control over property, depend on the cumulative outcome of interminable conflicts particular to each economy. Where, as in the advanced capitalist countries, markets have long existed, however, the emergence of the most fundamental rules of exchange appears so inevitable and those rules

5. Ibid., 389.
6. Ibid., 609–10, 491.

change so slowly and with such an air of self-evidence that markets appear to create themselves.

To make a market in the sense I intend here is a more deliberate act. It is to create and maintain orderly conditions under which controls over assets of particular kinds can be exchanged and combined in novel ways. Market making in this sense depends on and may require elaboration of the background rules of exchange in a particular economy. But (assuming that all transactions are voluntary) it also depends on the capacity to imagine some way in which redeployment of assets would make at least some parties to the exchange better off while worsening the condition of none. Those who make markets, therefore, must be able to value assets in various conditions and discover how to redeploy them in the most valued way.

What I want to suggest is that Morgan and Company achieved its dominant position in U.S. banking by making a market in the control of transportation and industrial companies, that the power to make such markets depended on respect for boundary conditions on the outcomes of market transactions and was in this sense self-limiting, and that a reputation for integrity was a necessary but far from sufficient condition for the exercise of this power. J. P. Morgan and his partners seem to have glimpsed the possibilities of this role and acquired the expertise to exploit it during the 1880s as they pursued the family's established business of selling American railroad securities to investors in the United States and Great Britain. By the beginning of that decade, Morgan was abandoning the earlier strategy of financing only well-established railroads,[7] and underwriting the debt for the construction or completion of "unbuilt" roads, whose value fluctuated depending on changing estimates of the costs, progress, and probable returns of the work-in-progress as well as the general condition of the financial markets. To manage these risks the firm had to learn to use its own resources and syndicates of underwriters, which it rapidly formed to buffer securities in roads such as the Oregon and Transcontinental against market turmoil.[8] The new expertise in the management of the securities markets drew the firm by middecade into the reorganization of bankrupt or faltering lines. As in the case of the Philadelphia and Reading in 1886, these restructurings required creation of the usual financial apparatus, the careful assessment of the road's affiliated properties (coal in this instance), and renegotiation of its leases on connecting lines. But also and more importantly, the restructuring created an agreement with the road's chief competitor (the Pennsylvania Railroad) to divide traffic in the region so as to "maintain paying rates," organization of an anthracite coal pool to stabilize prizes in *that* industry, and formation of a three-man committee (effectively headed by Morgan) representing the five-year voting trust that had final authority over management's decisions during the period of reorganization. The debt of the reor-

7. Ibid., 221–22.
8. Ibid., 249–53.

ganized line proved easily marketable precisely because Morgan and Company knew the road's finances in detail and because key revenue flows had been rendered more predictable by the reorganization itself. This experience, together with the reorganizations of the Baltimore and Ohio and the Chesapeake and Ohio in this same period must have confirmed what J. P. Morgan plainly suspected: The reorganization of companies was remunerative in itself and the ideal way to maintain a dominant position in the market for corporate securities. But the reorganization of a company depended on the reorganization, in whole or part, of its and allied industries.[9] From here the industrial reorganizations of the following decades were just around the corner.

I underline three aspects of this market-making activity in support of the contention that it was self-disciplining and created barriers to entry that included but were not limited to a reputation for integrity and reliability. First, the vast possibilities for self-dealing inherent in market making were checked at least in part by the obligation of reorganized companies to service their bonded debt. If Morgan and Company tolerated overpayment for the constituent properties of the new combines, whether because of greed or because of good-faith misjudgment of their potential profitability, then, as we saw, this could be detected and penalized by the financial markets. The Morgan power to reorganize firms opened the door to great riches, but as the frantic efforts of equivalent modern investment bankers such as Kohlberg, Kravitz, and Roberts to keep debt service on their companies current reminds us, it is not a license to steal. Morgan, recall, became an expert in industrial reorganization by first becoming an expert in the reorganization of bankrupt railroads. If he could not keep companies he created out of bankruptcy, what was he good for?

Second, the ability of Morgan and Company to make a market in firms depended on possession of highly specialized kinds of knowledge and disposition over diverse but complimentary resources, including political influence, all of which constituted barriers to entry into the market for corporate reorganization. To envision corporate restructuring as Morgan and Company did was to imagine simultaneously not only redistribution of properties and the means of financing and redistribution but also a new market order and a governance structure for monitoring it. To evaluate assets, it was necessary to consider their use in different settings, which required imagination of new governance structures, which required elaboration of new kinds of property, access to pools of capital, and so on. It was the combination of all these capacities, not any one alone, that I think allowed Morgan and Company to dominate the market for corporate reorganization. Participants in that market turned to the firm, it seems to me, not because it was more trustworthy than other securities dealers, but precisely because it could do things securities

9. Ibid., 259–66.

dealers could not—and this because it possessed, as investment bankers would say today, a technology that the others lacked. To see how specialized this technology was, recall the near disastrous results when Morgan and Company applied it to new problems, as in the case of the IMM and the New Haven. If it was dangerous for the leading maker of the market in corporate reorganization to move from one industry to another, imagine how forbidding it must have seemed to enter the general line of business in the first place.

Third, to say this does not imply that a reputation for integrity did not also operate as a barrier to entry to the Morgan and Company's field of operations or as a check on the firm's dealings. I already noted that the firm was only as good as its ability to insure that Morganized companies serviced their debt, and in fact went to extraordinary lengths to avoid bankruptcies. My point is simply that a reputation for knowledgeable integrity alone leaves a lot unexplained about Morgan and Company's place in the banking industry. Indeed, it is only when that reputation is interpreted in the light of the partners' widely acknowledged role as experts in corporate reorganization that the firm's ability to prosper despite the miserable performance of several Morganized common stocks becomes comprehensible. Morgan made companies, effectively warranted them against failure, and stood behind the warranty; and the securities industry evidently knew it. But it could not make companies because it was or was reputed to be more trustworthy than its competitors, any more than it could have done so if it had a less savory reputation than they.

## For a Less Constraining View of Constraints in History

As I noted at the outset, Chandler and De Long both intend to explain the general discipline that puts economic power to productive use when perfect competition does not. For Chandler, the disciplinary mechanism is technology; for De Long, the need to acquire and maintain a reputation for trustworthiness. Here I want to extend and conclude the discussion by indicating how pursuit of such arguments, whatever their precise form, leads to a characterization of economic constraints that obstructs understanding of how different economies change in history.

The difficulty is that, to be believable as a parsimonious explanation of constraint in any particular time or place, arguments of this type have to create the impression that they hold everywhere and always. They suggest, indeed, that economies will prosper to the extent that their institutions conform to the demands of the alleged constraints; and insofar as it also presumed—as it typically is—that pursuit of individual self-interest slowly pushes whole economies in the direction of prosperous outcomes, views of this kind wind up suggesting that all industrial economies will adopt similar, efficiently constrained forms of organization. Chandler's *Scale and Scope,* as well as his earlier project with Herman Daems,[10] argues, for example, that successful

10. Alfred D. Chandler, Jr., and Herman Daems, *Managerial Hierarchies* (Cambridge: Harvard University Press, 1980).

corporations in industries with economies of scale developed similar managerial structures, first in the United States and then in Germany, France, and Great Britain. Analogously De Long argues that the superior long-term performance of economies—Germany, Japan, and American in the Gilded Age—monitored by "financial capitalist" institutions, such as the Morgan bank, as compared to economies (Great Britain) that did not develop them is strong circumstantial evidence that those institutions contributed significantly to productive efficiency. His concluding remark that the intellectual "children and grandchildren" of the Progressives, and notably Lester Thurow, are discovering the virtues of a financial system that their doctrinal forebears reviled reinforces the impression that he believes "financial capitalism" to be a transhistorical—meaning "right," the quotation marks being, in this case, my doing—solution to the problem of allocating capital in an industrial market economy.

One obvious shortcoming of this view is that it reduces the practically and theoretically pressing question of why some economies fail to develop the institutions needed to meet the highest competitive standards to the question, What noneconomic disturbances retarded growth? For if by assumption the creation of such institutions is the natural outcome of the individual pursuit of self-interest under the appropriate economic (market and technological) conditions, then only some exogenous, noneconomic perturbations can obstruct what Adam Smith called the "natural progress of opulence."[11] Thus Chandler follows Donald Coleman in explaining the failure of pre-World War I British firms to expand and move into new industries as the result of management's attachment to a gentlemanly disregard for growth, a "value" so strong and attractive that it dominated the behavior of even those managers who were not gentlemen. The failure of U.S. corporations to keep pace with their Japanese competitors is attributed to their unprecedented, imprudent, and implicitly fainthearted attempt to escape the growing international competition of the 1960s by diversifying into unrelated businesses—attractive because of their high growth rates but so unfamiliar as to be treacherous to control—rather than defending their areas of core expertise.[12] In the same spirit, De Long explains the destruction of "financial capitalism" in the United States in the interwar years as the result of a rise in populist sentiment in Congress, the panic created by the Great Depression, and the success of marginally scrupulous door-to-door salesmen of stocks and bonds who "were able to directly tap savings that would otherwise have flowed into the life insurance and banking systems, and would presumably have reached the capital market in the hands of more sophisticated money managers." What are economic historians doing if they spend half their time appealing to some aspect of high economic theory to explain why things should go right and the other half pointing to things beyond the economy to explain why they do not?

11. Adam Smith, *The Wealth of Nations* (New York: Modern Library, [1776] 1937), book 3, chap. 1.
12. Chandler, *Scale and Scope*, 292, 622.

A second, related shortcoming is that views of generally efficient and very constraining constraints make it impossible to pose, let alone answer, questions about the ways the institutional embodiment of a particular economic regime—"financial capitalism" or mass production—influence the subsequent development of an economy. In the logic of De Long's argument, "financial capitalism" in Gilded Age America is theoretically indistinguishable from "financial capitalism" in pre–World War I Germany. Yet there plainly were important differences between the two. The forty-five employees of Morgan and Company had to steal time for monitoring from the time needed for deal making; and monitoring, perhaps predictably, got short shrift after the initial period of reorganization.[13] The meandering policies of U. S. Steel— now putting a price umbrella over its competitors, now driving them to the wall through rationalization and cost cutting—is the emblem of the bank's distant control.

The Deutsche and other German great banks did notably more monitoring. For one thing, they themselves grew by amalgamation with regional banks that had often grown up with the largest firms in their respective local economies. For another, the great banks had so many industrial participations—as De Long observes, Deutsche directors alone sat on the boards of 159 companies in 1912 (note 27)—that their officials could become experts in the substance of particular industries.[14]

Perhaps, as seems likely to me, this difference had an effect. Perhaps differences in monitoring had negligible effects on corporate structure. The only way to decide is to take seriously the possibility that it might have. This requires regarding the bank not just as trustworthy, but as trustworthy at doing something in a particular setting. Following the earlier discussion of an alternative view of the Morgan bank, this something might be making a market for the control of firms in Germany and the United States. The advantage of this formulation is that it captures the core constraints common to what might be called the property-transition regime specific to each country without making those constraints determinative of outcomes. Put another way, an analysis of this kind makes it possible to avoid a fruitless distinction between universal compulsions and local, historical accidents without reducing economic history to chronicle writing or sterile application of high theory.

One of the great opportunities, as I see it, of the new economic information broadly understood is precisely to understand the way the views and strategies of the economic actors as structured by the economy's manifold connection to

13. Carosso, *The Morgans*, 486–87. IMM was, significantly, the exception. Here the partners continued to watch matters closely, although to little effect (ibid., 486,491).
14. J. Riesser, *The German Great Banks and Their Concentration in Connection with the Economic Development of Germany* (Washington, DC: Government Printing Office, 1911); Martin Gehr, "Das Verhältnis zwischen Banken und Industrie in Deutschland seit Mitte das 19. Jahrhundert bis zur Bankenkrise von 1931 unter besonderer Berücksichtigung des industriellen Grosskredits," inaugural diss., Faculty of Law and Economics, Eberhard-Karls-Universität zu Tübingen, Germany, 1959.

political and social life shape economic outcomes—and, I cannot help adding, *vice versa*. Stopping short of that will mean merely reproducing old results and old statements in new language. Because, like De Long, the New Cambridge Business Historians are drawn by the aesthetic of theoretical parsimony yet alive to the historicity of economic development, they can play an important part in making sure that the occasion is not lost. I suspect that in the end their reputation will depend not least on their success in that.

# Contributors

Charles W. Calomiris
Department of Finance
The Wharton School
University of Pennsylvania
3620 Locust Walk
Philadelphia, PA 19104

J. Bradford De Long
Department of Economics
Littauer Center G-20
Harvard University
Cambridge, MA 02138

Bengt R. Holmstrom
Yale School of Organization and
    Management
Box 1A
New Haven, CT 06520

David A. Hounshell
Department of History
Carnegie-Mellon University
Pittsburgh, PA 15213–3890

H. Thomas Johnson
School of Business
Portland State University
Portland, OR 97207

Naomi R. Lamoreaux
Department of History
Box N
Brown University
Providence, RI 02912

Margaret Levenstein
Department of Economics
The University of Michigan
Ann Arbor, MI 48109–1220

Daniel M. G. Raff
Baker Library 110
Harvard Business School
Soldiers Field Road
Boston, MA 02163

Charles F. Sabel
Department of Political Science
E51–101B
Massachusetts Institute of Technology
50 Memorial Drive
Cambridge, MA 02139

Barry Supple
St. Catharine's College
Cambridge University
Cambridge CB2 1RL, U.K.

Peter Temin
Department of Economics
Room E52–373A
Massachusetts Institute of Technology
50 Memorial Drive
Cambridge, MA 02139

Peter Tufano
Baker Library 332
Harvard Business School
Soldiers Field Road
Boston, MA 02163

JoAnne Yates
Sloan School of Management
Room E52–545
Massachusetts Institute of Technology
50 Memorial Drive
Cambridge, MA 02139

# Name Index

# Subject Index